VOLUME 3

Lesotho

Revised Edition

Deborah Johnston

Compiler

CLIO PRESS
OXFORD, ENGLAND · SANTA BARBARA, CALIFORNIA
DENVER, COLORADO

British Library Cataloguing in Publication Data

Johnston, Deborah
Lesotho. – Rev. ed. – (World bibliographical series; v. 3)
1. Lesotho – Bibliography
I. Title
016.9′6885

ISBN 1–85109–247–1

ABC-CLIO Ltd.,
Old Clarendon Ironworks,
35A Great Clarendon Street,
Oxford OX2 6AT, England.

ABC-CLIO Inc.,
130 Cremona Drive,
Santa Barbara,
CA 93116, USA.

Designed by Bernard Crossland.
Typeset by Columns Design Ltd., Reading, England.
Printed and bound in Great Britain by Bookcraft (Bath) Ltd., Midsomer Norton.

THE WORLD BIBLIOGRAPHICAL SERIES

This series, which is principally designed for the English speaker, will eventually cover every country (and many of the world's principal regions), each in a separate volume comprising annotated entries on works dealing with its history, geography, economy and politics; and with its people, their culture, customs, religion and social organization. Attention will also be paid to current living conditions – housing, education, newspapers, clothing, etc.– that are all too often ignored in standard bibliographies; and to those particular aspects relevant to individual countries. Each volume seeks to achieve, by use of careful selectivity and critical assessment of the literature, an expression of the country and an appreciation of its nature and national aspirations, to guide the reader towards an understanding of its importance. The keynote of the series is to provide, in a uniform format, an interpretation of each country that will express its culture, its place in the world, and the qualities and background that make it unique. The views expressed in individual volumes, however, are not necessarily those of the publisher.

VOLUMES IN THE SERIES

1 *Yugoslavia*, Rev. Ed., John J. Horton
2 *Lebanon*, Rev. Ed., C. H. Bleaney
3 *Lesotho*, Rev. Ed., Deborah Johnston
4 *Zimbabwe*, Rev. Ed., Deborah Potts
5 *Saudi Arabia*, Rev. Ed., Frank A. Clements
6 *Russia/USSR*, Second Ed., Lesley Pitman
7 *South Africa*, Rev. Ed., Geoffrey V. Davis
8 *Malawi*, Rev. Ed., Samuel Decalo
9 *Guatemala*, Rev. Ed., Ralph Lee Woodward, Jr.
10 *Pakistan*, David Taylor
11 *Uganda*, Rev. Ed., Balam Nyeko
12 *Malaysia*, Ian Brown and Rajeswary Ampalavanar
13 *France*, Rev. Ed., Frances Chambers
14 *Panama*, Eleanor DeSelms Langstaff
15 *Hungary*, Thomas Kabdebo
16 *USA*, Sheila R. Herstein and Naomi Robbins
17 *Greece*, Richard Clogg and Mary Jo Clogg
18 *New Zealand*, R. F. Grover
19 *Algeria*, Rev. Ed., Richard I. Lawless
20 *Sri Lanka*, Vijaya Samaraweera
21 *Belize*, Second Ed., Peggy Wright and Brian E. Coutts
23 *Luxembourg*, Carlo Hury and Jul Christophory
24 *Swaziland*, Rev. Ed., Balam Nyeko
25 *Kenya*, Rev. Ed., Dalvan Coger
26 *India*, Rev. Ed., Ian Derbyshire
27 *Turkey*, Merel Güçlü
28 *Cyprus*, Rev. Ed., P. M. Kitromilides and M. L. Evriviades
29 *Oman*, Rev. Ed., Frank A. Clements
30 *Italy*, Lucio Sponza and Diego Zancani
31 *Finland*, J. E. O. Screen
32 *Poland*, Rev. Ed., George Sanford and Adriana Gozdecka-Sanford
33 *Tunisia*, Allan M. Findlay, Anne M. Findlay and Richard I. Lawless
34 *Scotland*, Eric G. Grant
35 *China*, Peter Cheng
36 *Qatar*, P. T. H. Unwin

37 *Iceland*, Rev. Ed., Francis R. McBride
38 *Nepal*, John Whelpton
39 *Haiti*, Rev. Ed., Frances Chambers
40 *Sudan*, Rev. Ed., M. W. Daly
41 *Vatican City State*, Michael J. Walsh
42 *Iraq*, Second Ed., C. H. Bleaney
43 *United Arab Emirates*, Frank A. Clements
44 *Nicaragua*, Rev. Ed., Ralph Lee Woodward, Jr.
45 *Jamaica*, K. E. Ingram
46 *Australia*, Second Ed., I. Kepars
47 *Morocco*, Rev. Ed., Anne M. Findlay and Allan M. Findlay
48 *Mexico*, Rev. Ed., George Philip
49 *Bahrain*, P. T. H. Unwin
50 *The Yemens*, G. Rex Smith
51 *Zambia*, Anne M. Bliss and J. A. Rigg
52 *Puerto Rico*, Elena E. Cevallos
53 *Namibia*, Stanley Schoeman and Elna Schoeman
54 *Tanzania*, Rev. Ed., Colin Darch
55 *Jordan*, Ian J. Seccombe
56 *Kuwait*, Rev. Ed., Frank A. Clements
57 *Brazil*, Solena V. Bryant
58 *Israel*, Second Ed., C. H. Bleaney
59 *Romania*, Andrea Deletant and Dennis Deletant
60 *Spain*, Second Ed., Graham J. Shields
61 *Atlantic Ocean*, H. G. R. King
62 *Canada*, Ernest Ingles
63 *Cameroon*, Mark W. DeLancey and Peter J. Schraeder
64 *Malta*, John Richard Thackrah
65 *Thailand*, Michael Watts
66 *Austria*, Denys Salt with the assistance of Arthur Farrand Radley
67 *Norway*, Leland B. Sather
68 *Czechoslovakia*, David Short
69 *Irish Republic*, Michael Owen Shannon
70 *Pacific Basin and Oceania*, Gerald W. Fry and Rufino Mauricio
71 *Portugal*, P. T. H. Unwin
72 *West Germany*, Donald S. Detwiler and Ilse E. Detwiler
73 *Syria*, Ian J. Seccombe
74 *Trinidad and Tobago*, Frances Chambers
75 *Cuba*, Jean Stubbs, Lila Haines and Meic F. Haines
76 *Barbados*, Robert B. Potter and Graham M. S. Dann
77 *East Germany*, Ian Wallace
78 *Mozambique*, Colin Darch
79 *Libya*, Richard I. Lawless
80 *Sweden*, Leland B. Sather and Alan Swanson
81 *Iran*, Reza Navabpour
82 *Dominica*, Robert A. Myers
83 *Denmark*, Kenneth E. Miller
84 *Paraguay*, R. Andrew Nickson
85 *Indian Ocean*, Julia J. Gotthold with the assistance of Donald W. Gotthold
86 *Egypt*, Ragai, N. Makar
87 *Gibraltar*, Graham J. Shields
88 *The Netherlands*, Peter King and Michael Wintle
89 *Bolivia*, Gertrude M. Yeager
90 *Papua New Guinea*, Fraiser McConnell
91 *The Gambia*, David P. Gamble
92 *Somalia*, Mark W. DeLancey, Sheila L. Elliott, December Green, Kenneth J. Menkhaus, Mohammad Haji Moqtar, Peter J. Schraeder
93 *Brunei*, Sylvia C. Engelen Krausse and Gerald H. Krausse
94 *Albania*, William B. Bland
95 *Singapore*, Stella R. Quah and Jon S. T. Quah
96 *Guyana*, Frances Chambers
97 *Chile*, Harold Blakemore
98 *El Salvador*, Ralph Lee Woodward, Jr.
99 *The Arctic*, H. G. R. King
100 *Nigeria*, Robert A. Myers
101 *Ecuador*, David Corkhill
102 *Uruguay*, Henry Finch with the assistance of Alicia Casas de Barrán
103 *Japan*, Frank Joseph Shulman
104 *Belgium*, R. C. Riley
105 *Macau*, Richard Louis Edmonds
106 *Philippines*, Jim Richardson
107 *Bulgaria*, Richard J. Crampton
108 *The Bahamas*, Paul G. Boultbee
109 *Peru*, John Robert Fisher
110 *Venezuela*, D. A. G. Waddell

111 *Dominican Republic*, Kai Schoenhals
112 *Colombia*, Robert H. Davis
113 *Taiwan*, Wei-chin Lee
114 *Switzerland*, Heinz K. Meier and Regula A. Meier
115 *Hong Kong*, Ian Scott
116 *Bhutan*, Ramesh C. Dogra
117 *Suriname*, Rosemarijn Hoefte
118 *Djibouti*, Peter J. Schraeder
119 *Grenada*, Kai Schoenhals
120 *Monaco*, Grace L. Hudson
121 *Guinea-Bissau*, Rosemary Galli
122 *Wales*, Gwilym Huws and D. Hywel E. Roberts
123 *Cape Verde*, Caroline S. Shaw
124 *Ghana*, Robert A. Myers
125 *Greenland*, Kenneth E. Miller
126 *Costa Rica*, Charles L. Stansifer
127 *Siberia*, David N. Collins
128 *Tibet*, John Pinfold
129 *Northern Ireland*, Michael Owen Shannon
130 *Argentina*, Alan Biggins
131 *Côte d'Ivoire*, Morna Daniels
132 *Burma*, Patricia M. Herbert
133 *Laos*, Helen Cordell
134 *Montserrat*, Riva Berleant-Schiller
135 *Afghanistan*, Schuyler Jones
136 *Equatorial Guinea*, Randall Fegley
137 *Turks and Caicos Islands*, Paul G. Boultbee
138 *Virgin Islands*, Verna Penn Moll
139 *Honduras*, Pamela F. Howard-Reguindin
140 *Mauritius*, Pramila Ramgulam Bennett
141 *Mauritania*, Simonetta Calderini, Delia Cortese, James L. A. Webb, Jr.
142 *Timor*, Ian Rowland
143 *St. Vincent and the Grenadines*, Robert B. Potter
144 *Texas*, James Marten
145 *Burundi*, Morna Daniels
146 *Hawai'i*, Nancy J. Morris and Love Dean
147 *Vietnam*, David Marr and Kristine Alilunas-Rodgers
148 *Sierra Leone*, Margaret Binns and Tony Binns
149 *Gabon*, David Gardinier
150 *Botswana*, John A. Wiseman
151 *Angola*, Richard Black
152 *Central African Republic*, Pierre Kalck
153 *Seychelles*, George Bennett, with the collaboration of Pramila Ramgulam Bennett
154 *Rwanda*, Randall Fegley
155 *Berlin*, Ian Wallace
156 *Mongolia*, Judith Nordby
157 *Liberia*, D. Elwood Dunn
158 *Maldives*, Christopher H. B. Reynolds
159 *Liechtenstein*, Regula A. Meier
160 *England*, Alan Day
161 *The Baltic States*, Inese A. Smith and Marita V. Grunts
162 *Congo*, Randall Fegley
163 *Armenia*, Vrej Nersessian
164 *Niger*, Lynda F. Zamponi
165 *Madagascar*, Hilary Bradt
166 *Senegal*, Roy Dilley and Jerry Eades
167 *Andorra*, Barry Taylor
168 *Netherlands Antilles and Aruba*, Kai Schoenhals
169 *Burkina Faso*, Samuel Decalo
170 *Indonesia*, Sylvia C. Engelen Krausse and Gerald H. Krausse
171 *The Antarctic*, Janice Meadows, William Mills and H. G. R. King
172 *São Tomé and Príncipe*, Caroline S. Shaw
173 *Fiji*, G. E. Gorman and J. J. Mills
174 *St. Kitts-Nevis*, Verna Penn Moll
175 *Martinique*, Janet Crane
176 *Zaire*, Dawn Bastian Williams, Robert W. Lesh and Andrea L. Stamm
177 *Chad*, George Joffé and Valérie Day-Viaud
178 *Togo*, Samuel Decalo
179 *Ethiopia*, Stuart Munro-Hay and Richard Pankhurst
180 *Punjab*, Darshan Singh Tatla and Ian Talbot
181 *Eritrea*, Randall Fegley
182 *Antigua and Barbuda*, Riva Berleant-Schiller and Susan Lowes with Milton Benjamin
183 *Alaska*, Marvin W. Falk
184 *The Falkland Islands*, Alan Day
185 *St Lucia*, Janet Henshall Momsen

186 *Slovenia*, Cathie Carmichael
187 *Cayman Islands*, Paul G. Boultbee
188 *San Marino*, Adrian Edwards and Chris Michaelides
189 *London*, Heather Creaton
190 *Western Sahara*, Anthony G. Pazzanita
191 *Guinea*, Margaret Binns
192 *Benin*, J. S. Eades and Chris Allen
193 *Madrid*, Graham J. Shields

For my husband, Kevin,
with love and gratitude for your support

Contents

INTRODUCTION xv

GLOSSARY xxxiii

SELECTED THESES AND DISSERTATIONS ON LESOTHO xxxv

THE COUNTRY AND ITS PEOPLE 1

GEOGRAPHY 3
General 3
Maps and atlases 5

GEOLOGY 6

TOURISM AND TRAVEL GUIDES 8
General 8
Colonial guides and travellers' accounts 9

FAUNA AND FLORA 11
Fauna 11
Flora 13

PREHISTORY AND ARCHAEOLOGY 16

HISTORY 18
General 18
Early history 19
Kingdom of Moshoeshoe I (1824-70) 20
Cape Rule (1871-83) 22
Late colonial period (1884-1966) 23

BIOGRAPHIES, AUTOBIOGRAPHIES AND MEMOIRS 26

Contents

POPULATION 29
General 29
Urbanization and urban growth 30

LANGUAGE 32

RELIGION 35

SOCIAL CONDITIONS 38
Social differentiation and poverty 38
Social surveys 42
Food and nutrition 44

WOMEN AND GENDER ISSUES 47

SOCIAL SERVICES, HEALTH AND WELFARE 52
Health 52
Indigenous health systems 56
Adult and child welfare 57

POLITICS 62
General 62
Pre-independence 63
Post-independence 65

CONSTITUTION, LEGAL SYSTEM AND HUMAN RIGHTS 68

ADMINISTRATION AND GOVERNMENT 73
General 73
Donor agencies 77

INTERNATIONAL RELATIONS 80

ECONOMY 84

FINANCE AND BANKING 88

TRADE 90
Internal 90
External 93

INDUSTRY 95
General 95
Energy 98

AGRICULTURE 101
General 101
Land 104
Forestry and woodlots 106
Fieldcrops and horticulture 107
Livestock 111

HUMAN RESOURCES AND EMPLOYMENT 114
General 114
Migrant labour 116

THE LABOUR MOVEMENT AND TRADE UNIONS 122

STATISTICS 124

ENVIRONMENT 125
General 125
Land degradation and soil erosion 127

EDUCATION 130
General 130
School system, teaching and teacher training 131
University education 133
Vocational, adult and non-formal education 134

RESEARCH AND DEVELOPMENT 136

LITERATURE 139
Literary criticism 139
Poetry 140

THE ARTS 142
Rock art 142
Visual art and design 143
Architecture 143
Crafts 145
Music 146
Theatre 147

CULTURE, CUSTOMS AND FOLKLORE 148
Folklore 148
Culture, customs and dress 149

SPORT AND RECREATION 153

MUSEUMS AND ARCHIVES 155

MASS MEDIA AND BOOKS 156
Newspapers 156
Printing and publishing 157

PERIODICALS 158

ENCYCLOPAEDIAS AND DIRECTORIES 160

BIBLIOGRAPHIES 162

INDEX OF AUTHORS 167

INDEX OF TITLES 173

INDEX OF SUBJECTS 189

MAP OF LESOTHO 198

Introduction

The Kingdom of Lesotho is a small, mountainous country (30,350 square kilometres) completely surrounded by South Africa. It is similar in size to Belgium and slightly larger than the American state of Maryland. Like many developing countries, Lesotho's statistical output is not without errors. However, it is worth presenting a statistical introduction to the country. An inter-censual estimate places the 1995 population at approximately 2.1 million, increasing at an annual rate of about 2.8 per cent. While the urban population is also growing fast, the country remains predominantly rural. In 1995, it was estimated that 83 per cent of the population lived in rural areas. However, data for the pre-drought year of 1990 show that agriculture accounted for only 20.9 per cent of Gross Domestic Product.

A large proportion of the male labour force works in South Africa, principally in the mining sector. Given the nature of South African influx regulations, this migration is oscillating, i.e. the migrant regularly returns home. Thus, the working population has not had the option to permanently migrate to the urban areas of South Africa. As will be discussed below, migrant remittances are an extremely important contribution to Lesotho's Gross National Product (GNP). In 1990, Lesotho's average per capita GNP of US$530 was one of the highest among low-income countries. However, the number of miners has declined in recent years, while the labour force has continued to grow. No other significant sources of alternative employment have emerged, and Lesotho appears to be experiencing an employment crisis of major proportions.

Out of the data arises the complex picture of a predominantly rural-based population, where agriculture accounts for less than a quarter of output and there is a strong historical trend for male labour migration. These trends will be explained in subsequent sections of the introduction. The people of Lesotho, the Basotho, are relatively homogeneous in terms of culture and there is a single national language, Sesotho. In addition, a large number of culturally and ethnically similar people live in South Africa, and the Sotho-speaking people as a whole are usually described as the Southern Sotho. In order to avoid confusion, this book will use the terms Sesotho and Basotho to refer to *de jure* citizens of Lesotho, reserving the term Sotho to describe the wider linguistic group. A strong sense of national identity prevails, despite Lesotho's economic dependence on South Africa and the cultural links with South Africans. Economic dependence has been most obvious in the large number of migrants from Lesotho to South Africa's mines, and the lack of industrial development in Lesotho itself. This lack of domestic development, contrasting so greatly with South Africa's industrial wealth, has contributed to the present concern over unemployment.

Presently, the people of Lesotho stand at a crossroads. Given the economic problems faced, some sort of regional federation with the newly democratic South Africa may be advisable. However, the cost would be the loss of national sovereignty. While practically limited due to the regional dominance of South Africa, this hard-won sovereignty is cherished by the Basotho people and will not be easily thrown over. The discussion below is intended to introduce the reader to Lesotho's past history and its present situation. The introduction is divided into four sections: the country; its population; its history; and the economy.

The country

Lesotho is completely surrounded by South Africa, being bordered by three South African provinces. This emergence of this anomalous situation was the result of a particular confluence of social and political forces, described below. The boundaries of Lesotho evolved in the mid-1800s and are the result of conflict between the Basotho people, Afrikaner settlers and the colonial authorities. To the north and west, the Caledon or Mohokare River separates Lesotho from the Free State Province. The eastern mountain escarpment provides a natural boundary with Kwazulu-Natal Province, while the south-western boundary with the Eastern Cape largely follows a boundary fence.

Lying between 28 degrees and 31 degrees south and 27 degrees and 30 degrees east, Lesotho is outside the Tropics. It has a temperate climate and is situated on average 1,500 metres above sea level. At 1,000 metres above sea level, Lesotho has the highest lowest point of any country in the world. Coupled with climatic factors, this altitude results in Lesotho being free from tropical disease. However, only one quarter of Lesotho is suitable for agricultural production, the rest being traversed by the Maloti mountains. The mountainous areas in the east of the country decline to the strip of arable land in the west, which contains most of the population and the urban centres. Lesotho's mountains form part of South Africa's Drakensburg range, and reach heights of 3,000 metres above sea level. Thabana-Ntlenyana is the highest mountain in Southern Africa at 3,481 metres. Unfortunately, Lesotho's mountains appear to contain few minerals. While coal has been found in scattered locations, it has yet to be developed. The most established diamond-mine, at Letseng-la-Terai, was closed in 1982, as it proved costly to work and had relatively low yields. A few other diamond-bearing areas exist, but none are involved in production on any significant scale.

Lesotho is divided into four major ecological regions: the Lowlands, the Foothills, the Mountains and the Senqu River Valley. The Senqu, or Orange, River originates in Lesotho's north-eastern highlands and is one of the largest rivers in Southern Africa. In general, the mountain areas are water-rich, although this water is relatively inaccessible as rivers run too far below the level of the surrounding fields to allow significant irrigation at a reasonable cost. Thus, there have been few schemes to harness this water for the benefit of the country. One scheme, the Lesotho Highlands Water Project, aims to sell Lesotho's water to South Africa. The project, still under construction, is a M10 billion scheme to dam water for use in South Africa and eventually to provide hydro-electric power in Lesotho. The concept has been discussed since Lesotho achieved independence in 1966. However, no concrete steps were taken until the military coup of 1986, discussed below, as the previous government wanted to reduce Lesotho's dependence on South Africa. There is some unhappiness over the degree to which the project has benefited the people of Lesotho in terms of employment and development. However, it is generally recognized that the royalties from the sale of water provide the government with funds that could be used for developmental purposes.

Lesotho has four distinct seasons. The spring planting season occurs between August and October. The summer months of November to January generally experience the heaviest rainfall. Autumn comprises the period February to April, while the winter months of May to July bring frost and sometimes heavy snow. The temperature in the Lowlands varies from a minimum of –6 degrees celsius or less to a maximum of 32 degrees celsius in summer. However, the mountain areas exhibit a much wider range in temperatures, although rarely achieving the maximum temperatures of the Lowlands.

Rainfall is highly variable, and several observers have attempted to identify a cyclical trend to explain the pattern of droughts and downpours that Lesotho experiences. However, weather patterns have been so diverse that there is disagreement about whether any identifiable pattern can be detected. Rainfall also varies within Lesotho, although this distribution is more predictable. The northern regions of the country persistently experience better rain than the southern regions. For example, in the 1992-93 farm season, recorded rainfall varied from 800 mm in the northern foothills to only 333 mm in the southern town of Semonkong. Consequently, the northern farming areas have better crop yields than the south of the country. Apart from the variability of rainfall, Lesotho's farmers also have a range of other environmental hazards to deal with. Particularly damaging are the unpredictable occurrences of hail and frost.

Lesotho's limited arable land resources were discussed at the beginning of this section. Growth in rural landlessness is evident from available statistics. Morojele's 1960 study found that 8.5 per cent of rural households were without fields. Agricultural census data from 1980 found that landlessness had risen to just over 20 per cent of rural households, while the Household Budget Survey of 1986/87 found that 24 per cent of rural households had no fields. However, access is uneven between villages, as access to arable land depends partly on topography. While some villages have larger access to arable land, they are unlikely to experience an inflow of households as an allocation of land is rarely made to recent arrivals in the general climate of land shortage. Even in the late 19th century, Eldredge described the difficulty of relocation between villages in Lesotho. Land allocation in rural areas has also been affected by chiefly favouritism despite attempts to regulate landholding. In addition, female-headed households have tenuous access to land. If never married, the women are not eligible for a land-allocation according to custom. If divorced, they lose access to land and, if widowed, their ability to continue to hold land depends on the goodwill of their husband's family.

Landlessness has been most visibly driven by population growth, which will be discussed in the next section. The number of people per hectare of arable land has increased sharply from 565 persons per square kilometre of arable land in 1986 to 748 in 1992. Productive arable land has also been lost from soil erosion, a problem worsened by the climatic extremes discussed above. It is estimated that approximately 1,000 hectares are lost to soil erosion each year, and the landscape is visibly scarred by sheet- and gully-erosion. Such gullies, locally called *dongas*, criss-cross arable land in the Lowlands, often dividing fields. Some *dongas* are several metres wide and have destroyed established footpaths. Several factors have encouraged this soil erosion, but the historical processes, discussed below, which forced ever denser settlement on a land ill-designed for crop production are foremost in this environmental change. Economic and social pressures have led to continued cultivation of the land without attention to the environmentally-damaging consequences. A vicious cycle has begun in which topsoil, exposed by over-cultivation, is washed away in heavy rain. The underlying soil is also washed away and *dongas* form. The run-off water from further rainfall is funnelled by these channels, cutting ever deeper gullies. In the mountains, sheet erosion occurs as a result of uncontrolled grazing and attempts to cultivate on mountain slopes. Barren rockfaces appear as the shallow soils are washed away in the heavy summer rains.

The absence of trees worsens the soil erosion problem, particularly in the mountain areas. However, trees have never been widespread naturally, and, before extensive habitation, it appears that Lesotho was predominantly a grassland with few indigenous trees. Today, these indigenous trees are rarely found, their existence limited to remote valleys. 'Invader' or introduced trees, such as the weeping willow and the white poplar, are more commonly seen, although they also remain sparse. A common site in villages are varieties of the aloe, and of particular interest is the spiral aloe (*Aloe polyphylla*) which is found only in Lesotho. This is a protected species in Lesotho, and can only be found on steep basalt slopes.

Records show that wild animals of various kinds were prevalent in Lesotho in the first half of the 19th century. Missionaries reported the existence of zebra, wildebeest and ostriches. However, game hunting by white hunters and population growth led to the annihilation of many animal species in the area. In the 1870s, the last lion was killed and hippos were eradicated from the Senqu River. However, jackal, baboons and some small buck continue to survive in Lesotho's mountain areas, although they are rarely seen. On a positive note, Lesotho has maintained a varied bird population and its butterflies have long attracted the attention of collectors.

Population

Earlier it was stated that the Basotho share a wide range of linguistic and cultural similarities with Sotho-speakers in South Africa. Within Lesotho itself, the population is relatively homogeneous, although a number of Xhosa-speaking people live in the southern districts. Sesotho is the national language, while English is the language used in both government and business, and is also the medium of instruction in secondary schools. The Basotho are predominantly Christian, the main churches being Roman Catholic, Lesotho Evangelical and Anglican. There are also other smaller Christian Churches. However, the Christian Church in Lesotho appears to be deeply divided, with a long history of enmity between the major churches. There is also an Islamic Centre and a Bahai Temple.

The population surveys carried out in 1966, 1976 and 1986 give the following figures: 965,913; 1,216,815; and 1,606,000. However, there are a large number of absentees from the country at any particular point in time. Thus, the resident, or de facto, population is usually much smaller. This de facto population increased from 852,000 in 1966 to 1,443,000 in 1986. The vast majority of absentees are resident in South Africa, and migration often takes place for employment purposes, given the paucity of employment opportunities within Lesotho (discussed in the final section). In addition, migration takes place for social purposes (i.e. visiting family) and for education.

Intercensal growth rates are calculated for both the de facto and the *de jure* populations. The respective *de jure* growth rates for the periods 1956-66, 1966-76 and 1976-86 were 1.4 per cent, 2.0 per cent and 2.6 per cent. This increase has occurred for a number of reasons. Firstly, permanent migration outside Lesotho is negligible, due to South African legal restrictions. Second, while fertility has remained constant, mortality has been declining rapidly. The crude birth rate in 1992 was 3.72 per cent, while the crude death rate was 1.18 per cent. In 1990, life expectancy at birth was 53.7 years, a rise from 41.6 in 1960. This compares well to the sub-Saharan average in life expectancy which was 51.8 years.

The de facto population growth rates between 1956 and 1966 were 2.9 per cent, 2.25 per cent between 1966 and 1976 and 3.1 per cent beween 1976 and 1986. The higher de facto intercensal growth rates appear to be due to declining migration to South Africa. This decline follows a number of restrictions on immigration from Lesotho to South Africa that have been implemented over time. In particular there have been a number of restrictions on female migrants, starting with the South African Native Laws Amendment Act of 1952, which limited the ability of African women in general to reside in an urban area. A few Basotho women with documentary proof were allowed to remain under section 10 of the Act, which provided residence rights for people with appropriate residence and employment records. However, most foreign women did not qualify and fell instead under section 12 of the Native Laws Amendment Act, which gave the South African government direct powers over the granting of their residence- and work-permits. Applications from Basotho women for permission to reside in an urban area were to be refused as being against policy.

In 1963, these restrictions were reinforced by the imposition of border regulations, following the introduction of the South African Aliens Control Act. Prior to this Act, there had been no border control posts between South Africa and the then Basutoland. The Act made it an offence for a foreign African to enter South Africa without a travel document issued by his own country and recognized by the South African government. If not recruited to work in the mines or agriculture, prior permission was needed. A large drop in the number of female absentees was recorded in Lesotho Census data, with the number of recorded female absentees falling from 41,992 in 1956 to 19,550 in 1966. The number of male absentees also fell but less sharply. These measures have both limited the amount of migration to South Africa and have also forced migrants to move clandestinely. A large number of labour migrants from Lesotho are likely to have been illegal, particularly female migrants The South African Institute of Race Relations (SAIRR) reports that 10,000 illegal immigrants were repatriated to Lesotho in 1989. It has been estimated that 10,000-30,000 women work illegally in the Republic of South Africa as domestic, factory- and farm-workers.

However, not all migration has been illegal. Work on South Africa's mines is the most visible form of legal migration, and, indeed, is probably the largest single form of labour migration. However, its labour force share has fallen consistently since the 1970s. In 1976, approximately 42 per cent of the male labour force was employed on the mines. By 1986, this had fallen to 33 per cent and for the early 1990s, the share of the workforce in mining employment may be as low as 20 per cent. This fall in the importance of mining employment has been the result of two separate trends. Firstly, the size of the male labour force has increased rapidly as a result of population growth. Earlier we saw the high rates of population growth in Lesotho and these have translated into a rapid growth of the male labour force, which increased from 228,890 in 1966 to 367,973 in 1986.

However, mining employment has not kept pace with the growth in potential recruits although there was a surge in numbers of Basotho employed in the mid-1970s. This was due to a desire on the part of the mines to switch to more reliable labour sources, following drastic reductions in the number of miners from Malawi and Mozambique in 1974. The Chamber of Mines data show that the average number of Basotho miners rose from 80,951 in 1966 to 121,062 in 1976. During this period, the number of miners from South Africa and Swaziland also increased significantly. Greater supply from these areas was only achieved by large wage increases, facilitated by a rapid rise in the gold price in the early 1970s. Between 1972 and 1980, mine wages improved by 320 per cent in real terms.

Greater supply also permitted employers to stabilize the workforce, as regulations on contract renewal became stricter. This stabilization led to an increase in contract length and the use of re-employment certificates for miners. This movement towards 'career mining' has also led to a reduction in the average number of miners on the mines, because of the significant reduction in labour turnover. At the same time, the number of novices on the mines fell from 16.5 per cent in 1975 to 2.9 per cent in 1990. This stabilization has led to the situation where the mine work force has become more permanent, but also more exclusive. A situation has emerged where the chances of employment for a man seeking minework are very small. Indeed, this situation has been worsened in recent years by retrenchments that have reduced the number of Basotho labour to around 100,000 mine workers. Retrenchment has occurred because of a concentration of Basotho workers on mines with poor productivity. The total number of gold mining jobs in South Africa as a whole fell from 477,397 in 1986 to 324,441 in 1992, and it has been estimated that the mines could lose another 150,000 jobs in the 1990s. Basotho workers have also been highly involved in trade union activity and a significant number were dismissed after a major strike in the late 1980s.

Unusually, women in Lesotho are particularly well educated. A survey in 1985 found that 70 per cent of women were functionally literate compared to 46 per cent of men. The educational advantage for women can be explained by two factors. Firstly, young boys are often used to look after animals in rural areas. This necessitates long absences from home, when animals are taken to remote mountain pastures, and boys are often forced to delay or forego schooling. Secondly, mining has dominated male employment opportunities. Mining jobs have required a relatively low level of education and young men were encouraged to leave school at an early age. The reduction in opportunities for mining employment may lead to a reversal of this educational differential. However, in 1991, the male/female enrolment ratio was 83:100 in primary schools, while the ratio in the National University was 89:100.

Primary school in Lesotho covers seven years of basic education The official primary school population is from age 6 to 12 years, although due to late starts and retakes, the actual primary school population can often be older than this. For the majority of the population, a primary education is the termination of formal schooling. Secondary school education is for four to five years for pupils from about age 13 to age 17 years. Technical and vocational education is provided at the Lerotholi Polytechnic, Leloateng Trades School, Technical School of Leribe, and five other vocational schools. There are two tertiary education institutions in Lesotho: the National University of Lesotho and the National Teacher Training College.

Educational enrolment has risen rapidly. In 1981, there were 288,472 pupils enrolled at all levels of education in the country. This enrolment rose to 401,531 in 1990. Teacher numbers have not increased at the same rate, although the absolute number of teachers has increased. Overall, teaching staff rose by 30.6 per cent from 6,943 in 1981 to 9,070 in 1990. Hence, the overall pupil-teacher ratio had changed from 41.5:1 in 1981 to 44.3:1 in 1990.

It is difficult to draw an accurate picture of the health of the Basotho people from clinic and hospital records, as a large proportion of people will approach traditional or spiritual healers for the treatment of certain ailments. However, hospital records do give a general indication of major trends and areas of concern. While normal deliveries and pregnancy problems are the main reason for women to be admitted to hospitals, admission records show that a large number of men are admitted for injuries resulting from violence. Hypertension is an important disease among older women and tuberculosis among older men. Indeed, TB is the number one killer of adults, fostered by hardship on the mines, poverty and overcrowding. In a recent outpatient survey, 29 adults were diagnosed as having TB out of every 10,000 people over the age of 14. A worrying trend is the recent increase in younger people found with the disease, a shift which appears to be attributable to the AIDS virus. By June 1993, there had been only 264 diagnosed cases of AIDS since 1986. However, the rate of infection appears to be rising rapidly. By the end of 1991, the number of HIV-positive individuals was estimated to be between 5,000 and 10,000. Worryingly, a study of women attending ante-natal clinics in Maseru in 1993 found that 5.2 per cent of expectant mothers were HIV-positive. Concern over the spread of HIV-infection is heightened by the lack of public awareness about the disease and its prevention.

In contrast, there has been a clear improvement in child health over time. An important indicator of children's health is the proportion of children who are less than 80 per cent of the normal weight for their age. In Lesotho, this fell from 22.8 per cent in 1987 to 13.4 per cent in 1991. The incidence of drought in 1992 is likely to have led to a rise in this indicator for later years. Another good indicator of child health is the infant mortality rate, which fell from 116 deaths per 1,000 live births in 1967/68 to 63 deaths in 1991. However, due to drought, the rate rose slightly in 1992 to 75 deaths per 1,000 births.

In interpreting the health and education indicators presented above, it must be remembered that household poverty in Lesotho is differentiated by geographic region, class and the gender of the household head. Income is inequitably distributed between rural and urban areas, and also within these areas. The 1991 joint report by the government of Lesotho and UNICEF on the situation of women and children found that many fields were left fallow because households could not afford the high cost of agricultural inputs and that 'this is particularly true of elderly and female-headed households'. Eckert found that 22 per cent of farm households were 'resource destitute landholders', with only land and no cattle, tools or outside incomes, and usually no males in the family.

The history of Lesotho

Settlement occurred in the region to the north of Lesotho as early as 900 AD. During the period 900 to 1400 AD, these Iron Age communities appear to have experienced great economic and cultural change. Cattle became central to economic life and settlement styles also changed in response to population pressures. It is also likely that there was some change in social organization, with the emergence of a chiefly class. Sotho-speaking people can be identified in the region as early as the 14th century, although it was several centuries before Lesotho itself was settled. The period 1400 to 1700 was one of rapid settlement of what is now the South African Transvaal and Free State. Sotho-speakers gradually settled this region, organized as relatively autonomous clans. The Bafokeng clan appears to have led much of the Sotho settlement in this area, living peacefully with other groups, including the indigenous 'bushmen'. Another Sotho clan, the Bakoena settled in the northern Free State in the 1500s, and the Sotho-speaking Batlokoa and Bataung also established themselves in the Free State during this period.

These Sotho clans shared both language and customs, but were often in conflict. Sotho chiefdoms rose and fell, but did not unite the various Sotho-speaking people. However, this is not to suggest that, because there was no more complex form of social organization, Sotho society did not evolve. Recently, a number of authors have shown that Sotho society was not static. External influence from other African communities was important, leading to the absorption of outside cultures, and to a certain degree the Sotho engaged in trade with their neighbours. Some of these neighbouring people were, themselves, involved with international trade via Mozambique. Elsewhere, this trade led to greater political centralization as some chiefs monopolized trade routes. The southern Sotho, however, experienced (limited) centralization only during the late 18th century.

Over time settlement spread towards the south, and, by 1800, the southern frontier of Sotho residence reached the Caledon River. The following three decades were, however, a time of great difficulty for the Sotho clans. Records show that there was a severe drought between 1790 and 1820, and the period 1820 to 1830 also saw attacks on the residents of this area. These attacks came from two sources. First,

Dutch expansion in the Cape led to the migration of a number of groups who wished to avoid incorporation. These groups, which generally consisted of people of mixed race, led raids against the communities settled in the area. Second, there were attacks by groups displaced through political changes in the East of the country. Zulu expansion had disturbed a number of communities, who, in turn, attacked other communities for the purpose of acquiring land, crops and cattle. This period has been termed the *lifaqane* by the Basotho, the term meaning 'forced displacement'.

The drought and these attacks left many Sotho-speaking communities weakened and without the means for survival, but, under a Sotho leader named Moshoeshoe, the Basotho rallied and regrouped. King Moshoeshoe I is accredited as the founder of the Basotho nation, as he was fundamental in organizing the loosely federated southern Sotho communities to withstand the chaos of the early 1800s. Born in 1786, he was a member of a minor chiefly family of the Bakoena clan and was named Letlama, only earning the praise-name Moshoeshoe (meaning 'the one who shaves his enemy') as a result of his participation in daring cattle raids. An important early influence on Moshoeshoe was the diviner and political leader, Mohlomi, who lived amongst the Bakoena clan in the late 18th and early 19th century and attracted many disciples, including the young Letlama. Letlama was politically ambitious and wanted to achieve power, but was taught the principles of fairness and good leadership from Mohlomi. By the time of Mohlomi's death in 1815, Letlama had been named Moshoeshoe and had also forged links with many important families of the Bafokeng clan by marriage. By making such politically astute marriages, Moshoeshoe had managed to acquire a large number of supporters.

Moshoeshoe settled the mountain stronghold of Thaba-Bosiu in 1824 with a large group of Sotho-speakers. Further Sotho refugees were accepted into the community to live under Moshoeshoe's protection and leadership. The Bakoena and Bafokeng clans dominated this group of Sotho, and Moshoeshoe strengthened linkages with these and other groups through intermarriage. He also loaned cattle to destitute refugees and assisted them to marry, which traditionally required a certain amount of resources on the part of the man. Through these actions, Moshoeshoe ensured that his new subjects had the ability to provide for their own livelihoods, and at the same time developed strong ties of political allegiance.

Moshoeshoe was known for his diplomacy and fairness. In addition, he demonstrated considerable foresight, for example, in recognizing the potential of French missionaries as emissaries to the colonial authorities. In 1833, the first missionaries arrived in Lesotho, from the

Société de Missions Evangéliques in Paris. These missionaries assisted Moshoeshoe in his foreign relations, particularly in his appeals to the British government for protection against the encroachment of Dutch settlers, who began to settle in the south-western part of Moshoeshoe's domain in the 1840s. As an attempt to solve these boundary disputes, the Napier Treaty was drawn up in 1843 by the Governor of the Cape Colony and signed by Moshoeshoe. This Treaty represented an agreement on the boundaries of the Basotho nation between the colonial government of South Africa, settler farmers and King Moshoeshoe. However, it was subsequently broken by settler communities, who captured large tracts of land during wars with the Basotho in the 1860s.

Moshoeshoe's plea for Lesotho's protection as a British Colony was answered only in 1868 after much of the Basotho land had been lost to settlers. This territorial loss was confirmed by the 1869 Treaty of Aliwal North, in which the Free State retained fertile land to the west of the Caledon (Mohokare) river. From that time, the British considered Lesotho to be a colony, although the Basotho themselves considered the country to be a protectorate. The British decision to incorporate what they called Basutoland into their colonial empire appears to have been heavily influenced by their concern over the power of settlers in the region.

Moshoeshoe I died in 1870, having overseen these dramatic transitions. He left a people that had shown their ability to rapidly adapt to climatic and life-style differences, and who had shown great dynamism in doing so. During the 1870s, the establishment of diamond mines at the South African town of Kimberley provided a market for Basutoland's grain, as well as employment for many Basotho men. Colin Murray notes that in 1873, Basutoland exported 100,000 bags of grain and 2,000 bags of wool.

Unfortunately, the death of Moshoeshoe also emphasized serious divisions that existed among the Basotho over succession, religion and colonial allegiance. In 1880, a rebellion by Chief Moorosi, based in Basutoland's southern districts, was triggered by a series of disputes over the succession to King Moshoeshoe. These disputes were escalated by the transference of the country to the Cape Colony authorities in 1871. Moorosi's uprising was put down by Basotho troops, but only after the threat of further land confiscation by the Cape Colony if they did not. The Gun War, 1880-81, followed soon after and again was proof of conflict between the chiefs on the subject of colonial annexation. This war was precipitated by the Cape Parliament's attempt to implement the Peace Preservation Act in Basutoland. The Act required the disarmament of Africans and included not only guns, but also spears and assegais. At the same time, the Cape Parliament proposed the annexation of Lesotho's southern Quthing District. These proposals led to an uprising by many of Lesotho's chiefs, although some remained loyal to the Cape Colony. The war ended in stalemate and the disannexation of Basutoland from the Cape Colony. The colony was returned to direct British rule in 1884.

With the resumption of direct British rule, a less interventionist style of government was pursued. The British ruled indirectly through the chiefs and maintained Moshoeshoe's successors as the 'paramount chief'. For almost five decades, the only formal policy of administration was one of law and order. Almost no attention was paid to the development of the country or its people; on the whole, initiatives concerning education, health and agriculture were left to the churches.

It was only after 1935 that the British government began to invest more resources in Basutoland. Recognizing the limited ability to raise government revenue, a common customs union was created with South Africa, in which Basutoland received a proportion of the customs receipts collected in South Africa. These custom receipts included those collected on goods being imported into Basutoland, and to reflect this, a customs revenue sharing formula was developed. Net exports of maize continued until about 1920, but the boom years were over by the middle of the 1880s. This decline in agricultural exports was due to drought, the heavy taxes imposed on imports, competition from American and Australian grain, and the exhaustion of Lesotho's farmlands. Periods of severe natural disaster left large numbers of families destitute, and, between 1936 and 1957, more than 150,000 Basotho left Lesotho to settle in South Africa.

In 1952, many politically conscious Basotho joined a common independence movement, the Basotuland African Congress, which later changed its name to the Basotuland Congress Party (BCP). Political parties were first formally allowed in 1958. In the same year, a group of chiefs and commoners broke away from the BAC and formed the Basotuland National Congress (BNP). In the 1965, pre-independence elections, the BNP, headed by Chief Leabua Jonathan, won 50 per cent of parliamentary seats. In 1966, after nearly a century of British rule, Basutoland gained full independence as the Kingdom of Lesotho. A Westminster-style constitution was adopted, which placed the then Paramount Chief Moshoeshoe II as the constitutional monarch. Shortly after independence, a constitutional crisis ensued and King Moshoeshoe II had to accept a non-political role as a titular head of state with limited legislative powers. Since this period, the role of the monarch has remained controversial.

After independence in 1966, Lesotho followed a turbulent political path, being troubled by internal political dissent and external pressure from an apartheid South Africa. The results of elections held in 1970 were suppressed and the country was plunged into a state of emergency. The state of emergency was imposed by Chief Jonathan after election results showed that the BCP had won the majority of the vote. All opposition was crushed by force and the country thrown into turmoil.

In the immediate post-independence period, the BNP had close relations with South Africa. However, in 1976 Lesotho refused to recognize the newly created South African homeland of Transkei. From this point, Lesotho's relationship with South Africa deteriorated and the BNP developed close relations with many Eastern bloc countries. Greater opposition to apartheid brought Lesotho increasing amounts of international aid. However, it also precipitated a number of politically inspired incursions sponsored by the South African government, who accused the Lesotho government of harbouring outlawed African National Congress members. On 9 December 1982, South Africans launched a raid which killed 42 people in Maseru, many of whom were unrelated to the ANC. In late 1985, after a second raid in which nine people were killed, South Africa closed its borders with Lesotho. Lesotho's dependence on imported foodstuffs, petroleum and electricity placed it an economically fragile situation. In addition, the South African government threatened to deport Basotho working in South Africa.

Matters reached an impasse, until a military coup, motivated by these difficulties, overthrew the government early in 1986. Lesotho was ruled by a military government from the mid-1980s until 1993, when the first democratic elections were held since independence. In these elections, the BNP lost every constituency, despite having formed the government for twenty years since independence. The BCP were elected into power, with Dr Ntsu Mokhehle as prime minister.

The economy

Several characteristics of Lesotho's economy must be noted. The Gross National Product (GNP) is substantially larger than the Gross Domestic Product (GDP). In 1991, the real GNP (based on 1980 prices) was M657.3 million, while real GDP was M445.5 million. The gap between the two is largely accounted for by migrant remittances, and so this gap has narrowed in the last two decades due to the factors affecting migrant labour discussed above. The share of migrant remittances in Gross National Income has fallen from over 50 per cent in 1984/85 to approximately 40 per cent in 1992/93. Real GDP and GNP per capita grew rapidly in the late 1980s, due largely to an increase in small industries in the urban centres. Between 1985 and 1990, the average annual growth rates achieved were 5.5 per cent for real GDP and 2.1 per cent for real GNP. However, this growth slowed down in the early 1990s.

The annual inflation rate, which before 1970 was below 5 per cent, rose rapidly to 17 per cent in 1992. Inflation is effectively imported from South Africa and there is little effective control due to the need to keep the Lesotho currency, the Maloti, on a par with the South African Rand. Lesotho is a member of the Common Monetary Area, which links the currencies of Lesotho and Swaziland with the South African Rand. Thus, Lesotho's monetary policy is heavily influenced by events in South Africa. As a result of inflation, most salaries in the public sector are worth less today than they were in 1966.

There is widespread economic dependence on South Africa; about 95 per cent of Lesotho's imports come from South Africa, while over 55 per cent of exports are destined for there. Earlier, Lesotho's dependence on South African labour markets was noted. In addition, government income is dominated by receipts from the Southern African Customs Union, which provides for pooling of customs and excise duties for sharing among the member countries of South Africa, Lesotho, Botswana, Swaziland and Namibia. These receipts have accounted for more than 50 per cent of total Government revenue, excluding grants, in recent years.

Recent economic developments in Lesotho have been overwhelmingly negative. Not only has migrant employment fallen, but domestic production has been hard hit by a number of adverse factors. The impact of a world recession has reduced demand for Lesotho's exports. In the early 1990s, manufactured exports accounted for 74 per cent of total exports, compared to 31 per cent in 1986. This growth was driven by Lesotho's free access to the American and European Community markets. But it was precisely this openness that left Lesotho vulnerable to changes in its export markets.

Lesotho still has to recover from the droughts of 1990/91 and 1991/92, which greatly reduced agricultural output and increased rural poverty. However, it must be remembered that even in ordinary years, the population of Lesotho is no longer food self-sufficient on a household basis. A recent poverty mapping exercise used FAO standards of subsistence, and found that, on average, 81 per cent of households produced less than the minimum necessary for self-sufficiency. The situation was far worse in years of drought. The harvests of 1990/91 and 1991/92 were the worst for twenty years. Cereal crop production was 66,000 tons in 1990/91, compared to almost 240,000 in 1989/90. The effects of drought were worse in Lesotho's arid southern districts, which consistently experiences crop failures higher than elsewhere. A survey of drought conditions in 1992 found that the southern Lowlands and Foothills and the whole of the country's Mountain area did very poorly, with almost every sub-area showing between 90 per cent and 100 per cent of the households not meeting the subsistence criterion. In addition, cattle, sheep and goat holdings are particularly concentrated and to complicate matters there is a positive relationship between land and livestock holdings, with the largest herds/flocks occurring with the largest landholders. The Household Budget Survey found that 28 per cent of rural households had no poultry and 44 per cent had no cattle, goats or sheep.

These statistics illustrate the myth that Lesotho is an agricultural country. Despite its large rural population, the vast majority of households are dependent on wage employment, which has led to great concern about unemployment, poverty and welfare. The employment situation has deteriorated rapidly in the last few years, and the unemployment rate has risen to 36 per cent in 1992 from 23 per cent in 1985. However, skilled labour remains in short supply, worsened by labour outflows, and leads to bottlenecks in the economy.

The unemployment crisis illustrates the structural weakness of Lesotho's economy, as well as the vulnerability of Lesotho to external factors. In an effort to reduce this vulnerability and to restructure the economy, the government adopted a structural adjustment programme. The first Structural Adjustment Programme started in 1988, with the aim of improved revenue raising measures, tighter controls on government expenditure and efforts to revitalize the underlying economy. However, despite socio-economic problems, Lesotho has controlled its financial situation. The national debt has been kept under control, and the country has maintained a debt service ratio of 4.2 per cent of exports of goods and services, a ratio which is enviable among other developing countries. Broad balancing of Lesotho's balance of payments has been facilitated by migrant remittances and donor assistance.

In 1988, foreign aid per capita was the third highest among the low-income countries of the world, and this high rate of development assistance has continued in subsequent years. However, recent anecdotal evidence suggests that donors are moving their attention elsewhere, which seems to be due to political changes in the region and in the donor-countries. It is well-known that most First World countries are down-sizing their aid budgets. At the same time, there have been significant political changes in the region, with the move to democratically elected governments in both South Africa and Namibia. Lesotho, no longer a front-line state, is likely to find the international aid environment less welcoming in the future.

The bibliography

This bibliography attempts to be as comprehensive as possible. All works are in English and have been chosen with their worldwide availability in mind. This has led to the exclusion of some publications that are difficult to find, except where they are of lasting significance. As there are a limited number of recently published books, considerable attention has been paid to journal articles, university publications and government reports. A considerable amount of work published by Sechaba Consultants has been included in this bibliography, as it has been unique in covering certain topics or because it is particularly up-to-date. The work of Sechaba Consultants can be obtained at source from: Sechaba Consultants, Private Bag A84, Maseru 100, Lesotho. Individual entries have been arranged by subject and, within sections, entries have been cited alphabetically by title (ignoring the definite and indefinite article). Emphasis is on contemporary and 20th-century items and there has been particular attention to have a full coverage of the situation of women. A section is also included on literature, with a focus on works of literary and poetic criticism.

Standard Sesotho orthography has been used in annotations or descriptions. This is different to the orthography used for Sesotho in South Africa, and is also different to early usage, evident in spellings from the colonial period, such as: Basuto, Sesuto, etc. However, all titles have been reported as published. Sesotho has two commonly used diacritical marks. One is an apostrophe used before an initial 'm' or 'n' to indicate a deleted letter of the same kind. For example, the title used for women is 'me, meaning m-me. The second diacritic occurs in the aspirated 'ts' sound, written tš. It should also be noted that Sesotho contains some unusual pronunciations. Of particular importance is the pronunciation of the letters 'li' and 'lu' as 'di' and 'du'. A short glossary has been included, but generally explanations are given in the text.

Acknowledgements

Although I accept sole responsibility for any errors or omissions in this book, there are many individuals whose assistance was greatly appreciated. Of particular help were John Gay and David Hall, of Sechaba Consultants. Also of assistance was Philip Cole. Thanks must go to the library staff of the Institute of Southern African Studies, University of Lesotho. Lindy-Lou was of great assistance in negotiating with the libraries of the University of Witwatersrand. Particular thanks is given to Kevin Braim, whose support and assistance makes him a full partner in this bibliography.

Glossary

basotho	Collective noun for the people of Lesotho
kopano	Group, usually a self-help or religious group
lekhotla	Chief's court, comprising the chief, his advisors and village elders
letsema	Gathering for work, traditionally called by a chief
lifaqane	Period of social turbulence, war and cattle raiding in the early 19th century
lira	or *tšimo ea lira*, 'field of enemies'. This field was customarily the one used to provide food for the chief and his warriors in times of war
litema	Decorative patterns used on the walls of houses
lithoko	Praise poetry
Maloti	Mountainous area of central and eastern Lesotho
matsema	Plural of *letsema*
mosotho	Citizen of Lesotho
sesotho	Language of Lesotho, may also be used as an adjective referring to anything characteristic of the Basotho, e.g. *sesotho* music

Selected Theses and Dissertations on Lesotho

R. L. Betz. 'Organizing to help rural groups: income generation and rural development in the Third World', PhD thesis, University of Massachusetts, 1984.

A. Blair. 'Patterns of infant care in Lesotho', PhD thesis, University of Nottingham, 1989.

Joe William Carvalho. 'Agriculture and economic development in Lesotho: analysis using a social accounting matrix', PhD thesis, Washington State University, 1988.

L. B. Cobbe. 'Women's income generation and informal learning in Lesotho: a policy-related ethnography', PhD thesis, Florida State University, 1985.

Elizabeth A. Eldredge. 'An Economic History of Lesotho in the Nineteenth Century', PhD thesis, University of Wisconsin, Madison, Wisconsin, 1986.

Judith S. Gay. 'Basotho women's options: a study of marital careers in rural Lesotho', PhD thesis, University of Cambridge, England, 1980.

P. Graham. 'Incorporating nutrition into agricultural development projects: a model and case study', PhD thesis, Colorado State University, 1988.

Judy Kimble. 'Migrant labour and colonial rule in Southern Africa: the case of Basutoland, 1870-1930', PhD thesis, University of Essex, 1985.

Steven W. Lawry. 'Private herds and common land: issues in the management of communal grazing land in Lesotho, Southern Africa', PhD thesis, University of Wisconsin, Madison, 1988.

M. L. Maxwell. 'Innovations in teacher education in developing countries: a case study', PhD thesis, University of Massachusetts, 1983.

R. I. M. Moletsane. 'Complementary functions of formal and non-formal education in Lesotho', PhD thesis, University of Massachusetts, 1977.

R. I. M. Moletsane. 'A literary appreciation and analysis of collected and documented Basotho miners' poetry', Master's Dissertation, University of the Orange Free State, South Africa, 1982.

Colin Murray. 'Keeping house in Lesotho', PhD thesis, University of Cambridge, England, 1976.

Timothy Kevin Charles Quinlan. '*Marena a Lesotho*: chiefs, policies and culture in Lesotho', PhD thesis, University of Cape Town, South Africa, 1975.

R. E. Rodman. 'Educative and empowering development: comparative case studies for four rural Basotho communities participating in an alternative development approach in Lesotho', PhD thesis, Georgia State University, College of Education, Georgia, 1984.

Mafa Sejanamane. 'Security and small states: the political economy of Lesotho's foreign policy – 1966-1985', PhD thesis, Dalhousie University, Halifax, Canada, 1987.

E. K. Thaele-Rivkin. 'Women in national development in a predominantly female population: the case of Lesotho', PhD thesis, Syracuse University, 1990.

Caroline Wright. 'Unemployment, migration and changing gender relations in Lesotho', PhD thesis, University of Leeds, 1993.

The Country and Its People

1 **The guide to Lesotho.**

David P. Ambrose. Johannesburg: Winchester Press, 1974. 2nd ed. 370p. maps.

Intended for both visitors and residents, this book includes an extensive general description, covering geography, geology, climate, flora, fauna, population, language, history, village life, the agricultural cycle, and other topics. Hotels and other forms of accommodation are listed, and there are extensive sections on each of the towns and districts. Itineraries along main roads and mountain tracks are described, together with several mountain climbs. Other sections cover government, chieftainship, the economy, bird watching and numerous other topics more briefly. Despite its age, this book will continue to be useful to the traveller and researcher alike. For more detailed information, see the series of Oxfam guides written by the same author. Individual guides cover: *Ha Khotso rock paintings and the Mountain Road* (1966, revised 1969, 1972); *Roma* (1966, revised 1971); *Butha-Buthe District* (1967); *Ramabanta's* (1967); *Mohale's Hoek District* (1969); *Qacha's Nek District* (1969); *Semonkong* (1970); *Mokhotlong District* (1970); *Mafeteng District* (1971); *Maseru* (1973); and *Teyateyaneng and Berea District* (1974), all published in Roma, Lesotho, by the University of Botswana, Lesotho and Swaziland.

2 **Lesotho.**

A. Oberholzer. *Prisma*, vol. 7, no. 3 (March 1992), p. 6-11.

A non-academic overview of the country and its history. The author provides a short discussion of the economic situation, with particular emphasis on agriculture and crafts.

3 **Lesotho.**

Dirk Schwager, Colleen Schwager. Cape Town: Schwager, 1986. 3rd ed. 141p. bibliog. 1 map.

A photographic essay on Lesotho, which provides a short history and information on geography, economy, agriculture, religion and tourism. These sections will be useful for the general reader but are of varying standard. While the historical overview is well written, the section on economics is too brief and weak on migrant labour, and some of the information on industry and tourism outdated. However, these deficiencies are overshadowed by the excellent colour photographs of both landscapes, including mountain ranges and national parks, and people.

4 **Lesotho's long journey: hard choices at the crossroads.**

Sechaba Consultants. Maseru: Sechaba Consultants, Irish Aid, 1995. 207p. 4 maps. bibliog.

An ambitious report that reviews the history of Lesotho, present-day conditions and scenarios for the future. For quick reference, the report has been organized into stand-alone topics, such as 'Land Use', 'Social Services' and 'The Economy'. It contains recent data and up-to-date information on economic and political trends. For this reason, it is invaluable for all readers interested in events since the decline of migrancy and the return to democracy. It makes a particularly good attempt at analysing the situation of women in terms of custom and the law. The section on donor aid draws together rarely seen information on the magnitude of aid and its uses. This is a good, general knowledge text, aimed particularly at a non-academic readership.

5 **A short history of Lesotho: from the late Stone Age until the 1993 elections.**

Stephen J. Gill. Morija, Lesotho: Morija Museum and Archives, 1993. 266p. bibliog. 16 maps.

An excellent history of Lesotho, which will be useful for those interested in the country's past and present. It is the first comprehensive history of Lesotho to be published for forty years and includes over eighty illustrations to assist the reader. Chapter one discusses the settlement of Southern Africa from the first Iron Age, c.200 AD. Chapter two examines Sotho culture, politics and spiritual understanding. Chapter three discusses the unification of the Sotho under Moshoeshoe I in the 19th century. Chapters four and five look at the colonial period and the growing incorporation and dependence of Lesotho. Chapter six analyses the period between independence and the 1993 elections. The book concludes with an assessment of the future challenges facing the nation.

Geography

General

6 **Agroclimatology of Lesotho.**
G. C. Wilken. Fort Collins, Colorado: Colorado State University, Department of Economics, Lesotho Agricultural Sector Analysis Program, 1978. 31p. bibliog. 2 maps. (Discussion Paper, no. 1).

The author describes the characteristics of agroclimatology in Lesotho, including temperature, rainfall and wind. Particular attention is paid to environmental hazards and climatic risk. Recommendations are also made for future agroclimatic research.

7 **Climatological Bulletin.**
Maseru: Ministry of Works, Hydrological and Meteorological Services Branch, Jan. 1975- . monthly.

Contains observations on rainfall and temperature, together with occasional information on other climatological factors. While useful in the assessment of climatic trends, this publication is likely to be of interest primarily to the specialist researcher.

8 **Global climate change and agricultural productivity in Southern Africa.**
R. E. Schulze, G. A. Kiker, R. P. Kunz. *Global Environmental Change*, vol. 3, no. 4 (1993), p. 330-49.

This article embarks on a regional food security study, covering South Africa, Lesotho and Swaziland. The study begins with the contention that crop production will have to expand at three per cent per annum until the year 2035 to keep pace with food demand. The authors map the distributions and inter-annual variabilities of maize yields, as well as the distributions for future climate scenarios. These scenarios are developed to simulate changes in carbon dioxide, solar radiation, temperature, evaporation and precipitation. The results of modelling climate change show a large dependence on rainfall and its seasonal variation. The overall effect of an increase in both temperature and carbon dioxide was to increase the efficiency of water use by maize and to increase yields in some areas.

9 **Land capability guide to safe land use and crop suitability ratings for Lesotho.**

Ministry of Agriculture. Maseru: Ministry of Agriculture Conservation Division, 1977. 62p.

A list of land capability units divided into eight broad classes. Each land capability unit is a geographic area of similar soil potential. In this case, the units were categorized according to soil erosion risk, soil drainage, soil quality and length of growing season. Each unit is also rated on a four-point scale for twelve common Lesotho crops. The guide was developed through group participation by representatives of the Crop Division, Conservation Division, Thaba-Bosiu Rural Development Project, Thaba-Tseka Project and Senqu Project.

10 **The land resources of Lesotho.**

M. C. Bawden, D. M. Carroll. Tolworth, England: Land Resources Division, Directorate of Overseas Surverys, 1968. 89p. maps. (Land Resource Study, no. 3).

Discusses the physical and human aspects of Lesotho's environment. The report divides the country into twenty-seven 'land systems' and into seven areas on the basis of agricultural potential. It contains numerous plates and maps and also three separate maps (scale – 1:250,000) in an endpaper folder, showing land systems, soils and agricultural potential.

11 **Lesotho: a geographical study.**

P. Smit. Pretoria: Africa Institute, 1967. 44p. maps. bibliog.

A thorough geographical study, accompanied by several maps, and divided into separate sections on physical background, population, agriculture and land use. The section on population includes details of population changes since 1891, and calculations of the percentage of migrant labourers. Under agriculture and land use, there is consideration of erosion, land use, crop yields and stock farming together with shorter sections on mining and industries, communications and water resources.

12 **Rainfall oscillations in Lesotho and the possible impact of drought in the 1980s.**

J. B. Eckert. Fort Collins, Colorado: Colorado State University, Department of Economics, Lesotho Agricultural Sector Analysis Program, 1980. 20p. bibliog. (Discussion Paper, no. 10).

This report hypothesizes that there is a twenty-year drought cycle in Lesotho. It then makes a number of recommendations concerning government action for drought-readiness, which include the development of research programmes focusing on improved water management, as well as legal initiatives surrounding water rights.

Maps and atlases

13 **Atlas for Lesotho.**
David P. Ambrose, J. W. B. Perry. Johannesburg: Collins Longman Atlases, 1973. 72p. maps.

This general atlas also contains three pages of maps showing special features of Lesotho including: population; rainfall; and land use and agriculture.

14 **Lesotho/Maseru map.**
Maseru; Pinetown, South Africa: Braby, 1993. 1 sheet. 2 maps.

This map includes both a map of Lesotho and of Maseru. The latter includes a street index. Road types and places of interest are also denoted.

Geology

15 **Dolerite dykes in Basutoland with special reference to the geomorphological effects of the dykes and their economic significance.**

Louis Meijs. Roma, Lesotho: Pius XII College, Papers no. 1, 1960. 54p. bibliog.

Describes the geomorphology of the dykes and their economic importance. The latter includes the use of dykes as pathways up the mountain slopes, the use of dolerite as a road-surfacing material, and the possibilities of dam-building with the dyke as a foundation.

16 **Report on the geology of Basutoland.**

Edited by G. M. Stockley. Maseru: Basutoland Government, 1947. 114p. 1 map.

A report on the first systematic geological survey made in 1938-40, whose publication was delayed by the Second World War. As well as a detailed discussion of each of the beds in the geological succession, there are also sections on economic geology (including coal, kimberlite, water supply, and agriculture), and on palaeontology (by L. D. Boonstraand and W. B. Edwards). Among the appendices is one by T. B. Kennan on place-names and their meaning.

17 **Secondary mineral zonation in the Drakensberg Basalt Formation, South Africa.**

J. N. Dunlevey, V. R. Ramluckan, A. A. Mitchell. *South African Journal of Geology*, vol. 96, no. 4 (December 1993), p. 215-20.

The authors report on the secondary minerals present in the Drakensberg Formation at the Sani Pass, which forms the border of Lesotho and South Africa. Information on the composition of these basaltic lavas is presented in both statistical and diagrammatic fashion. This article will appeal to the specialist researcher in geology.

18 **Short general report on the geology of the extreme northern and north-eastern portion of Basutoland.**
F. A. Venter. In: *An ecological survey of the mountain area of Basutoland.* Edited by R. R. Staples, W. K. Hudson. London: Crown Agents for the Colonies, 1938, p. 47-56.

This report appears as Annexure A to the Staples and Hudson report. Analyses of rocks and soils are given and there is some speculation about mineral deposits.

Tourism and Travel Guides

General

19 **Southern Africa, Lesotho and Swaziland: a travel survival kit.**
Richard Everist, Jon Murray. Hawthorn, Australia; Oakland, California; London; Paris: Lonely Planet Publications, 1993. 558p. 2 maps (Lesotho).

Twenty-four pages of this publication are devoted to Lesotho, including a brief but accurate history and a useful language guide. Detailed information is provided on major towns and there is a selection of colour photographs. In addition, the book contains a short guide to flora and fauna in the region.

20 **Southern Africa on a budget: the essential guide for the adventurous traveller.**
Jennifer Stern. Cape Town: Struik, 1994. 368p. 2 maps (Lesotho).

Offers twenty pages on Lesotho, including sections on outdoor sports, accommodation for the budget traveller and information on the Sesotho language. This is generally a helpful guide, although the information on the major towns is somewhat limited.

21 **Visitor's guide to Lesotho: how to get there, what to see, where to stay.**
Marco Turco. Halfway House, South Africa: Southern Book Publishers, 1994. 192p. 1 map.

A tourist guide to Lesotho, giving a description of the country and sites of interest. The book begins with a twenty-six page information guide on: health; security; cost; documentation and customs regulations; and issues affecting the female traveller. Other sections cover: travel to and within Lesotho; Maseru; historial sites; areas of natural beauty; and activities such as pony-trekking and hiking. This is a useful guide; however, some of the information on shops and hotels is outdated, and the inclusion of photographs would have improved the publication.

Colonial guides and travellers' accounts

22 **Andrew Smith's journal of his expedition into the interior of South Africa, 1834-1836: an authentic narrative of travels and discoveries, the manners and customs of the native tribes, and the physical nature of the country.**

Edited by William F. Lye. Cape Town: Balkema for South African Museum, 1975. 323p. 1 map.

Written between 20 July 1834 and 3 July 1835, this journal was first published in its present form only in 1975. Andrew Smith trained as a doctor and was sent to South Africa in 1821 by the British Army. At the time, the Cape authorities knew little about the interior of the territory, and, in 1832, the South African Literary and Scientific Institution began preparations for an expedition under the directorship of Smith. The expedition, consisting of forty members, set out in August 1834 and returned in January 1836. The party spent some time with Moshoeshoe, the founder of Lesotho, and Casalis, a pioneer missionary to the area, and the author comments on Moshoeshoe's character and describes Morija and Thaba-Bosiu. The publication concludes with an excellent annotated index, and contains several sketches of the countryside and people.

23 **The High Commission Territories in South Africa: Pt. II Basutoland.**

Sir John Houlton. *Geographical Magazine*, vol. 26, no. 3 (July 1953), p. 132-38. 1 map.

Sir John Houlton was a senior British civil servant, with a distinguished career in India. He travelled widely in Southern Africa shortly before this article was published. The purpose of his visit appears to have been to assess the potential for independence of the three British territories in the region: Basutoland, Swaziland and Bechuanaland. The article provides a general account of Lesotho's history, starting from its origins in the *lifaqane* period. Written in a popular style, it covers British attitudes towards the country, its social structure and its economy. A number of black-and-white photographs of the landscape and people are included.

24 **Missionary excursion.**

Thomas Arbousset, edited and translated by David Ambrose, Albert Brutsch. Morija, Lesotho: Morija Museum and Archives, 1991. 219p. maps.

This previously unpublished manuscript describes a trip taken from Thaba-Bosiu to the Maliba-matso river basin in 1840 by Moshoeshoe and Arbousset, a pioneer missionary. David Ambrose and Albert Brutsch have translated and edited this travelogue, which now also includes numerous illustrations, maps and notes.

25 **A narrative of a visit to the Mauritius and South Africa.**
James Backhouse. York, England: Linney, 1844. 2 vols.

Contains a valuable account of a visit by two members of the Society of Friends, James Backhouse and George Washington Walker, to Lesotho in 1839. The narrative includes descriptions of the country at the time, encounters with wild animals, etc. The author attended the funeral of one of Moshoeshoe's wives, who was buried according to Christian rites, much against the wishes of the tribe, but on the orders of Moshoeshoe himself.

26 **A tour in South Africa.**
J. J. Freeman. London: John Snow, 1851. 492p. 1 map.

Freeman includes a detailed account of visits to Thaba-Bosiu and Morija, in a work which devotes some fifty pages to Lesotho and the Conquered Territory. The map of the Orange River Sovereignty shows the boundaries between chiefs.

27 **Twelve hundred miles in a waggon.**
Alice Blanche Balfour. London: Arnold, 1896. 265p. maps.

Pages 40-59, entitled 'Journey to Basutoland', include a description of visits to Maseru, Berea, Roma and Masopha's village, in 1894. The work also includes illustrations of *dongas* (soil erosion) at Berea and Qiloane and of Basotho riding on oxen.

The guide to Lesotho.
See item no. 1.

A backpackers guide to Lesotho.
See item no. 522.

Fauna and Flora

Fauna

28 **The amphibia of Southern Africa.**

J. C. Poynton. *Annals of the Natal Museum*, vol. 17 (Nov. 1964), p. 1-334.

Includes illustrations, distribution maps and extensive discussion and references. Of the 127 forms described, 6 toads and 13 frogs are recorded for Lesotho.

29 **Animals of Lesotho: snakes of Lesotho.**

T. Sohl Thelejane. *Lesotho: Basutoland Notes and Records*, vol. 5 (1965-66), p. 32-40.

This article begins with a general discussion, followed by a check-list of snakes found in Lesotho. Sixteen species are recorded, of which thirteen had been collected personally by the author. Sesotho names are included, as well as recorded localities and other notes for each species.

30 **Birds of Lesotho: a guide to distribution past and present.**

Kurt Bond. Pietermaritzburg, South Africa: University of Natal Press, 1993. 108p. bibliog. 8 maps.

A guide to the historical and current status of bird species in Lesotho. This is the most recent guide of its kind and includes detailed directions to good bird-watching sites. Bond has also compiled a comprehensive bibliography on the subject, presenting publication details and, occasionally, annotations.

31 **Catalogue of the birds of Basutoland.**
Charles Frédéric Jacot-Guillarmod. Cape Town: Percy Fitzpatrick Institute of African Ornithology, 1963. 111p. (South African Avifauna Series, no. 8).

The standard list of the birds of Lesotho, based particularly on the observations of Charles Jacot-Guillarmod ('Mamathe's area), Walter P. Stanford (Lowland and Qacha's Nek) and Gordon Maclean (Maloti). For each of 258 birds, the family, genus, species and race are given, together with Sesotho name and notes on distribution. A supplement, adding ten new species, was edited by J. P. Murray and J. M. Winterbottom: *Some MS notes on Basutoland birds* (Cape Town: Percy Fitzpatrick Institute of African Ornithology, 1964. 10p. [South African Avifauna Series, no. 21]).

32 **The fish of the Orange River.**
R. A. Jubb. *Civil Engineer in South Africa*, vol. 14, no. 2 (Feb. 1972), p. 89-93.

Jubb provides a systematic list of species of both indigenous and exotic fish inhabiting the headwaters of the Orange River, together with detailed information about each one.

33 **Garden birds of Southern Africa.**
Peter Ginn, Geoff McIlleron. Ferreirasdorp, South Africa: Chris van Rensburg Publications, 1980. 52p.

Identifies garden birds in the region, including a number which are present in Lesotho. Unfortunately, no distribution maps have been compiled.

34 **More garden birds of Southern Africa.**
Peter Ginn, Geoff McIlleron. Ferreirasdorp, South Africa: Chris van Rensburg Publications, 1981. 52p.

A companion to item no. 33, this book contains additional information on garden birds in the region. Distribution maps are not provided.

35 **A preliminary fish survey of the Caledon River system.**
R. D. Marshall. *Civil Engineer in South Africa*, vol. 14, no. 2 (Feb. 1972), p. 96-97.

This brief article lists seven species of fish from thirteen collecting sites, four of which are located on the Lesotho border.

36 **Reptile fauna of the Katse Dam catchment area and a biogeographical assessment of species composition in the Lesotho Highlands.**
P. Mouton, J. H. van Wyk. *Koedoe*, vol. 36, no. 1 (1993), p. 67-78.

A survey of reptile fauna in the Katse Dam catchment area, in northern Lesotho. The Katse Dam is part of the Lesotho Highlands Water Project area and an assessment is made of reptile species composition in this area. The authors make some suggestions on the possible impact of the dam on reptile fauna once it is full.

37 **Waterbirds of Southern Africa.**
Peter Ginn, Geoff McIlleron. Ferreirasdorp, South Africa: Chris van Rensburg Publications, 1982. 143p.

Identifies a number of Southern African waterbirds and presents some distribution maps.

Flora

38 **The aloes of South Africa.**
Gilbert Westacott Reynolds. Johannesburg: Trustees [of] The Aloes of South Africa Book Fund, 1950. 520p. maps. bibliog.; Cape Town: Balkema, 1974. 2nd ed. 534p. maps.

This *magnum opus* contains much historical information on early botanical explorers and includes descriptions of the aloe species of Lesotho. The first edition includes seventy-seven colour plates, but these are reproduced in black-and-white in the second edition. Pages 194-96 on *Aloe polyphylla* (Spiral Aloe) comprise a drawing and photographs, including one of Maphotong village, Roma valley.

39 **The bogs and sponges of the Basutoland mountains.**
Amy Jacot-Guillarmod. *South African Journal of Science*, vol. 58, no. 6 (June 1962), p. 179-82. bibliog.

Describes the plant life of peat bogs and hillside seepage areas.

40 **Botanical exploration in Basutoland.**
Amy Jacot-Guillarmod. *South African Journal of Science*, vol. 63, no. 3 (March 1967), p. 81-83.

Jacot-Guillarmod presents the history of plant collectors in Lesotho, the present location of their collections and a list of their publications.

41 **Classification of the eastern alpine vegetation of Lesotho.**
C. D. Morris, N. M. Tainton, S. Boleme. *African Journal of Range and Forage Science*, vol. 10, no. 1 (April 1993), p. 47-53.

Reports on the botanical composition of vegetation communities in the alpine catchments of Lesotho. Five such communities were analysed using botanical data and the authors conclude that they represent particular topographical positions. This article presents a wide variety of both statistical and diagrammatic information, and will be useful for the specialist researcher.

42 **A contribution to the flora of the Leribe Plateau and environs with a discussion of the floras of Basutoland, the Kalahari and the South-Eastern regions.**

E. P. Phillips. *Annals of the South African Museum*, vol. 16, no. 1 (June 1917), p. 1-379.

For a long time the standard publication on the flora of Lesotho, this work is based on a collection made over a period of nineteen years by Mme Dieterien at Leribe Mission. In his introduction, Phillips proposes an Eastern mountain region to include Lesotho and its immediate surroundings. The plant species of this region are listed, including complete descriptions of forty-one new species. For all species, where possible, the Sesotho name is given together with its meaning and the local uses of the plant.

43 **Flora of Lesotho (Basutoland).**

Amy Jacot-Guillarmod. Lehre, German Federal Republic: J. Cramer, 1971. 474p. bibliog. (Flora et Vegetatio Mundi, vol. 3).

A standard work which covers history, topography, climate and ecology. There are also notes on early collectors, a gazetteer, and an analysis of the flora by genus and species. The main check-list of flora, which is unillustrated and without a key, is followed by a glossary of scientific names to Sesotho and vice versa. An extensive section covers the use of plants, and an 188-item list of references cites most publications on the botany of Lesotho.

44 **Flora of Southern Africa: the genera of Southern African flowering plants. vol. 1: Dicotyledons. vol. 2: Gymnosperms and Monocotyledons.**

R. Allen Dyer. Pretoria: Department of Agricultural Technical Services, 1975-76. 1,040p.

This is now a standard work, covering the flora of Lesotho and consisting of each genus grouped under families. Volume two of Dyer's work was completed with the assistance of A. Amelia (Obermeyer) Mauve, A. E. Loxton and P. Goldblatt. In addition to the two volumes, there is a separately published sixty-page *Key to families and Index to the genera of Southern African flowering plants*, published in 1977. The key is intended for students and herbarium workers. Pages 31-60 of the key are a reprint of the index at the back of the main work.

45 **The Forest Arboretum of trees and shrubs of Lesotho: notes on the establishment of species represented, together with field records of their present occurrence and growth potential in Lesotho.**

E. D. May. Maseru: Ministry of Agriculture, Forestry Division, 1992. 2nd ed. 86p.

The forest arboretum was established in late 1989. This publication provides descriptions of species present and their prevalence and growth prospects. Both Sesotho and Latin names for trees and shrubs are included.

46 **Grasses of southern Africa: an identification manual with keys, descriptions, classification and automated identification and information retrieval from computerized data.**
Edited by O. A. Leistner. Pretoria: Botanical Research Institute, 1990. 437p. maps.

Contains information on grasses in the region. Details are presented on the species of Lesotho grasses, although Sesotho names are not provided.

47 **Notes on *Aloe polyphylla*.**
Amy Jacot-Guillarmod. *Lesotho: Basutoland Notes and Records*, vol. 8 (1969), p. 30-36.

A description of the spiral aloe, a plant which is found only in Lesotho. Instructions for growing the plant from seed are included.

48 **Some medicinal, magic and edible plants of Lesotho.**
Mary Nthoana Tau. *Lesotho: Lesotho Notes and Records*, vol. 9 (1970-71), p. 13-19.

Includes photographs of forty-six species of plants, together with their species and Sesotho names, and a description of their use in traditional diet, herbalism or magic.

49 **Trees of Southern Africa covering all known indigenous species in the Republic of South Africa, South-West Africa, Botswana, Lesotho and Swaziland.**
Eve Palmer, Norah Pitman. Cape Town: A. A. Balkema, 1972. 3 vols.

The standard work on trees in the area of Southern Africa. Of approximately 1,000 trees described and illustrated, some 40 are from Lesotho. Information provided includes Sesotho names and medicinal uses.

50 **Veld types of South Africa with accompanying veld type map.**
J. P. H. Acocks. Pretoria: Botanical Research Institute; Department of Agricultural Technical Services, 1975. 2nd ed. 128p. maps, (Memoirs of the Botanical Survey of South Africa, no. 40).

Acocks describes and illustrates four veld types for Lesotho. The work includes six maps, one of which, with a scale of 1:1,500,000, is separate from the text, in the endpapers.

Prehistory and Archaeology

51 **The archaeology of Tloutle rock-shelter, Maseru District, Lesotho.**
P. J. Mitchell. *Navorsinge Van Die Nasionale Museum Bloemfontein*, vol. 9, no. 4 (1993), p. 77-128.

The results of an archaeological research programme in western Lesotho. This work establishes a cultural-stratigraphic sequence for the Later Stone Age of this part of southern Africa and provides a basis from which to investigate the land-use and social systems of Holocene hunter-gatherers in this area. The results of the excavation of the Tloutle rock-shelter are reported here in detail. Interpretations are offered for the use of the site and the Tloutle sequence is compared with others from adjacent parts of southern Africa.

52 **Iron Age communities of the southern highveld.**
T. M. O. C. Maggs. Pietermaritzburg, South Africa: Council of the Natal Museum, 1976. 326p.

Based on a University of Cape Town doctoral thesis, in which settlements between the Senqu (Orange) and Vaal rivers are classified into four main types by features visible in aerial photographs. Detailed excavations of seven sites are described. The remaining chapters include background material and analysis of the results, with frequent references to the history of Basotho clans and to modern Basotho village life.

53 **Moshebi's Shelter: excavation and exploitation in eastern Lesotho.**
P. L. Carter. *Lesotho: Basutoland Notes and Records*, vol. 8 (1969), p. 13-23.

The excavation in the late 1960s at a painted site near Sehlabathebe (Qacha's Nek district) yielded both Late and Middle Stone Age deposits. The article also describes possible Late Stone Age population distribution in the area and a map shows the location of nearly 100 painted sites. Also on excavations in eastern Lesotho, see: *The dating of industrial assemblages from stratified sites in Eastern Lesotho*, by P. L. Carter, J. C. Vogel (*Man* [UK], vol. 9 [1974], p. 557-70).

54 **New radiocarbon dates from Sehonghong rock shelter, Lesotho.**
P. J. Mitchell, J. C. Vogel. *South African Journal of Science*, vol. 90, no. 5 (May 1994), p. 284-88.

This study contains radiocarbon dates on excavations at the Sehonghong rock shelter in eastern Lesotho. The authors review earlier information on the site and investigate its cultural stratigraphy.

55 **Ntloana Tsoana: a Middle Stone Age sequence from western Lesotho.**
P. J. Mitchell, J. M. Steinberg. *South African Archaeological Bulletin*, vol. 47, no. 155 (June 1992), p. 26-33.

A report on Middle Stone Age assemblages from western Lesotho. The authors provide comparisons with similar assemblages in eastern Lesotho.

56 **Recent Holocene archaeology in Western and Southern Lesotho.**
P. J. Mitchell, R. Yates. *South African Archaeological Bulletin*, vol. 49, no. 159 (June 1994), p. 33-52.

Provides the results of excavations at four small rock shelters in Lesotho, dated to the second half of the Holocene period. There are significant differences in settlement patterns between the early and late Holocene. The authors consider the evidence for interaction between hunter-gatherers and agro-pastoralists.

57 **Revisiting the Robberg: new results and a revision of old ideas at the Sehonghong rock shelter, Lesotho.**
P. J. Mitchell. *South African Archaeological Bulletin*, vol. 50, no. 161 (June 1995), p. 28-38.

The Sehonghong rock shelter in eastern Lesotho is a key site for understanding the late Pleistocene period. This paper describes artefact assemblages discovered from excavations conducted in 1992. The evidence suggests a shift in site use from a hunting station to a home base.

58 **A tentative history of Lesotho palaeontology.**
David Ambrose. *NUL Journal of Research*, Occasional Publication no. 1, 1991. 38p. bibliog. 1 map.

Lesotho's importance to palaeontology derives from the wealth and relative accessibility of its fossil remains. These reveal important events in evolutionary history and a large number of scientific articles have been devoted to them. Ambrose cites a selection of the most important of these articles and presents the history of palaeontological discovery.

History

General

59 **The Basutos; the mountaineers and their country; being a narrative of events relating to the tribe from its formation early in the nineteenth century to the present day.**

Sir Godfrey Lagden. London: Hutchinson, 1909. 2 vols. 9 maps.

A painstaking, well-written and sympathetic history of Lesotho until 1909, dealing in detail with the 19th-century wars, border disputes and negotiations. The author was in Lesotho from 1880 until 1901 and for the last eight of these years was Resident Commissioner. The book contains seventy photographs, and is one of the best sources of published photographic material for this early period.

60 **From granary to labour reserve: an economic history of Lesotho.**

Colin Murray. *South African Labour Bulletin*, vol. 6, no. 4 (1980), p. 3-20.

Describes broad historical changes in the economy and society of Lesotho. Murray presents information on Lesotho's transformation from a dynamic, agricultural economy to a labour reservoir for South Africa. Presently, a large number of citizens of Lesotho migrate to find employment in South Africa, due to a lack of local job opportunities and a decline in the quantity and quality of agricultural land in Lesotho. Murray argues that this process of impoverishment accompanied and was engendered by the enrichment of white settlers in South Africa. On the same subject, Murray has also written *From granary to labour reserve: an analysis of Lesotho's economic predicament* (Cambridge, England: Cambridge University, 1976. 38p. mimeo.).

61 **The rise of the Basuto.**

Geoffrey Tylden. Cape Town: Juta, 1950. 270p. 1 map. bibliog.

A standard work covering the period 1824-1950, which is particularly detailed on military history. The author discusses the initial settlement by Moshoeshoe of the area that is now Lesotho. The wars over territory and the boundary disputes of the mid-

19th century are chronicled, and particular attention is paid to the colonial dispute of the 1870s onwards. During this period a number of disputes occurred over succession and colonial allegiance, discussed here in the context of overall political and social changes. Tylden lived and worked in the country for many years and writes knowledgeably of the terrain and the people.

62 **Transformations on the Highveld: the Tswana and Southern Sotho.**
William F. Lye, Colin Murray. Cape Town: David Philip; Totowa, New Jersey: Barnes & Noble Books; London: Global Book Resources, 1980. 158p. bibliog.

A history of the Tswana and Southern Sotho. Murray and Lye discuss the historical transformation of these ethnic groupings into the former 'homeland' areas of South Africa and the modern-day states of Lesotho and Botswana. Chapters two and three discuss the emergence of the Sotho states. The next three chapters consider the political and economic changes that occurred in response to the arrival of settlers and the imposition of colonialism. Two chapters are devoted to Sotho kinship structures and ritual belief. The final chapter deals with the contemporary economic predicament of the Sotho people.

Early history

63 **History of the Basuto: ancient and modern.**
D. Frederic Ellenberger, translated by J. C. Macgregor. Morija, Lesotho: Morija Museum and Archives, 1992. rev. ed. 394p. 1 map.

A facsimile reprint of the original 1912 edition, which is a standard reference work concerning the history of the Basotho from earliest times until 1833. It covers the pre-*lifaqane* and *lifaqane* periods, based on reports of eye-witnesses, oral traditions and historical records, and also discusses the origins of Basotho clans. This edition contains supplementary materials by Stephen J. Gill: 'The life and work of D. F. Ellenberger'; 'Reconstructing the history of the Basotho'; and 'A review of the settlement of Southern Africa'. Originally written as a French manuscript by D. F. Ellenberger, the book was translated, with considerable freedom, by his son-in-law J. C. Macgregor: *History of the Basuto: ancient and modern* (London: Caxton, 1912; New York: Negro Universities Press, 1969. 396p.).

64 **The Sotho-Tswana peoples before 1800.**
Martin Legassick. In: *African societies in South Africa: historical studies.* Edited by Leonard Thompson. London: Heinemann, 1969, p. 86-125. maps.

Includes maps of the distribution of the Sotho-Tswana people before 1500, in the 16th to 18th centuries and around 1800. This paper deals with these periods in the history of the Sotho-Tswana people, during which there was a great deal of population movement and social change. In particular, there was expansion to the south and west. Legassick sets the stage for the subsequent period of chaos and warfare, known as the *lifaqane*.

Kingdom of Moshoeshoe I (1824-70)

65 **Basutoland records.**

George McCall Theal. Cape Town: W. A. Richards, 1883. 3 vols. Reprinted, Cape Town: Struik, 1964. 3 vols. maps. bibliog.

Contains 2,194 documents and letters on the period 1833-68, providing a useful history of that time. Three subsequent volumes, which cover the period 1868 and 1869, were never printed but exist in manuscript form at the archives in Cape Town. Each volume covers a particular period, and the introductions to each volume contain useful summaries of these periods. The reprint contains a biographical sketch of Theal by R. F. M. Immelman, a bibliography of Theal's works and a forty-page index.

66 **An economic history of Lesotho in the nineteenth century.**

Elizabeth A. Eldredge. PhD thesis, University of Wisconsin, Madison, Wisconsin, 1986. 403p.

Presents detailed evidence on the Basotho economy in the 19th century. This is a significant achievement and Eldredge uses some imaginative and otherwise obscure sources. The study diverges from other historical economic work by analysing broader trends rather than concentrating solely on the interaction between European and African society. Instead she places 19th-century political and economic change within a longer process of evolution, beginning her analysis with the relations between the Sesotho-speaking peoples and their Tswana and Nguni neighbours in the 17th century. This thesis and its bibliography will be extremely useful for those investigating the early economy of the area that is now Lesotho.

67 **History of the Basutus of South Africa.**

Joseph Millerd Orpen. Cape Town: Saul Solomon, 1857. 143p.

The first published history of the Basotho from 1815 until 1857. Orpen based the history in part on the collection of official correspondence kept by Moshoeshoe at Thaba-Bosiu, and the work is very sympathetic to the Basotho cause. Although the book was originally published anonymously, the author's identity soon became well-known; Orpen was arrested at Smithfield in March 1858 and deported from the Orange Free State.

68 **The passing of Sotho independence, 1865-1870.**

Anthony Atmore. In: *African societies in Southern Africa: historical studies.* Edited by Leonard Thompson. London: Heinemann, 1969, p. 282-301. maps.

This is a detailed analysis of events leading up to Cape Government rule of Lesotho, with some material based on oral history. It also includes a map of the different Lesotho boundaries between 1865-71.

69 **Reluctant empire: British policy on the South African frontier, 1834-1854.**

John S. Galbraith. Berkeley, California: University of California Press, 1963. 293p. bibliog.

The author provides information on the organization of the Basotho by Moshoeshoe in the first half of the 19th century, and the subsequent boundary disputes. In particular, Galbraith deals with the Napier Treaty, which was drawn up in 1843 by the Governor of the Cape Colony and signed by Moshoeshoe. This Treaty represented an agreement on the boundaries of the Basotho nation between the colonial government of South Africa, settler farmers in the South African Free State and King Moshoeshoe. However, the Treaty was subsequently broken by settler communities, who captured large tracts of land during wars with the Basotho in the 1860s. This territorial loss was confirmed by the 1869 Treaty of Aliwal North, in which the Free State retained fertile land to the west of the Caledon (Mohokare) river.

70 **South Africa: a reprint of the 1878 edition.**

Anthony Trollope, with an introduction and notes by J. H. Davidson. Cape Town: Balkema, 1973. 504p.

Trollope visited the Orange Free State Republic in the latter half of 1877 and briefly summarizes much of its history, including the wars with the Basotho. The history of the Basotho is treated separately and the author comments very critically upon the gullibility of missionaries, while making heavy use of material from Casalis' *The Basuto or, twenty-three years in South Africa* (q.v.).

71 **A South African kingdom: the pursuit of security in nineteenth-century Lesotho.**

Elizabeth A. Eldredge. Oakleigh, Australia; Cambridge, England; New York: Cambridge University Press, 1993. 250p. 2 maps. bibliog. (African Studies Series, no. 78).

Provides a critical reference work on 19th-century Lesotho. Eldredge argues that the overriding interest of the Basotho during this period was the pursuit of security in the face of political threats and environmental challenge. While showing that women were dominated by men in the pre-colonial period, she argues that Basotho society was relatively homogeneous in terms of both economic assets and power. A rich description of local agriculture, iron-working and craft industry is offered and Eldredge documents the extent of industry and trade in pre-colonial Lesotho. Chapter thirteen, 'Economy, politics, migrant labour and gender', provides an assessment of the motives of migrant labourers and argues that much less migration of this period was coerced than other authors have claimed. While Eldredge's argument about the relative homogeneity of Basotho society has been criticized by other authors, this remains an important text for those interested in Basotho history.

72 **Towards an understanding of the political economy of Lesotho: the origins of commodity production and migrant labour 1830- c.1885.**

Judy Kimble. MA thesis, National University of Lesotho, Lesotho, 1978. 327p.

A landmark study of Lesotho's early colonial experiences. Kimble analyses the pattern of market production and migration that resulted from contact with both colonial and settler forces. She argues that the internal, highly hierarchical structure of Basotho society was crucial in shaping these external relationships. She has since been criticized for some of her assumptions; Eldredge in particular (see item no. 71) disputes that chiefs had coercive power in the early 19th century, and instead argues that individuals had greater freedom of choice within society. Despite these criticisms, Kimble's thesis remains a classic work on the early political economy of Lesotho, and will be useful for those studying this historical period.

73 **Women in production: the economic role of women in 19th-century Lesotho.**

Elizabeth A. Eldredge. *Signs*, vol. 16, no. 4 (1991), p. 707-31.

Discusses the economic role of women in 19th-century Lesotho. Eldredge provides a great deal of detail on the economic activities of women during this period. By reference to the nature of these activities and the types of constraint placed upon women, she discusses the nature of women's subordination.

Cape Rule (1871-83)

74 **Fighting a two-pronged attack: the changing legal status of women in Cape-ruled Basutoland, 1872-1884.**

Sandra B. Burman. In: *Women and gender in Southern Africa to 1945*. Edited by Cherryl Walker. Cape Town: David Philip; London: James Currey, 1990, p. 48-75. bibliog.

Burman discusses the legal changes affecting women during the period of Cape Rule in Lesotho, concluding that the effect of these changes on women were ambiguous. While some women suffered, many of the changes that took place which were not to women's advantage were in fact already underway before the advent of Cape Rule. While the new administration attempted to introduce individual rights for women, there was some conflict as the administration also allowed the continuation of customary law.

75 **Government by proxy: ten years of Cape Colony rule in Lesotho, 1871-1881.**

J. Makibinyane Mohapeloa. Morija, Lesotho: Sesuto Book Depot, 1971. 116p. maps. bibliog. (University of Botswana, Lesotho and Swaziland Local Studies Series, no. 1).

A useful account of the period of Cape Rule, including the Gun War of 1880-81. This war was precipitated by the Cape Parliament's attempt to implement the Peace Preservation Act in the then Basutoland. The Act required the disarmament of Africans and included not only guns but also spears and assegais. At the same time, the Cape Parliament proposed the annexation of Lesotho's southern Quthing District. These proposals led to an uprising by many of Lesotho's chiefs, and the war ended in stalemate and the disannexation of Basutoland from the Cape Colony. The book is divided into two sections and deals with the general history of the period and the social and economic history. The latter includes a portion on education and mission work at the time. Much use has been made of archival material and the Blue Books covering the years under discussion.

76 **The justice of the Queen's Government: the Cape's administration of Basutoland 1871-1884.**
S. B. Burman. Leiden, Netherlands: Africa Studies Centre, 1976. 132p.

Contains a useful commentary on events, accompanied by reproductions of selected archival materials, for the period 1871-84. Burman reports on selected incidents before, during and after the Moorosi war and the Gun War. The rebellion by Chief Moorosi in 1880 was precipitated by a series of disputes over succession to King Moshoeshoe, who had died in 1870. These disputes were escalated by debates over annexation to the British and then transference to the Cape Colony in 1871. Moorosi's uprising was put down by Basotho troops, but only after the threat of further land confiscation by the Cape Colony if they did not. The Gun War followed soon after and again showed conflict between the chiefs on the subject of colonial annexation (see item no. 75 for more details on this conflict). This book includes previously unpublished material relating to the period.

Late colonial period (1884-1966)

77 **1960 agricultural census, Basutoland.**
Clifford M. H. Morojele. Maseru: Agricultural Department, 1963-65. 8 vols.

A very detailed description of agriculture in Lesotho in statistical form. Part four includes a good account of the types of crops cultivated in Lesotho and their distribution. Part seven exists only as a preliminary mimeographed report, and the compiler has not seen part eight. The preparation of the final volumes was not completed, owing to the transfer of the author from government service to the FAO in Rome. The volumes cover the following topics: part one, Census methodology (120p.); part two, Households and families (88p.); part three, Agricultural holdings (88p.); part four, Crop acreage, yield and production (104p.); part five, Land classification and farming practices (64p.); part six, Agricultural implements and storage facilities (76p.); part seven, Livestock and poultry (unpublished); and part eight, Agricultural population (unpublished).

78 **'Desirable or undesirable Basotho women?' Liquor, prostitution and the migration of Basotho women to the Rand, 1920-1945.**
Philip L. Bonner. In: *Women and gender in Southern Africa to 1945*. Edited by Cherryl Walker. Cape Town: David Philip; London: James Currey, 1990, p. 221-50. bibliog.

The author demonstrates that Basotho women contributed disproportionately to the flow of women to the South African Rand. Bonner suggests that this was the result of the uneven impact of labour migrancy and specific characteristics internal to Basotho society. He shows that the attempt by municipal and central authorities to control women's illicit brewing of beer was an attempt to gain some control over the process of black urbanization. Control over women proved unobtainable in this period, mainly because they were not obliged to carry passes, which was itself the result of resistance by women to pass legislation. Lack of government control over women in both Basutoland and South Africa also weakened the control of Basotho men over Basotho women, and had important repercussions on Basotho migrant culture in the towns.

79 **An ecological survey of the mountain area of Basutoland.**
R. R. Staples, W. K. Hudson. London: Crown Agents for the Colonies, 1938. 68p. maps.

This survey, carried out as a result of the recommendations of the Pim Report, provides information on vegetation types and the effects of overgrazing, as well as recommendations on how best to protect and utilize mountain pastures and fields.

80 **The economics of independence.**
Julius G. Malie. *Basutoland Quarterly*, vol. 1, no. 2 (March 1966), p. 8.

Comments on the financial position of pre-independence Lesotho and discusses problems of agriculture, land tenure and industrialization.

81 **Labour migration in Basutoland, c.1870-1885.**
Judy Kimble. In: *Industrialisation and social change in South Africa: African class formation, culture and consciousness 1870-1930.* Edited by Shula Marks, Richard Rathbone. London; New York: Longman, 1982, p. 19-141. bibliog.

Kimble seeks to explain Basotho participation in the labour markets of Southern Africa during the 1870s. The central argument is that the structural conditions prevailing in Basutoland at that time ensured that large numbers of adult men began to sell their labour power. Kimble pays particular attention to the role of chiefly power and increasing commoditization to explain the rise in migrant labourers. While she has been criticized for her lack of attention to the decisions made by migrants themselves, this remains an important historical work on the Basotho social structure and the emergence of migration. For more detail, see her doctoral dissertation: *Migrant labour and colonial rule in Southern Africa: the case of Basutoland, 1870-1930* (PhD thesis, University of Essex, 1985).

82 **Land tenure in Basutoland.**
Vernon George John Sheddick. London: HMSO, 1954. 196p. (Colonial Research Studies, no. 13).

This book results from field studies undertaken in 1947-49. It includes a detailed account: of the Basotho social system and socio-ecological setting; of settlement and residence patterns; of agricultural practices; and of animal husbandry and land tenure. There are useful sections on the history and administration of the government reserves, and on land occupied by traders and missionaries. The chieftainship is discussed in detail, including the origin of the main wards and administrative areas, and the rights of chief to *lira* (fields) and *matsema* (labour). Throughout the book there is a variety of tables of agricultural statistics, and the photographs of agricultural practices include some taken from the air. The Commonwealth Relations Office's foreword indicates the Basutoland Government's disagreement with some of Dr Sheddick's conclusions.

83 **Lesotho, Botswana and Swaziland: the former High Commission Territories in Southern Africa.**
Richard P. Stevens. London: Pall Mall Press, 1967. 294p. bibliog.

Pages 14-97, entitled 'From Basutoland to Lesotho', trace the history of Lesotho from the point of view of administrative and political developments up to 1966. Part six of the section on Lesotho deals with the country's economy and was written by H. G. Henry.

84 **'Runaway wives': Basotho women, chiefs and the colonial state, c. 1890-1920.**
Judy Kimble. London: University of London, School of Oriental and African Studies, Centre for African Studies, 1983. 20p. bibliog. (Women in Africa Discussion Paper).

Discusses the extent to which women migrated in the late 19th and early 20th centuries. Kimble shows that, contrary to other accounts, women did not get 'left behind' while men migrated; she finds rather that women did begin to move into towns and enter into wage labour alongside, and independent of, their men. This occurred with a particular form of landlessness and marginalization common to women under colonial rule. Women lost some degree of their rights to land, but also found that there was less control by senior family members or chiefs over their labour. However, their movement off the land was constrained by the political and juridical intervention of the colonial state and the chieftainship.

85 **Trade, accumulation and impoverishment: mercantile capital and the economic transformation of Lesotho and the conquered territory, 1870-1920.**
Timothy Keegan. *Journal of Southern African Studies*, vol. 12, no. 2 (April 1986), p. 196-216.

Keegan discusses the economic transformation of Lesotho following its incorporation into South Africa. He finds that mercantile capital was central to this transformation, which saw a pattern of impoverishment arise in Lesotho.

A short history of Lesotho: from the late Stone Age until the 1993 elections.
See item no. 5.

Iron Age communities of the Southern Highveld.
See item no. 52.

Maseru: an illustrated history.
See item no. 99.

Biographies, Autobiographies and Memoirs

86 **Among Boers and Basutos and with Barkly's Horse: the story of our life on the frontier.**
Fanny Barkly. London: Remington, 1893. 270p.

An account of the life of a magistrate's wife in Lesotho between 1877-81. A. C. S. Barkly served at Advance Post, Mohale's Hoek and Mafeteng. The book is of interest for its accounts, taken from contemporary newspaper reports, of Moorosi's War and the Siege of Mafeteng in the Gun War. It also describes life in Lesotho from the viewpoint of a Victorian lady.

87 **The Basutos or, twenty-three years in South Africa.**
Eugène Casalis. London: Nisbet, 1861. 355p.

An English translation of a work published in French in 1859. The author was one of the three pioneer missionaries to the Basotho in 1833. The book is of great value in giving details of the customs and way of life of the Basotho at the time, containing much useful historical material.

88 **A chief is a chief by the people.**
Stimela Jason Jingoes, recorded and compiled by John Perry, Cassandra Perry. London: Oxford University Press, 1975. 260p. maps.

Jingoes was a distinguished commoner, born in 1895. Based on oral recollections, this book covers his life up to the early 1950s. His childhood exploits and working life are recounted, including a description of mine work. Of greatest interest to the reader is the later period of his life, which was spent serving the chieftainship. Jingoes discusses the role of chiefs, traditionally exemplified in the saying that 'a chief is a chief by the people', which means that the chieftainship and the people serve each other. However, Jingoes argues that this relationship has changed significantly in practice. The book has little in the way of analytical content, but is useful as a description of one man's understanding of social change. Black-and-white photographs and illustrations of Lesotho and the Basotho people are provided, including several of Jingoes himself.

89 **Correspondence of Lieut.-General the hon. Sir George Cathcart, K. C. B., relative to his military operations in Kaffraria until the termination of the Kafir War, and to his measures for the future maintenance of peace on that frontier and the protection and welfare of the people of South Africa.**

Sir George Cathcart. London: Murray, 1856. 401p. maps. Facsimile reprint, New York: Negro Universities Press, 1969.

Contains much information on the Basotho, including a verbatim report of an interview between Moshoeshoe and Cathcart, and the latter's report on the Battle of Berea (1852). The publication also contains the text of Moshoeshoe's letter to Cathcart after the battle.

90 **Fourteen years in Basutoland.**

John Widdicombe. London: Church Printing Co., 1891. 312p.

A description of the first fourteen years (1876-90) of the Anglican mission of 'Thlotse Heights', the modern Hlotse, where the Revd Widdicombe's was the first building. The book contains a detailed account of the siege and battles at Hlotse during the Gun War, and the subsequent civil war between chiefs. Widdicombe also published a similar item with a supplementary chapter on the Hlotse Anglican Mission (1890-95): *In the Lesuto: a sketch of African mission life* (London: S. P. C. K., 1895. 352p. 1 map).

91 **Moshoeshoe, Chief of the Sotho.**

Peter B. Sanders. London: Heinemann, 1975. 350p. bibliog.

King Moshoeshoe I is accredited as the founder of the Basotho nation. Born in 1786, he was fundamental in organizing the loosely federated southern Sotho communities to withstand the chaos of the early 1800s, known as the *lifaqane*. This was a period of massive displacement of people, during which communities were attacked, and land and cattle lost. Moshoeshoe led one such group to the area that is now Lesotho, settling the mountain stronghold of Thaba-Bosiu in 1824. From there he was able to forge links with other groups and so increase his power base. Moshoeshoe anticipated the encroachment of South African settlers and applied for Lesotho's protection as a British Colony; however, he died in 1870, having reached only partial agreement on the terms of British annexation. This is a comprehensive biography and an established standard work which has been compiled from oral traditions as well as archival and published sources. Originally in part an Oxford DPhil thesis, it contains a valuable bibliography which includes a survey of the relevant archival material and Government publications. The appendix contains a brief article on 'Oral tradition among the Sotho' in which the author discusses the development of oral traditions and their reliability.

92 **Moshoeshoe I: profile.**

Edited by Ntsu Mokhehle. Maseru: Khatiso ea Lesotho, 1976. 72p.

The sayings of Moshoeshoe and descriptions of encounters with the founder of Lesotho, from a variety of published sources and oral traditions, are reproduced in this work.

93 **My life in Basutoland: a story of missionary enterprise in South Africa.**

Eugène Casalis, translated by J. Brierly. London: Religious Tract Society, 1889. 293p. Facsimile reprint, Cape Town: Struik, 1971. 100p.

An English translation of a work published in French c.1880. Only the second half of the book deals with Lesotho, but it contains an especially detailed account of the missionaries' life and work in the period 1833-36.

94 **Sketches of life and sport in South-Eastern Africa.**

Charles Hamilton, edited by F. G. H. Price. London: Chapman & Hall, 1870. 268p.

The author visited Thaba-Bosiu and met Moshoeshoe. He hunted lion and other animals in the country and gives interesting details of the wildlife that existed in Lesotho in the 19th century. Pages 246-68 deal with Lesotho.

95 **Survival in two worlds: Moshoeshoe of Lesotho 1786-1879.**

Leonard Thompson. Oxford: Clarendon Press, 1975. 392p. bibliog.

A perceptive biography of Moshoeshoe I, who was instrumental in the founding of the kingdom of Lesotho. In the context of the chaos of the *lifaqane* period, Moshoeshoe settled many southern Sotho communities in the area now known as Lesotho. This book makes extensive use of archival, published and oral sources, and includes an extensive bibliography. A more detailed summary of Moshoeshoe's life is included in the introduction of this bibliography and in item no. 91.

Population

General

96 **Law and population growth in Lesotho.**
Sebastian Poulter, William McClain, J. B. K. Kaburise, J. Mugambwa, D. Milazi. Roma, Lesotho: National University of Lesotho, Faculty of Law, Law and Population Project, 1981. 96p. bibliog.

Argues that any sound population policy requires a prior understanding of the effects of the existing law. A large proportion of Lesotho's laws date from a period when little thought had been given to population policy. Thus, it is unsurprising that many laws seem to be out of keeping with the Government's stated objective of cutting annual population growth. The authors propose changing several existing laws. However, on one particular matter of concern, abortion, this report contains no specific proposal for law reform, as it recognizes that the sensitive nature of the subject places it outside the academic arena.

97 **Population and development in Southern Africa: the 1980s and beyond.**
I. Sembajwe. In: *Southern Africa in the 1980s and beyond: Institute of Southern African Studies 1980-1990.* Edited by the Institute of Southern African Studies. Roma, Lesotho: University of Lesotho, Institute of Southern African Studies, 1993, p. 136-55. bibliog.

Lesotho is one of the countries discussed in this regional overview of population trends. Sembajwe presents data on overall population growth, age structure and birth/death rates. The paper links population growth to socio-economic development and provides a regional comparison for population statistics.

98 **Population census analysis report, 1986.**
Lesotho Government. Maseru: Bureau of Statistics, 1991. 4 vols.

The results of the 1986 census are presented together with detailed explanations of the compilation of key statistics. Comparisons with previous census returns are made.

Urbanization and urban growth

99 **Maseru: an illustrated history.**
David Ambrose. Morija, Lesotho: Morija Museum and Archives, 1993. 256p. 13 maps. bibliog.

This work is the only comprehensive history of Maseru. The origins and growth of the city are documented from prehistory to modern times. Ambrose examines both the physical infrastructure of Maseru and its interaction with the society it serves. The study includes a detailed map section and a selection of aerial photographs.

100 **Migrancy, dependency and urban formation in Lesotho: a case study.**
Chris Peters. MA thesis, School of Development Studies, University of East Anglia, England, 1993. 82p.

Peters reports on the urbanization process in Maseru, presenting a statistical picture of the urban population and their migration history. He argues that the rapid urbanization is linked to Lesotho's dependent relationship on South Africa, which precludes rural development, and investigates the role of local government. This thesis will be especially interesting to those involved in urban planning.

101 **Report on the socio-economic study carried out in Leribe town for the Urban Upgrading Project.**
Sechaba Consultants. Maseru: Sechaba Consultants & Lesotho Housing and Land Development Corporation, 1990. 65p.

Presents the results of a study in urban Leribe. Data is presented in the form of tables, and the report is divided into five subsections: household membership; access to facilities; tenancy details (where applicable); dwelling type; and site type (including details of rent, etc.). The purpose of the study was to gather basic socio-economic data on an urban area and to establish an approach to urban analysis in conjunction with other studies for urban planning and development. A ten per cent sample was constructed. Greater verbal analysis would have been helpful, but otherwise this is a useful report on socio-economic conditions for an urban population. A similar report exists for Mohales Hoek (see item no. 102).

102 **Report on the socio-economic study carried out in Mohales Hoek town for the Urban Upgrading Project.**
Sechaba Consultants. Maseru: Sechaba Consultants & Lesotho Housing and Land Development Corporation, 1990. 69p.

Presents the results of a study in Mohales Hoek. Data is presented in the form of tables, and the report is divided into five subsections: household membership; access to facilities; tenancy details (where applicable); dwelling type; and site type (including details of rent, etc.). The purpose of the study was to gather basic socio-economic data on an urban area and to establish an approach to urban analysis in conjunction with other studies for urban planning and development. A ten per cent sample was constructed. Greater verbal analysis would have been helpful, but otherwise this is a useful report on socio-economic conditions for an urban population. A similar report exists for urban Leribe (see item no. 101).

103 **Report on the socio-economic survey carried out in Butha-Buthe Town for the department of Housing of Ministry of Interior, Chieftainship Affairs and Rural Development.**
Sechaba Consultants. Maseru: Sechaba Consulting & Lesotho Housing and Land Development Corporation, 1992. 65p. 2 maps.

The data is presented in two parts: data for the town as a whole; and data for the various districts. A sample of ten per cent of urban residents was obtained and data collected on previous place of residence, schooling, occupation, ownership, plot size and household income. A similar report exists for Maputsoe (see item no. 104).

104 **Report on the socio-economic survey carried out in Maputsoe for the Department of Housing of Ministry of Interior, Chieftainship Affairs and Rural Development.**
Sechaba Consultants. Maseru: Sechaba Consultants & Lesotho Housing and Land Development Corporation, 1992. 75p. 2 maps.

The data is presented in two parts: data for the town as a whole; and data for the various districts. A sample of ten per cent of urban residents was obtained and data collected on previous place of residence, schooling, occupation, ownership, plot size and household income. A similar report exists for Butha-Buthe town (see item no. 103).

105 **Some characteristics of the urban informal sector in Southern Africa: the case of Lesotho.**
Emil Katona. KwaDlangezwa, South Africa: University of Zululand, 1993. 34p. bibliog. (Publication Series A, no. 49).

Katona investigates the urban informal sector in Lesotho, concentrating on the economic characteristics of this sector, and particularly on the nature of income.

Language

106 **Basotho children's early development of speech.**
Michael Connelly. *African Studies (South Africa)*, vol. 46, no. 2 (1987), p. 229-39.

This article uses data from a longitudinal survey of four Basotho children to discuss the development of speech among children of different cultures. The data on Basotho children's development suggests strongly that language development takes place earlier in Lesotho than in Europe and the United States.

107 **Elements of Southern Sotho.**
R. A. Paroz. Morija, Lesotho: Sesuto Book Depot, 1957. 2nd ed. 283p.

A graded textbook aimed at English-speaking persons wishing to learn Sesotho and intended to replace Jacottet's *A practical method to learn Sesuto* (see item no. 113). The book divides into four roughly equal parts: an outline of Sesotho sounds and of the grammatical structure, enabling the student to build short and simple sentences; a more thorough study of the grammar, enabling the student to read simple texts and to engage in conversation; completion of grammar sufficient for normal speech and reading; and notes on syntax and peculiarities of the Sesotho language. Each of the forty lessons contains translation exercises, some of the later ones selected from Sesotho literature. The book concludes with Sesotho-English and English-Sesotho vocabularies.

108 **Everyday Sesotho grammar.**
M. R. L. Sharpe. Morija, Lesotho: Sesuto Book Depot, 1951. 158p.

A useful, simple grammar for newcomers to the language, containing graded translation exercises with solutions. A sequel was produced by the author: *Everyday Sesotho reader* (Morija, Lesotho: Sesuto Book Depot, 1952. 85p.).

109 **A grammar of the Sesuto language.**
Edouard Jacottet, Z. D. Mangoaela, edited by C. M. Doke. *Bantu Studies*, vol. 3, special number (1927), 209p.

Edited by C. M. Doke after Jacottet's death, and printed at Morija, this was the standard work on Sesotho grammar for many years. The introduction (by Jacottet) also provides a most valuable account of earlier works on Sesotho grammar with reference to landmarks in Lesotho publishing history, and details of Sesotho dictionaries and Sesotho literature.

110 **The language situation in Lesotho today: a preliminary survey.**
T. Lynn. *NUL Journal of Research*, vol. 4 (1994), p. 1-59.

An overview of the language situation in Lesotho. The first part of the paper deals with the treatment of Sesotho by previous writers. This section also outlines varieties of Sesotho based on geography, class and gender. The rest of the paper considers the other languages in use in Lesotho. This paper will be helpful for those interested in the varieties of language spoken in Lesotho.

111 **The meaning of Sesotho.**
David B. Coplan. *NUL Journal of Research*, vol. 2 (1992), p. 1-56.

A discussion of meaning and trends in the modern use of Sesotho.

112 **Orthographical rules for Sesuto together with the report of the conference on Sesuto orthography, 1906.**
Edouard Jacottet. Morija, Lesotho: Sesuto Book Depot, 1970. 16p.

A reprint of the standard work on Sesotho orthography. The orthography adopted in 1906 has remained in use in Lesotho unchanged since that time.

113 **A practical method to learn Sesotho, with exercises and a short vocabulary.**
Edouard Jacottet, additions by H. E. Jankie. Morija, Lesotho: Sesuto Book Depot, 1936. 324p. Reprinted, Gregg Press, 1968.

The original book by Jacottet was written in 1906 and apparently first published in 1907 (although later editions give 1912 as the date of the first edition). For many years it was the standard textbook for English-speaking people wishing to learn Sesotho, and it still fulfils a useful purpose in this regard. There are forty-four graded exercises in English and Sesotho, each preceded by an exposition of a portion of grammar. The original book concludes with a useful vocabulary. The second edition (1928, reprinted 1936) is expanded by more than one-third by incorporating material compiled by H. E. Jankie. The additions include chapters on doublets, synonyms, homonyms, proverbs, and phrases and idioms. There are also chapters on word derivation including lists of Sesotho words of English, Dutch and Xhosa origin. The etymology of many Sesotho words is given, including the word Basotho itself, and the Sesotho names of the months.

114 **Textbook of Southern Sotho grammar.**
Clement M. Doke, Sophonia Machabe Mofokeng. London: Longmans, 1957. 491p.

This standard work owes its origin to an attempt by Doke (assisted by René Ellenberger) to revise the grammar of Jacottet published in 1927. The book is not suitable for the beginning student wishing to learn Sesotho, for whom the textbooks by Jacottet, Paroz and Sharpe present alternative graded courses in Sesotho and are to be preferred.

Religion

115 **The birth of a church: the Church of Basutoland.**
Alex Berthoud. *International Review of Missions*, no. 150, vol. 38 (April 1949), p. 156-64.

Discusses the organization of the Lesotho Evangelical church and presents a brief account of its history. A similar article is available by the same author: *How the Church of Basutoland came into being* (*Basutoland Witness*, vol. 3, no. 3 [May-June 1949], p. 26-35).

116 **Blessed Joseph Gérard O. M. I., apostle to the Basotho (1831-1914): letters to the Superiors General and other oblates; spiritual writings.**
Edited by Yvon Beaudoin, translated by Roland Zimmer. Rome: General Postulation O.M.I., 1991. 269p.

Contains a number of letters and extracts from some of the spiritual writings of Father Gérard, the founder of the Catholic mission in Lesotho. The letters will be of particular interest to historians as they cover some of the most important events in the history of Lesotho.

117 **A century of mission work in Basutoland (1833-1933).**
Victor Ellenberger, translated by Edmond M. Ellenberger. Morija, Lesotho: Sesuto Book Depot, 1938. 382p. 1 map. (Centenary Jubilee of the Basutoland Mission, 1833-1933).

This detailed account of the first 100 years of the Paris Mission in Lesotho and the evolution of the Lesotho Church contains historical information about the history of the Basuto from 1833.

118 **Christianization and the African response among the Barolong and the Basotho, 1820-1890.**
L. B. B. J. Machobane. Roma, Lesotho: National University of Lesotho, Institute of Southern African Studies, 1993. 32p. bibliog. (Occasional Paper, no. 7).

Machobane finds that the two societies of the Basotho and the Barolong along the Caledon river generally had good relations with missionary groups. The chiefly class admired their secular usefulness and thus forged strong links. However, Machobane argues that this closeness had its costs, such as the loss of traditions. The missionaries had an unmistakingly imperialist character, and the author finds that a significant amount of passive resistance existed among both the Barolong and the Basotho.

119 **Domesticity and piety in colonial Lesotho: the private politics of Basotho women's Pious Associations.**
Marc Epprecht. *Journal of Southern African Studies*, vol. 19, no. 2 (June 1993), p. 202-24.

Analyses women's religious groups (*kopano*) during the colonial period. Epprecht finds that there was a considerable divergence between the stated ideology of these groups and their actual role. This divergence sometimes drew criticism from both the colonial authorities and the church administration. The author argues that the character of these groups can be explained by the otherwise limited public role women were allowed. In this context, involvement in a *kopano* provided women with a culturally acceptable degree of independence and action.

120 **Father Patrick Maekane M. B. K.**
Sister Theresia Mary. Morija, Lesotho: Church of the Province of Southern Africa, 1987. 54p.

A narrative history of the Anglican 'Community of the Servants of Christ', beginning in 1902 with the birth of the founder, Father Patrick. The pamphlet covers the period up to the 1980s, which saw great changes in Anglican worship in the region. The brief discussion of the recent period is particularly interesting in its presentation of the complex links between the Community, NGOs and the government.

121 **A history of Christian missions in Lesotho.**
Gordan M. Haliburton. Gaborone, Botswana: History Workshop, 1973. 33p. mimeo.

The author summarizes the history of many of the Christian denominations in Lesotho. Particular attention is paid to the three major denominations: the Société de Missions Evangéliques de Paris, established in 1933; the Roman Catholic Church, from the Congregation of the Oblates of Mary Immaculate, who arrived in 1862; and the Anglican Church, established in 1876. A number of minor Christian denominations have also been established. However, the Christian Church is Lesotho appears to be deeply divided and there has been long-standing enmity between the major churches.

122 **A history of Christian missions in South Africa.**
J. Du Plessis. London: Longmans & Green, 1911. 494p. 1 map. bibliog. Facsimile reprint, Cape Town: Struik, 1965.

When published, this was the best overall survey of 19th-century mission work in the subcontinent. Somewhat less than one-tenth of the total work deals with Lesotho, but this includes accounts of the work of the four missionary societies then active in Lesotho, with most detail on the Paris Mission. Appendix II includes, as Note U, a translation from *Proceedings of the Volksraad* (7 Feb. 1866), recording the decision of the Orange Free State Volksraad to expel the French missionaries. Note Y is entitled 'The Ethiopian Movement' and includes the history of the African Methodist Episcopal Church.

123 **Missionary work and the Sotho in the gold mine compounds, 1920-1940.**
Tshidiso Maloka. *South African Historical Journal*, no. 31 (November 1994), p. 28-54.

This article describes the activities of the Paris Evangelical Missionary Society among the Sotho in the gold mines compounds. Maloka considers the importance of religion in instilling an industrial work ethic.

124 **The P.E.M.S.: Church of Basutoland origin.**
Paul Germond. *South African Outlook*, vol. 95 (March 1964), p. 40-43.

A history of the development of the Lesotho Evangelical Church up to 1964. In 1964 the Paris Mission handed over its responsibilities to the Kereke ea Lesotho and from that time the remaining white missionaries would be under the jurisdiction of the Synod.

125 **The planting of Christianity in Africa.**
C. P. Groves. London: Lutterworth Press, 1954. 4 vols.

The standard work on mission history in the area. volume 2 (pages 147-52, 269-72) covers the Paris Mission in Lesotho, and the arrival of Catholics and Anglicans, and also provides brief historical background up to the 1880s. Volume four contains many references to Lesotho, the organization of the Lesotho Evangelical Church, and religion generally, up to 1954.

126 **Women in the Church of Basutoland.**
L. Bezençon. *Basutoland Witness*, vol. 3, no. 2 (March-April 1949), p. 16-19.

Examines the responsibilities of women in the Lesotho Evangelical Church.

The Basutos or, twenty-three years in South Africa.
See item no. 87.

Fourteen years in Basutoland.
See item no. 90.

My life in Basutoland: a story of missionary enterprise in South Africa.
See item no. 93.

Social Conditions

Social differentiation and poverty

127 **Africa misunderstood: or whatever happened to the rural-urban gap?**

Vali Jamal, John Weeks. London: MacMillan Press, 1993. 180p. bibliog.

Discusses the rural-urban income gap and argues that urban-bias is not as widespread as previously thought. However, one of the authors' case-studies is on Lesotho, where they do find a widening rural-urban gap, measured in terms of the ratio of unskilled wages on mines to farm income. There are a number of methodological flaws in the analysis, most notably that they fail to consider that a significant proportion of mine wages are remitted back to rural areas. Despite this, Jamal and Weeks present a valuable summary of macroeconomic and income data, which will be useful for readers investigating the importance of migration for household income. It should be noted, however, that their analysis ends in the first half of the 1980s and does not encompass the recent falls in the demand for migrant labour.

128 **Class, gender and the household: the development cycle in Southern Africa.**

Colin Murray. *Development and Change*, vol. 18, no. 2 (1987), p. 235-49.

Concentrating mainly on Lesotho, Murray links changes in household structure to changes in the economic situation of a community. He argues that an analysis of household formation and dissolution can help us understand patterns of inequality within rural areas, as well as the division of labour between men and women in the household.

129 **The cultural topography of wealth: commodity paths and the structure of property in rural Lesotho.**
James Ferguson. *American Anthropologist*, vol. 94, no. 1 (1992), p. 55-73.

In this critique of the conventional methods for measuring wealth, Ferguson uses the example of Lesotho to explain that the wealth-holdings of different households are incomparable in important ways, arguing that economic exchanges are governed by cultural, legal and moral factors. Different types of wealth have different cultural and social properties, and this means that households have different kinds of wealth. An alternative investigation of wealth should include the structure of property-holdings and an analysis of these 'commodity paths', which he defines as the channels facilitating commodity flow. This paper is useful for readers interested in rural socio-economic status.

130 **The effects of migrant labour: a review of the evidence from Lesotho.**
Colin Murray. *South African Labour Bulletin*, vol. 6, no. 4 (1980), p. 21-39.

Examines the relationship between migrancy, class formation and the structure of the household. Murray argues that this type of analysis suggests a causal connection between the problem of poverty and the system of labour migration. The paper provides demographic data and then discusses the evidence on differentiation in rural communities. Murray finds that this evidence contradicts the official orthodoxy of the 1970s, which suggested that the rural population of Lesotho was relatively homogeneous. See item no. 132 for a summary of the criticisms aimed at Murray.

131 **Enhancing the diversified strategies of the rural poor in Lesotho.**
P. Roy. *Rural Development in Practice*, vol. 1, no. 3 (1989), p. 5-11.

A study of the Local Initiatives Support Project (LISP) based in southern Lesotho. This project was designed to enhance the existing life-strategies of the rural poor, as it was argued that there are constraints to the introduction of new activities in terms of time and willingness. LISP has been concerned to improve agricultural productivity, develop off-farm sources of income and improve local water supply. These activities have involved the participation of local groups. It appears that the project activities have considerable local support and have been effective in increasing local income.

132 **Families divided: the impact of migrant labour in Lesotho.**
Colin Murray. Melbourne, Australia; Cambridge, England; New York: Cambridge University Press, 1981. 219p. 2 maps. bibliog.

A much-quoted text on the effect of migrant labour in Lesotho. The author analyses the impact of migration on family structure and agriculture, and argues that reliance on migrant remittances places women in a dependent position. He concludes that the migrant labour system puts pressure on social structures and, in fact, distorts these structures. Chapter one, 'From granary to labour reserve', affords crucial insights into the historical development of Lesotho and its transition from an agricultural exporter to a country dependent on migrant labour. Murray argues that the present situation of Lesotho cannot be understood in isolation from an analysis of the wider regional economy. Despite criticism of his failure to discuss class-based social stratification, this remains an essential text for scholars and historians. See also his unpublished PhD thesis: *Keeping house in Lesotho* (PhD thesis, University of Cambridge, England, 1976).

133 **Labour-related aspects of rural development in Lesotho.**
James H. Cobbe. Roma, Lesotho: National University of Lesotho, Institute of Labour Studies, 1982. 32p. bibliog. (Institute of Labour Studies, Discussion Paper, no. 6).

Investigates the effects of labour migration on agriculture, economic development and women. The author argues that agriculture in Lesotho is currently experiencing a self-sufficiency crisis; agricultural policy should thus concern itself with increasing productivity, through both traditional and non-traditional methods. Furthermore, rural development should be concerned with non-farm activities. Cobbe recognizes the likely decline in migration and argues that this makes an improvement in rural opportunities more urgent.

134 **Poverty and remittances in Lesotho.**
B. Gustafsson, N. Makonnen. *Journal of African Economics*, vol. 2, no. 1 (1993), p. 49-73.

Beginning with a general presentation on the economy of Lesotho, this article investigates the nature of poverty in Lesotho. Data from the 1985/86 Household Budget Survey is used to measure the extent of poverty and special attention is paid to the role of remittances. The results show that households headed by women are particularly likely to experience poverty. Remittances from migrant employment are found to have an important effect in reducing the extent of poverty in the country as a whole. This is a useful study for those interested in social welfare in a national context, and it makes particularly good use of data from the Household Budget Survey.

135 **Poverty eats my blanket: a poverty study: the case of Lesotho.**
Pieter J. T. Marres, Arie C. A. van der Wiel. Maseru: Government Printer, 1975. 112p.

The authors deal with measurements of poverty in general and its application to Lesotho in particular, by developing a poverty datum line for Maseru. A poverty datum line calculates a minimum income level for family subsistence, below which a household may be considered as living in poverty. The book also attempts to gauge the extent of poverty in Maseru, and includes a number of relevant economic statistics.

136 **Poverty in Lesotho: a mapping exercise.**
John Gay, Debby Gill, Thuso Green, David Hall, Mike Mhlanga, Manthatisi Mohapi. Maseru: Sechaba Consultants, 1991. 189p. 33 maps. bibliog.

The first publication that has attempted to give statistical measures of poverty on a country-wide basis. The authors combine data from other studies with the results of their own survey to give detailed statistics on measures of poverty. Chapter three, 'Statistical analysis and spatial distribution of poverty', constructs an index of poverty based on local definitions of basic needs. This work was submitted to the Food

Management Unit, Government of Lesotho, and is also available from Sechaba Consultants, Private Bag A84, Maseru 100, Lesotho.

137 **Poverty in Lesotho, 1994: a mapping exercise.**
John Gay, David Hall. Maseru: Sechaba Consultants, 1994, 162p.

Updates the earlier report compiled in 1991 (see item no. 136). This report uses a number of additional poverty indicators compared to the 1991 report. Some of these have worsened since 1991: there has been a fall in incomes, a reduction in employment and a deterioration in agricultural production.

138 **Research on the rural poor of Lesotho: preliminary indicators and future directions.**
G. J. Van Apeldoorn, S. D. Turner. Roma, Lesotho: National University of Lesotho, Institute of Southern African Studies, 1984. 61p. (Research Report, no. 5).

In this study data was collected on the socio-economic status of households in two foothill areas of Maseru district in 1983, and compared with data from other rural surveys in order to draw some conclusions about the nature of poverty in Lesotho. The authors find that the majority of households received no remittances from migrant workers, and that agricultural production was low. Thus, local off-farm employment was found to provide a significant source of income. The authors suggest that the poorest households display certain characteristics; many are headed by women and are smaller than average.

139 **Rural development in Lesotho.**
James H. Cobbe. *Journal of Contemporary African Studies*, vol. 2, no. 1 (1982), p. 113-40.

This article discusses the effect of labour migration on socio-economic structures in the rural areas of Lesotho. In addition, the author explores some of the implications of migration for rural development, paying particular attention to policy and planning. The paper is divided into the following sections: 'Background'; 'Economy and history'; 'The impact of migration on rural structures'; 'Effects of labour migration'; 'Rural social structure'; and 'Implications for rural development policy and planning'.

140 **Rural development in Lesotho.**
J. Trollip. Cape Town: University of Cape Town, Southern African Labour and Development Research Unit (SALDRU), 1981. 85p. bibliog. (Working Paper, no. 33).

Trollip discusses the issues surrounding rural development in Lesotho, in both theoretical and empirical terms. This paper provides a useful review of the rural development experience in Lesotho, although Trollip does not make strong policy recommendations.

141 **Rural differentiation and the diffusion of migrant labour remittances in Lesotho.**

Andrew D. Spiegel. In: *Black villagers in an industrial society.* Edited by Philip Mayer. Cape Town: Oxford University Press, 1980, p. 109-68. bibliog.

An interesting, descriptive account of the lives of rural people. Spiegel's analysis is based on fieldwork carried out in the late 1970s, and as such is rather outdated in its concentration on male migration to the mines, which fell in importance from more than half of the male workforce to approximately one third in 1990. Spiegel shows that farming in modern Lesotho is dependent on wage labour and in itself rarely provides a sufficient amount for subsistence. A variety of case-studies are presented and an arresting picture emerges of poverty and differentiation among the rural population. This is a particularly useful article for those interested in understanding the place of agriculture in rural Lesotho.

142 **Vandalism and uneven development: lessons from the experiences of the Lesotho Electricity Corporation and the Lesotho Telecommunications Corporation.**

Motlatsi Thabane. *NUL Journal of Research*, vol. 4 (1994), p. 59-85.

Vandalism is becoming a social problem in Lesotho and Thabane discusses the wider context in which acts of vandalism can be understood. It is argued that vandalism takes two distinct types: in one, groups of juveniles are involved in a destructive act, while in the second case, adults remove equipment to sell or use it. Both types are encouraged by the uneven nature of development in Lesotho, and thus Thabane argues that the solution to vandalism is largely out of the hands of the organizations that experience it.

Social surveys

143 **Household data for the Matelile ward, Mafeteng district: a compilation of secondary data.**

Philip Cole. Maseru: Cole Consulting & Ministry of Agriculture, Matelile Rural Development Project, 1993. 26p.

Cole provides a summary of existing data on the Matelile area. The major themes arising from these data sets are identified and discussed. Among the relevant characteristics, Cole discusses the position of women, investment in enterprises and crop production, and soil erosion. This is a helpful publication for researchers interested in an overview of this particular rural area of Lesotho.

144 **Household income and expenditure in rural Lesotho: a village-level case study.**
Judy S. Gay. Roma, Lesotho: National University of Lesotho, Institute of Southern African Studies, 1981. 89p. (Research Report, no. 1).

A study of sources and allocation of household funds conducted in a village in southern Lesotho. In addition, information was collected on household structure, economic assets and economic activities. Gay finds that migrant remittances are extremely important for some households, and that agriculture is universally insignificant as a source of income. In addition, she discusses the limited employment opportunities for rural women and the complex pattern of rural differentiation in Lesotho. Finally, suggestions are made for the development activities required to meet the needs of various types of rural household. Despite being slightly outdated in its discussion of migrant labour, Gay's work provides valuable budgetary information on rural households.

145 **Incomes, expenditure and consumption of Basotho households.**
Lesotho Government. Maseru: Bureau of Statistics, 1988. 2 vols.

Provides results of the National Household Budget Survey carried out between October 1986 and September 1987. The entire country was surveyed, and detailed tabulations can be found in the *Tabulation report*. For general results, see the volume titled *Main results from the household budget survey 1986/87*. In both volumes, data is presented on the four rural ecological zones as well as for urban areas. However, it is worth noting that some rural areas had a high level of non-reporting. Details on the methodological aspects of the survey are provided in a separate publication, *The 1986/87 household budget survey in Lesotho: methodological report* (Maseru: Bureau of Statistics, 1988).

146 **Report on the socio-economic conditions and needs of the people in the Ketane valley of Lesotho.**
Thuso Green, David Hall. Maseru: Unitarian Services Committee of Canada & Sechaba Consultants, 1990. 56p.

The Ketane valley is a remote area situated north-east of the southern town of Mohales Hoek. This study finds that the most important issue for local people is the building of a bridge. The lack of accessibility has led to a number of problems, including difficulties with schooling and farming. This report contains comprehensive data on the Ketane valley, which will prove valuable for those interested in the social and economic character of such remote areas.

147 **Socio-economic analysis of the Hololo Valley, Lesotho, 1978-1988.**
David Hall. Maseru: Hololo Valley Project & Transformation Resource Centre, 1988. 75p.

Presents data from a survey of villages in the catchment area of the Hololo river. This data includes information on household membership, wealth and landholding. It updates a survey carried out ten years previously, and thus gives an idea of the change in the socio-economic character of the area over time. However, the report would have been more useful if greater written analysis had been made.

Food and nutrition

148 **Drought relief and local organizations: report on the capacity of non-governmental organizations, Private Health Association of Lesotho and churches to participate in a drought relief operation.**
Michael Adams, Debby Gill, David Hall. Maseru: Sechaba Consultants, 1993. 57p.

Although the whole country was affected by drought in the early 1990s, some areas were worst hit than others. Households from the north-eastern and central mountains and the south-western lowlands were particularly badly affected. In addition, concerns have been raised about the fair and efficient distribution of drought aid. Donor agencies were involved in the importation of emergency food-aid and this study finds that only a limited number of NGOs were large enough to make a significant contribution to any drought relief programme. It was also found that only two hospitals, Tebellong and Scott, have the administrative capacity to manage emergency drought-relief operations. Thus the report recommends that a National Drought Relief Committee be set up to target interventions more effectively.

149 **Factors influencing food production in Lesotho and Swaziland.**
J. J. Sterkenburg. In: *Food systems in Central & Southern Africa.* Edited by J. P. Pottier. London: School of Oriental and African Studies, University of London, 1985, p. 246-64.

Investigates the nature of food production in Lesotho and Swaziland. Although superficially similar in size and geographic location, the two countries have distinct agricultural systems. A general description is given of food production in each country and then a comparison made. It is argued that poor ecological conditions and the availability of migrant employment in Lesotho have led to an undeveloped agricultural sector. Despite the fact that agricultural production is concentrated on staple food crops, imports of food are also high, in contrast with the agricultural system in Swaziland, which contains an export-producing, commercial sector. Finally two case-studies are offered to support these conclusions. One study is of farming systems in the Mafeteng District of Lesotho, while the other is from the Swazi Lowveld.

150 **Food and Nutrition Information Bulletin.**
Maseru: Ministry of Agriculture, Food and Nutrition Co-ordinating Office, 1984- . bi-monthly.

This bulletin provides an integrated picture of the food and nutrition situation through the use of statistical data derived from a number of different ministries, departments and other organizations. It also provides diagrams, maps and a certain amount of descriptive material. Information on domestic production and commercial imports is presented. Importantly, the report discusses factors which affect the distribution and consumption of the available food supply and the possible nutritional outcomes. This publication is aimed at those researching changes in health and poverty.

151 **Food and nutrition planning – the Lesotho approach.**
R. T. Learmonth. *Food and Nutrition*, vol. 6, no. 2 (1980), p. 2-6.

Learmonth discusses the establishment of the Food and Nutrition Coordinating Office. Founded in 1978, the office assists in projects that, either directly or indirectly, deal with food and nutrition. In addition, the office is attempting to develop a national food and nutrition programme and its progress in this regard is discussed.

152 **Home gardens nutrition program: 1989/90 baseline survey.**
Thope Matobo, Mampho Makhaola. Maseru: Ministry of Agriculture, Research and Nutrition Divisions, 1990. 37p.

Surveys the socio-economic and nutritional status of households living in the mountain districts of Thaba-Tseka and Qacha's Nek. The authors find that respondents rarely consumed food with other than carbohydrate value due to poverty. It was also found that approximately half of the respondents bought vegetables instead of producing them. This was a result of limited resources, especially the lack of garden tools. Given the small size of gardens, it was difficult to produce enough to consume or sell, and this problem was also aggravated by animal destruction and theft. This study provides an interesting picture of the nature of under-nutrition in Lesotho.

153 **Lesotho's food priorities.**
J. B. Eckert. *Food Policy*, vol. 8, no. 1 (1983), p. 76-81.

In this discussion of Lesotho's food priorities, Eckert provides a useful overview of the situation of food production and marketing in the early 1980s. Given the limited arable land and poor productivity, the country has a food deficit which is met both by imports and food aid. Food markets are highly monetized and food purchases are largely funded by migrant remittances. This report provides an interesting picture of the role of remittances in meeting food needs. However, the situation should be reassessed given the significant reduction in the prevalence of migrant employment since this study was published.

154 **The mediating effect of maternal nutrition knowledge on the association between maternal schooling and child nutritional-status in Lesotho.**
M. T. Ruel, J. P. Habicht, P. Pinstrupandersen, Y. Grohn. *American Journal of Epidemiology*, vol. 135, no. 8 (1992), p. 904-14.

Evaluates the effects of maternal nutritional knowledge using data collected on nutritional knowledge and socio-economic status. The authors found that a family's socio-economic status is crucial in explaining the influence of maternal schooling, and that maternal nutritional knowledge appeared important only for richer households. These results show that nutritional education cannot improve child nutritional status without additional action to help households that do not have access to a minimum level of resources.

155 **Resource guide for nutrition planning in Lesotho.**
J. H. Anderson. Fort Collins, Colorado: Colorado State University, Department of Economics, Lesotho Agricultural Sector Analysis Program, 1978. 41p. (Discussion Paper, no. 6).

Anderson provides information on both the current state and history of nutrition in Lesotho, suggesting that nutritional inadequacy can only be solved by a re-shaping of agricultural policy. Recommendations are made concerning nutrition policy. Despite the date of publication, this remains an important paper for those interested in nutritional issues.

156 **A sociological sketch of Sotho diet.**
Edmond Hugh Ashton. *Transactions of the Royal Society of South Africa*, vol. 27 (1939), p. 147-214.

Records the quantities and kinds of food consumed over a certain period. The information in the study was obtained while the author was conducting a sociological study of the Batlokoa of Mokhotlong.

157 **An update of the village drought survey: revised edition.**
John Gay, Deborah Gill, Thuso Green, David Hall. Maseru: Sechaba Consultants, 1992. 2nd ed. 34p. 1 map.

This is an update of a survey carried out earlier in the year for USAID. This report contains more information on the effect of drought. The authors find that household disposable income had fallen steadily and that many households were unable to buy food. Very few areas had a reasonable harvest and almost no families had enough food in storage to carry them through until the next harvest; begging from neighbours continued as did theft. While the number of deaths from malnutrition was small, there is evidence that hunger was affecting the population. In particular, children are being admitted to hospitals in increasing numbers for malnutrition-related diseases. For the earlier survey, see: *Village drought assessment survey: a report based on a survey of 213 villages in the ten districts of Lesotho* by Thuso Green, David Hall (Maseru: Sechaba Consultants, USAID, 1992. 30p. 5 maps).

Women and Gender Issues

158 **An analysis of the impact of labour migration on the lives of women in Lesotho.**

Elizabeth Gordon. In: *African women in the development process.* Edited by Nici Nelson. London; Totowa, New Jersey: Frank Cass, 1981, p. 59-76. bibliog.

Written at a time of overwhelming outmigration of Basotho men, this is a study of the lives of migrants' wives. Gordon disagrees with the view that these women achieve greater security and independence in the absence of husbands. Instead, her research suggests that the wives of migrants find themselves in difficulty in both their economic and personal affairs. Although the relative importance of male migration to the mines has waned since the mid-1980s, this paper remains a classic study of household decision-making and domestic friction. It also appears in a special issue of the *Journal of Development Studies* (vol. 17, no. 3 [1981]), entitled 'African women in the development process'.

159 **Basotho women migrants: a case study.**

Judith Gay. *IDS Bulletin*, vol. 11, no. 4 (1980), p. 19-28.

Literature on migration from Lesotho has concentrated on the impact of male migrant labour. However, the author shows that many Basotho women, impelled by a range of social and economic factors, also worked as migrants in South Africa during the early part of the century. Since the 1960s, women have been prohibited from legally migrating by 'influx control' measures, and Gay argues that the social life of rural Basotho women has been profoundly affected by this confinement to impoverished rural areas. Gay's article remains an important portrayal of the situation in the 1970s and a useful source of information on the legislation affecting female migrants.

160 **Basotho women's options: a study of marital careers in rural Lesotho.**
Judith S. Gay. PhD thesis, University of Cambridge, Cambridge, England, 1980. 320p.

This thesis examines women's lives in rural areas of Lesotho, and discusses women's access to cash income, as well as to homesteads, property and fields. Gay shows how rural women's options change with age and marital condition, but how, at all stages, these options are structured by Lesotho's position within the regional economy. Gay argues that the migrant labour system compels migrants' wives to be self-reliant; however, this leads to domestic conflict as migrant men attempt to reassert their authority on their return.

161 **Gender-related factors influencing the viability of irrigation projects in Lesotho.**
Pamela Johnson Riley, Naomi T. Krogman. *Journal of Asian and African Studies* (UK), vol. 28, no. 3 (1993), p. 162-79.

Argues that women should receive greater attention in the implementation of agricultural projects as they are the primary farm managers in Lesotho. Interviews were held with female farmers involved in irrigation projects to identify their interests and constraints. The study also discusses the constraints of male and female farmers involved in dryland agriculture. The authors find that a primary problem is the time constraint faced by female farmers, and suggest several ways that this could be eased, including education on issues of labour hiring and alternative strategies for child care.

162 **The implications of the sociocultural environment for women and their assumption of management positions: the case of Lesotho.**
Matora T. Ntimo-Makara. In: *Southern Africa in the 1980s and beyond: Institute of Southern African Studies 1980-1990.* Edited by the Institute of Southern African Studies. Roma, Lesotho: University of Lesotho, Institute of Southern African Studies, 1993, p. 52-69. bibliog.

This chapter highlights the situational, organizational and dispositional factors that affect the situation of women in Lesotho. The paper also reports on the developments that have taken place in the last decade to advance women. Many of these observations are based on a survey of women in senior management positions carried out by the author in 1985. In addition, data are also presented on the trends in higher education for women. This is an interesting article, offering a number of illuminating quotations from women managers.

163 **Legal constraints on women in development in Lesotho.**
Seitebatso M. Seeiso. Roma, Lesotho: National University of Lesotho, 1986. 19p. bibliog. (Institute of Labour Studies Discussion Papers, no. 8).

Describes the dual legal system of Lesotho, where customary law is practised alongside a civil code. The author examines the way in which women are prejudiced under law, particularly in marriage, and identifies specific laws which hamper women in business. As well as arguing that such laws should be repealed, the author suggests that an awareness programme could encourage women to appeal against discrimination.

164 **The legal situation of women in Lesotho.**
S. M. Seeiso, L. M. Kanono, M. N. Tsotsi, T. E. Monaphathi. In: *The legal situation of women in Southern Africa*. Edited by Julie Stewart, Alice K. Armstrong. Harare: University of Zimbabwe Publications, 1990, p. 47-74. (Women and Law in Southern Africa, vol. II).

An essential text on women and the law in Lesotho. This short paper covers the main areas of women's legal situation: marriage, divorce, health, law and employment. The authors conclude that women are doubly oppressed by the dual legal system, which recognizes both common and customary law; both legal systems appear to incapacitate women by placing them in inferior and vulnerable positions.

165 **Lesotho: a gender analysis.**
Debby Gill. Maseru: Sechaba Consultants, 1992. 60p. bibliog.

Offers statistics and information on gender covering a range of economic and social issues. After a general overview of some of the issues facing Lesotho, the report discusses these from the perspective of gender. This discussion covers the law, demography, service provision and participation in the labour market. Traditional gender roles and the government's attitude towards women are also considered, and there is a short section on donor agencies with women's programmes in Lesotho. This publication offers a good general guide to gender issues and gender-aware projects in Lesotho.

166 **Maintenance in Lesotho.**
P. Letuka, P. Mochochoko, M. P. Mamashela, M. Mohale, L. Mbatha. Harare: Women and Law in Southern Africa Research Project, 1991. 189p. 1 map. bibliog.

The author discusses the relationship between maintenance as described in the law and the situation in practice. A central theme in this analysis is the dual legal system operating in Lesotho. Relevant literature is surveyed and the results of a specially tailored research exercise are presented. The authors conclude that lack of maintenance is a major concern; among the relevant factors, they identify a serious lack of knowledge about the law, and more fundamentally, a reluctance to resort to the law that renders it operationally ineffective.

167 **A note on women, conflict and migrant labour.**
Kate B. Showers. *South African Labour Bulletin*, vol. 6, no. 4 (1980), p. 54-57.

Offers some insights into the domestic conflict resulting from the male migrant labour system. Within the household, the absence of men can lead to conflict around the allocation of resources and the delegation of authority. This appears to arise from the differing priorities and needs of the migrant and his family. However, the migrant labour system also subverts the traditional system of intra-household authority by placing a migrant's wife in a more secure position than her mother-in-law, to whom she was traditionally subservient. This is a brief but interesting discussion of the allocation and importance of migrant remittances.

168 **The persistence of women's invisibility in agriculture: theoretical and policy lessons from Lesotho and Sierra Leone.**
Constantina Safilios-Rothschild. *Economic Development and Cultural Change*, vol. 33, no. 2 (1985), p. 299-317.

Using information from Lesotho and Sierra Leone, the author shows that institutional and normative patterns render women's role in agriculture invisible despite statistics which show their significant involvement. Safilios-Rothschild makes a number of theoretical and policy conclusions. She argues that women farmers ought to be made more visible and should be integrated into agricultural development projects. The study shows, however, that women's integration into ongoing agricultural development programmes remains minimal in Lesotho. A longer paper is available on the same subject by this author: *The persistance of women's invisibility in agriculture: theoretical and policy lessons from Lesotho and Sierra Leone* (New York: Population Council, 1982. 31p. bibliog. [Working Paper, no. 88]).

169 **Struggling over scarce resources: women and maintenance in Southern Africa.**
Alice K. Armstrong. Harare: University of Zimbabwe Publications, 1992. 157p. 1 map. bibliog.

Part of the study 'Women and Law in Southern Africa', this volume presents an overview of maintenance law in the region. Despite the regional character of the publication, there is a significant amount of information on Lesotho, including details of both common and customary law. Interviews and case-studies were carried out to determine the extent and nature of conflicts over maintenance. Church groups and other civic organizations were also surveyed.

170 **Successful women's projects: the case of the Lesotho National Council of Women.**
M. K. Khabele, F. L. Moloi, L. A. Sebatane, G. Davenport. In: *Rural development and women: lessons from the field*, vol. II. Edited by S. Muntemba. Geneva: International Labour Organisation, World Employment Programme, 1985, p. 111-29. 1 map.

This chapter outlines the position of women in Lesotho, and then analyses the history, organizational structure and activities of the Lesotho National Council of Women (LNCW). The LNCW, run completely by women, encourages women's self-development through educational and productive activities. It aims to benefit rural women in five ways: household savings; nutrition; income generation; health; and socio-political change. It concludes with recommendations for the design of women's projects.

171 **Women and development in Lesotho.**
Judith S. Gay. Maseru: United States Agency for International Development, 1982. 84p. bibliog.

Provides information on the role, status and contribution of women in Lesotho. Particular reference is made to fields such as agriculture, health, education and rural development. This is a good overview of the position of women in Lesotho, but some aspects are rather dated.

172 **Women in Southern Africa.**
Christine N. Qunta. Johannesburg: Skotaville Publishers, 1987. 256p. 1 map. bibliog.

A collection of essays on women in Southern Africa with a brief review of the situation of women in Lesotho. Also included is a list of women's organizations active in Lesotho.

173 **Women, land and agriculture in Lesotho.**
P. Kishindo. Roma, Lesotho: National University of Lesotho, Institute of Southern African Studies, 1992. 8p. bibliog. (Paper no. 4).

Examines Basotho women's access to land and their role in agricultural production. The paper argues that women can be innovative in their use of land, particularly when widowhood leaves them with de facto control over its use. Unfortunately, despite the fact that the 1979 Land Act made it possible for women to acquire land in their own right, it has had little impact as controversy has prevented its implementation. The paper will be of interest not only to those researching the position of women but also to readers studying agriculture, as the author presents a detailed discussion of the land tenure system in Lesotho.

Class, gender and the household: the development cycle in Southern Africa.
See item no. 128.

The situation of children and women in Lesotho, 1994.
See item no. 206.

The situation of women and children in Lesotho, 1991.
See item no. 207.

Unemployment, migration and changing gender relations in Lesotho.
See item no. 406.

Basotho women and their men: statistics on women and men in Lesotho, 1993.
See item no. 411.

Social Services, Health and Welfare

Health

174 **Annual Report for the Ministry of Health and Social Welfare.**
Maseru: Ministry of Health and Social Welfare, 1965- . annual.

Includes extensive medical statistics, and data on various health and capacity indicators. This publication will be of interest to the specialist health researcher. The title varies.

175 **Assault, a burden for a rural hospital in Lesotho.**
A. A. van Geldermalsen. *Tropical and Geographical Medicine*, vol. 45, no. 1 (1993), p. 30-32.

This article presents the results of a survey of assault at a rural hospital in Lesotho in 1987. Results show a high prevalence of assault, with one fifth of adult men admitted due to such injuries. Murder rates also appeared high. The most common instruments of assault were found to be knives and sticks. Assault cases placed a heavy burden on hospital resources and the victims of assault required more care than other patients.

176 **A case-control study of the impact of improved sanitation on diarrhoea morbidity in Lesotho.**
D. L. Daniels, S. N. Cousens, L. N. Makoae, R. G. Feachem. *Bulletin of the World Health Organization*, vol. 68, no. 4 (1990), p. 455-63.

Discusses the impact of improved sanitation on a group of young children in the Mohale's Hoek district. The authors find that children under five years from households with a latrine experience significantly fewer episodes of diarrhoea than children from households without a latrine. The health impact was greater for households that practised better personal hygiene, and where the mothers had more education or were employed.

177 **Decentralization and primary health care in Lesotho.**
Malcolm Wallis. Roma, Lesotho: National University of Lesotho, Faculty of Social Sciences, 1982. 19p. (Staff Seminar Paper, no. 31).

Wallis discusses the future of primary health care (PHC) in Lesotho. He argues that community participation and decentralization should be central features in PHC provision, and identifies three problem areas in developing a decentralized PHC system in Lesotho. First, he considers the difficulty of involving the chieftainship in community participation schemes. He then comments on the problem of designing participatory institutions. Finally, the extent of 'urban-bias' in health care provision in Lesotho is evaluated.

178 **Diagnosis and management of acute respiratory infections in Lesotho.**
S. Redd, M. Moteetee, R. Waldman. *Health Policy and Planning*, vol. 5, no. 3 (1990), p. 255-60.

Acute respiratory infections account for a significant proportion of child deaths in Lesotho and this article presents the results of a survey of diagnosis and treatment in rural areas. The survey questioned doctors, nurses and nurse-clinicians in order to investigate the extent of compliance with World Health Organization recommendations on the management of such infections. Results show that medical practitioners require training in some areas and the article recommends that a national programme be developed for the treatment of acute respiratory infections.

179 **Disease in Lesotho: perception and prevalence.**
John Gay. Maseru: Ministry of Health, 1993. 86p.

Provides the results of a socially stratified survey on disease in Lesotho. Twelve socio-economic groups were chosen, covering well-paid urban professionals to poor rural inhabitants. Interestingly, these groups appeared to perceive certain diseases in the same way. Lack of money appeared to be an important constraint to obtaining health care.

180 **Drinking water source, diarrhoeal morbidity, and child growth in villages with both traditional and improved water supplies in rural Lesotho, southern Africa.**
S. A. Esrey, J. P. Habicht, M. C. Latham, D. G. Sisler, G. Casella. *American Journal of Public Health*, vol. 78, no. 11 (1988), p. 1,451-55.

A study of the effects on child health of improved water supply in ten villages in rural Lesotho. Growth and morbidity rates were compared for households who relied exclusively on improved water supplies and for households who supplemented these with water from traditional sources. Children whose families relied exclusively on improved water supplies for drinking and cooking grew faster than children whose families supplemented these sources. The difference was particularly apparent for children older than one year, due to the nature of various water-borne infections. Thus, the survey shows that improved water supplies can benefit children's health, but only if used exclusively.

181 **An evaluation of the Lesotho Planned Parenthood Association community based distribution.**

Jeanette Bloem. Maseru: Sechaba Consultants & Ministry of Health and Social Welfare, Lesotho Planned Parenthood Association (LPPA), 1993. 31p.

The LPPA has been executing a national Community Based Distribution (CBD) of Contraceptives programme with the aim of increasing family planning among the rural population. It aims to bring these services closer to the target population through the use of trained village health workers. This survey found that there was a high awareness of the project in the community. Moreover, contraceptive prevalence had increased, although there is resistance to condoms and CDB agents more frequently supplied the contraceptive pill. While religion and years of schooling seemed to have no significant influence on the use of contraceptives, other factors were important, such as age, marital status, socio-economic status, occupation and number of children.

182 **An evaluation of the Scott Hospital Community Based Distribution Family Planning Programme.**

David Hall. Maseru: Sechaba Consultants & Scott Hospital, 1992. 45p.

An evaluation of the Scott Hospital Community Based Distribution Family Planning Programme. The author reports findings from a community-level study on the use of and attitudes towards contraceptives. It appears that awareness of the project is high and positive attitudes towards contraceptives have risen quite dramatically since a study conducted in 1988. The percentage of those who used contraceptives had also risen, which appears largely attributable to the project. However, the report finds that health workers do not supply the contraceptive injection which is the method preferred by the majority of those studied.

183 **Getting the best value for money in health care.**

S. N. Banoub. *World Health Forum*, vol. 10, no. 2 (1989), p. 258-64.

The author discusses the efficiency of various health care strategies in Lesotho, beginning with a proposal to establish a college of medicine and teaching hospital. Given the small proportion of the rural population that presently have access to health care, it is argued that resources could be used more efficiently in developing primary health care. This article presents an overview of the health situation in Lesotho and will be useful as an introduction to health policy issues.

184 **Health and disease in south-eastern Lesotho: a social anthropological perspective of two villages.**

Marion Heap. Cape Town: University of Cape Town, Centre for African Studies, 1989. 133p. 2 maps. bibliog. (Communications, no. 16).

Primarily a descriptive study of the social dimensions of health and disease-coping strategies. Work was carried out in two villages in south-eastern Lesotho on local experiences of health and disease. The study concludes that the choice of medical service is highly related to cost and geographic proximity.

185 **Health and family planning services in Lesotho: the people's perspective.**
David Hall, Gwen Malahleha. Maseru: Ministry of Health, [n.d.]. 80p. 1 map. bibliog.

This undated report was probably carried out in the late 1980s. It provides a qualitative analysis of individual and household behaviour and attitudes to health using information collected at three research sites. Special attention was paid to women, and additional information was also collected from a small sample of village health workers and traditional practitioners. This is a useful survey for researchers in health practices.

186 **Health in Lesotho.**
Lesotho Government. Maseru: Ministry of Health, 1993. 131p. 2 maps. bibliog.

A rich survey of health in Lesotho, presenting up-to-date statistics on a wide range of health issues. Particularly useful is the concentration on the full spectrum of health practitioners, including traditional healers. The report argues that the decline in employment opportunities and growing economic stratification of the population has led to a multi-tier health system. Local attitudes and the classification of common diseases are discussed in terms of their implications for the health system.

187 **Human immunodeficiency virus and migrant labour in South Africa.**
Karen Jochelson, Monyaola Mothibeli, Jean-Patrick Leger. *International Journal of Health Services*, vol. 21, no. 1 (1991), p. 157-73.

This investigation of the impact of the migrant labour system on the transmission of the HIV virus has particular relevance for Lesotho, as the majority of both miners and prostitutes surveyed were from Lesotho. The authors find that the migrant system has created a market for prostitution in mining towns, and this, combined with the networks between urban and rural communities, is likely to worsen the problems of combating the HIV epidemic.

188 **Lesotho and Nepal: the failure of western 'family planning'.**
N. Kanno. In: *Reconstructing Babylon: essays on women and technology*. Edited by P. H. Hynes. London: Earthscan, 1990, p. 38-58.

Discusses the importance of social and cultural factors in understanding contraceptive activities. Historical beliefs about reproductive and contraceptive activities are shown to affect family planning practices, and the author argues that they largely explain the failure of 'western' family planning.

189 **Modelling access to a basic need: the provision of primary health care in rural Lesotho.**

P. A. Wellings. *South African Geographer*, vol. 11, no. 2 (1983), p. 127-48.

Wellings examines the relevance of geographical location in modelling access to primary health care. He presents a location-based model for this purpose, but then goes on to make a number of theoretical and practical criticisms. This article will be of interest to health planners and researchers interested in the use of geographic models to plan health care delivery. This article is also available under the same title as a University of Natal working paper (Working Paper no. 3, 1983. 45p.).

190 **The sexual behaviour and attitudes to AIDS of soccer players in Lesotho.**

Debby Gill. Maseru: Sechaba Consultants & CARE, 1994. 20p.

Investigates the knowledge and behaviour of players from Division A football teams in Lesotho. The young men in this study showed a high rate of condom use and some awareness of the problems of AIDS. However, researchers felt that many of them used condoms to prevent pregnancy rather than to prevent AIDS or sexually transmitted diseases. It was also found that condoms were not used consistently, although this may have been due to lack of availability. There is still some confusion over AIDS and its transmission; many of the players rated their chances of contracting AIDS as very low, but the results of the survey found that many were at high risk. Given the relatively high socio-economic and educational status of the players, the report argues that it should be possible to enable players to gain a better understanding of AIDS and thus act as motivators within their communities.

Indigenous health systems

191 **Medicine, magic and sorcery among the Southern Sotho.**

Edmond Hugh Ashton. Cape Town: University of Cape Town, School of African Studies, 1943. 33p. bibliog.

Ashton studies various aspects of sorcery and witchcraft among the southern Sotho. Although his focus is on the southern Sotho as a whole, and thus includes southern Sotho-speakers in South Africa, Ashton's study remains highly relevant for Lesotho. This is a thorough discussion of the linkages between health, medicine and the supernatural. Despite its age, it remains a standard work.

192 **Ritual and medicines: indigenous healing in South Africa.**

David Hammond-Tooke. Johannesburg: A. D. Donker, 1989. 166p. bibliog.

Although the discussion is directed at Sotho people in South Africa, this book makes many references to the place of health and disease in Sotho culture. As such, it is useful for an understanding of traditional attitudes towards disease and healing in

Lesotho. Hammond-Tooke offers an analysis of the relationship between the use of traditional healers and 'western' medical doctors. A long bibliography is appended.

193 **Sotho medicine.**

Mosebi Damane. *Lesotho Notes and Records*, vol. 10 (1973-74), p. 48-59.

Damane discusses traditional medicine in Lesotho, and provides a description of the various kinds of traditional doctors and their role in solving health and personal problems. Included is a discussion of the role of medicine-murder in witchcraft. Such murders occur because of the belief by some people that the use of human remains in 'medicine' or ritual has a particularly powerful effect. Also examined is the praise poetry associated with the use of divining bones. This will be a useful publication for those interested in customs and health.

194 **Suto (Basuto) medicines.**

J. M. Watt, Marie G. Brandwijk. *Bantu Studies* (South Africa), vol. 3 (1927-29), p. 73-100, p. 155-78, p. 297-319. bibliog.

An exhaustive description of some seventy Basotho medicinal plants, including for each its various names, distribution, uses, chemical composition and pharmacological action. References to botanical, medical and pharmacological literature are given for each plant, and an appendix lists the Sesotho names of the medicinal plants alphabetically together with their corresponding botanical species names.

Adult and child welfare

195 **Changes in body-weight in Basotho women: seasonal coping in households with different socioeconomic conditions.**

D. A. Himmelgreen, N. Romerodaza. *American Journal of Human Biology*, vol. 6, no. 5 (1994), p. 599-611.

Seasonal weight change is examined in women living in the Lesotho highlands. Households were divided into two types: female managed and multiple-parent. In addition, households were separated into those that were far from the district headquarters and those that were closer. No significant difference was found in body weight across seasons for female and multiple-parent households. However, women living in households far from the district headquarters had significantly lower body weight throughout the seasons and a greater fluctuation in body weight over time. This suggests that seasonality has a greater influence on body weight for those households that depend on subsistence agriculture than for those with greater involvement in the wage economy.

196 **Child rearing in Lesotho: some aspects of child rearing in the Teyateyaneng area.**

E. E. Bam. Roma, Lesotho: National University of Lesotho, 1984. 77p. bibliog.

A description of traditional child rearing practices using data from villages around Teyateyaneng, in the central-north lowlands. Information was collected on pregnancy, taboos and child care. The education of children and their social environment during the first two years of life were investigated. This book concludes with an assessment of the impact of women's education on child rearing.

197 **An evaluation of the Community Alcohol Rehabilitation Programme of Scott Hospital.**

Debby Gill, David Hall. Maseru: Sechaba Consultants, 1993. 62p.

The results of this survey show that alcohol abuse is perceived as a widespread problem in Lesotho. The Community Alcohol Rehabilitation Programme (CARP) is the first programme in the country developed to prevent alcohol abuse. This evaluation sought to measure the extent of awareness of CARP and the efficacy of the programme. The study finds that CARP has played an important role in pioneering prevention and rehabilitation of alcoholism. However, it is also argued that the programme should be revitalized and some recommendations for change are presented.

198 **Female alcoholism problems in Lesotho.**

M. Mphi. *Addiction*, vol. 89, no. 8 (1994), p. 945-49.

A short paper on the alcohol and alcohol-related problems of women in Lesotho. The author argues that the cultural position of women promotes a vicious circle where they become brewers of alcohol and then consumers. Excessive alcohol consumption can also be encouraged by marital difficulties. However, high alcohol consumption leads to social censure and, sometimes, the breakdown of a woman's marriage, which places her in an economically and socially vulnerable position. The author believes that greater training on female alcoholism should be given to health workers, and that greater research is needed.

199 **A longitudinal study of Basotho children, Volume 1. Off to a good start: a study of 400 Basotho one year olds.**

A. Blair. Roma, Lesotho: National University of Lesotho, Institute of Southern African Studies, 1986. 125p. bibliog. (Southern African Studies Series, no. 2).

This is the first volume of what is intended to be a four-volume study of Basotho children. This will be a longitudinal study over the first fifteen years of a child's life, and it provides a wide range of information on child care and socio-economic conditions. In order to be representative, the sample was drawn from an urban area, as well as from villages in the lowlands and mountains.

200 **Low-cost urban sanitation in Lesotho.**
Isabel C. Blackett. Washington, DC: International Bank for Reconstruction and Development, UNDP-World Bank Water and Sanitation Program, 1994. 37p.

Lesotho's low-cost urban sanitation programme is widely regarded as a successful, self-sustaining project. This document presents information on adoption and the reasons for success. Central to the project's achievements were an affordable latrine design, and insistence on a commitment by beneficiaries in terms of both time and money. The lessons learnt have relevance for other development projects and it is helpful that details of the advertisement campaign for the sanitation programme are provided.

201 **Maintenance payments for child-support in Southern Africa: using law to promote family planning.**
Alice K. Armstrong. *Studies in Family Planning*, vol. 23, no. 4 (1992), p. 217-28.

Armstrong seeks to demonstrate in this article that maintenance laws are relevant to family planning. By making men bear the costs of supporting their legitimate and illegitimate children, maintenance laws would encourage men to practice family planning. However, based on the evidence from a large-scale project on maintenance in southern Africa, Armstrong argues that maintenance laws are inadequate to counter the social norms that prevent women claiming support for their children. This article will be useful for researchers into family planning and the legal position of women. See item nos. 166 and 169 for other publications from the same project.

202 **Migrancy and male sexuality on the South African gold mines.**
T. Dunbar Moodie, Vivienne Ndatshe, British Sibuyi. *Journal of Southern African Studies*, vol. 14, no. 2 (January 1988), p. 228-56.

A descriptive analysis of male sexual experience on the South African mines, dealing with both heterosexual and homosexual behaviour. The paper argues that the particular form of homosexual behaviour on the gold mines can be explained by the character of proletarianization in southern Africa. The South African influx control system prevents a migrant's family from joining him at the mines, and, in the past, home-leave was relatively infrequent. This system encouraged some miners to engage in same-sex relationships. The authors argue that homosexuality as practised in the mines is a reflection of traditional heterosexual practices and is understood as such by miners. Such traditional practices involve non-penetrative sex between young adults, often, but not always, as a precursor to marriage. Thus, homosexual relationships on the mines are not seen as incompatible with heterosexual behaviour; however, this type of relationship is stigmatized in the migrants' home areas.

203 **Patterns of infant care in Lesotho.**
A. Blair. PhD thesis, University of Nottingham, England, 1989. 508p.

Investigates infant care practices in Lesotho. Questions were asked on early infancy care practices, including birth, language, play and nutrition. The results were analysed for three key groups: urban households of high socio-economic status; rural households of high socio-economic status; and rural households of low socio-economic status. A mixture of traditional and 'western' child care practices were observed. These did not vary much among households, except for urban areas, which have more 'westernized' practices.

204 **Preliminary findings from the national database on rural water supply.**
David Hall. Maseru: Ministry of Home Affairs, Village Water Supply Section, & Sechaba Consultants, 1993. 42p. 2 maps.

A national database on the country's water supply has been established to serve as a policy tool for the provision of sustainable water supplies in Lesotho. This database shows that many projects have taken place in urban areas but that despite this, rural water supply projects have only reached approximately fifty-seven per cent of the rural population. However, coverage varies significantly between districts and ecological zones. The coverage in the mountains is only twenty-six per cent of the population compared to eighty-six per cent in the Lowlands. Coverage in the Senqu River valley is forty-one per cent and in the foothills it is thirty-seven per cent. In addition, these success rates appear inadequate in terms of the policy aims of water provision.

205 **Rural water supply systems in Lesotho: findings from a nation-wide inspection.**
David Hall. Maseru: Ministry of Natural Resources, Department of Rural Water Supply & Sechaba Consultants, 1995. 91p. 2 maps.

Presents data on rural water supplies and level of service standards. Interestingly, the author finds that a large proportion of villages still use traditional water sources, consisting mainly of unprotected springs, which are used particularly in times of drought and breakdowns. However, the partial use of unprotected water sources will reduce the health impact of improved water systems.

206 **The situation of children and women in Lesotho, 1994.**
Edited by Debby Gill. Maseru: Sechaba Consultants & Unicef & Ministry of Planning, Economic and Manpower Development, 1994. rev. ed. 242p. 3 maps. bibliog.

Intended as an update of the earlier study (see item no. 207), this document has changed significantly to reflect newer data and far-reaching changes in the political situation. There is an analysis of Lesotho's place within the newly democratic South Africa, and on the new democracy in Lesotho itself. The first part of the report discusses general socio-economic factors, while the second part is mainly concerned with infrastructure. The specific situation of children and women is then discussed. Finally the report provides an overview of the law regarding women and children in Lesotho.

207 **The situation of women and children in Lesotho, 1991.**
Ministry of Planning, Economic and Manpower Development and Unicef Lesotho. Maseru: Government of Lesotho, Ministry of Planning, 1991. 2nd ed. 170p. 7 maps. bibliog.

Provides an analysis of the issues affecting women and children in Lesotho. Material on the health and education sectors is included, as is information on traditional attitudes and beliefs. A wide range of statistics is gathered on key social indicators.

208 **Sociocultural environment in Lesotho as it impinges on development: focus on children.**
Itumeleng Kimane. In: *Southern Africa in the 1980s and beyond: Institute of Southern African Studies 1980-1990*. Edited by the Institute of Southern African Studies. Roma, Lesotho: University of Lesotho, Institute of Southern African Studies, 1993, p. 38-51. bibliog.

Kimane discusses the position of children within the sociocultural environment of Lesotho. The paper first provides an overview of the legal issues surrounding children and then moves on to discuss child health using data on common childhood diseases. Finally, there is a short discussion on the political and economic characteristics of child welfare in Lesotho. This paper lacks any detailed theoretical or empirical analyses and instead presents a number of areas for future work. It may be useful for those interested in the research questions that can be generated in this field.

209 **Water, sanitation, hygiene and health in the Qabane Valley, Lesotho.**
David Hall, Michael Adams. Maseru: Sechaba Consultants, 1991. 102p. bibliog.

A survey of health and hygiene in the remote Qabane Valley, southern Lesotho. The authors discuss local attitudes to health and hygiene, and argue that health education is necessary for the effective use of improved water supplies. A local community drama group is presented as a successful case-study of the use of theatre for health education. Detailed socio-economic data and a wide range of information is collected on health and sanitation practices. This publication is useful for both health specialists and academic researchers.

Politics

General

210 **The Basotho nation-state: what legacy for the future?**
Richard F. Weisfelder. *Journal of Modern African Studies*, vol. 19, no. 2 (1981), p. 221-56.

Beginning with the observation that Lesotho's strong national identity has not forestalled domestic conflict nor solved economic problems, Weisfelder argues that the historical bases of Basotho identity remain substantial forces in promoting national solidarity and survival. However, he also finds that Lesotho has no option for separate development and considers this in the light of future democracy in South Africa.

211 **Crocodiles and commoners in Lesotho: continuity and change in the rule-making system of Lesotho.**
W. J. Breytenbach. Pretoria: Africa Institute, 1975. 136p. bibliog.

Based on a University of South Africa doctoral thesis, this book is an interdisciplinary study covering history, sociology and political science. It contains considerable material on chieftainship, and gives a detailed account of political developments from Moshoeshoe I to the Interim National Council of 1973. It also contains tabulated material on individual politicians and a useful bibliography.

212 **Lesotho and the struggle for Azania Africanist political movements in Lesotho and Azania: the origins and history of the Basutoland Congress Party and the Pan Africanist Congress.**
Bernard Leeman. London: University of Azania, 1985. 3 vols. 2 maps. bibliog.

A minutely detailed account of the links between the Basutoland Congress Party and the South African-based Pan Africanist Congress. Leeman's study covers the period 1780 to 1984, thereby surveying both the historical roots and the recent past of these organizations. In three slim volumes, this analysis will be useful reading for researchers into politics and the black consciousness movement in southern Africa. However, the work is heavily flavoured by the author's own commitment to Pan Africanism and this reduces confidence in some of his assertions. The publication is available from: The University of Azania, PAC Education Office, BCM Box 1618, London WC1N 3XX, England.

213 **Lesotho: historical legacies of nationalism and nationhood.**
Tefetso Mothibe. In: *Southern Africa after apartheid: prospects for the inner periphery in 1990s.* Edited by Sehoai Santho, Mafa Sejanamane. Harare: Southern Africa Political Economy Series (SAPES), 1991, p. 188-93. bibliog.

A short commentary on the creation of nationhood in Lesotho. Mothibe describes the changing nature of Lesotho's constrained independence, and argues that historical events have helped create a strong national pride. However, despite this cultural independence, Lesotho has not been able to escape the consequence of her incorporation into the South African economy.

Pre-independence

214 **Chiefdom politics and alien law: Basutoland under Cape rule, 1871-1884.**
Sandra B. Burman. New York: Africana Publishing, 1981. 250p. 6 maps. bibliog.

A study of early colonial rule in Basutoland, covering the period of the Gun War, when a successful revolt was led against Cape government rule. It is a well-documented record of conflicting interests among the Basotho chieftainship, which led to the initial placing of Lesotho under British rule and then the subsequent pattern of acquiescence and rebellion. Burman also draws a picture of conflict among the colonial authorities, and more interestingly between the government and missionary groups. Commonly, Christian Basotho are thought to have accepted colonial authority unquestionably, but Burman shows that there were important differences in opinion. While this book does not focus directly on the position of the commoners, Burman discusses the nature of chiefly power and the way in which it was constrained by the imposition of colonial legislation and economic change.

215 **'Clinging to the chiefs': some contradictions of colonial rule in Basutoland, c. 1890-1930.**
Judy Kimble. In: *Contradictions of accumulation in Africa: studies in economy and state.* Edited by Henry Bernstein, Bonnie K. Campbell. Beverly Hills, California; New Delhi, London: Sage Publications, 1985, p. 25-69. bibliog.

The first section of the paper deals with Moshoeshoe's kingdom from c. 1830 to annexation by the Cape Colony in 1868. The second section is concerned with British colonial domination from c. 1890 to 1930. From an analysis of these periods, Kimble identifies the initial ambivalence towards British rule on the part of the chiefs. The paper concludes with an attempt to demonstrate how the chieftainship had both changed through its articulation with the colonial state but also how it became central to the discourse of almost all competing political forces. Kimble argues that this analysis of the colonial period illuminates the character and dynamics of the pre-capitalist mode of production and the pre-colonial state in Lesotho.

216 **Democracy and indirect rule.**
Edmond Hugh Ashton. *Africa* (UK), vol. 17, no. 4 (Oct. 1947), p. 235-51.

Compares pre-colonial government in Lesotho and Botswana with that under the colonial administration. The author concludes that whereas the early form of government was fairly democratic, the result of indirect rule was to strengthen the power of chiefs and weaken control over them by the nation at large. Poor education and lack of economic development are factors which influenced this growth in the authoritarian rule of the chiefs.

217 **The political dilemma of chieftainship in colonial Lesotho with reference to the administration and court reforms of 1938.**
L. B. B. J. Machobane. Roma, Lesotho: National University of Lesotho, Institute of Southern African Studies, 1986. 36p. bibliog. (Occasional Paper, no. 1).

Lesotho's ill-defined constitutional status under the British Crown produced a parallel government, as the indigenous government remained in charge of internal affairs. The author argues that due to a combination of factors this system broke down. Resentful of chiefly abuse, commoners demanded political change and a reduction in the power of the chiefs. Thus, the 1938 reforms specifically defined the functions of the chieftaincy and so reduced its powers. A major drawback with this analysis is its failure to consider the effect of legislation on the growth of a royal aristocracy.

218 **Prophets with honour: a documentary history of Lekhotla la Bafo.**
Robert Edgar. Johannesburg: Ravan Press, [1987?]. 250p.

Edgar has assembled a collection of writings and songs from the Basotho rural protest movement, Lekhotla la Bafo. Accompanying the collection is a history of the group and an assessment of its legacy for present-day politics in Lesotho. This is an intriguing study of the resistance movement, which was founded after the Second World War and which continued to have influence until the 1960s.

219 **Women's 'conservatism' and the politics of gender in late colonial Lesotho.**
Marc Epprecht. *Journal of African History* (UK), vol. 36, no. 1 (1995), p. 29-56.

Investigates the widespread assumption that Basotho women tend to be politically 'conservative', while Basotho men are more politically sophisticated. Epprecht argues that these stereotypes stem from women's supposed domesticity, religiosity or love of tradition. He examines the actual history of Basotho women in politics in the late colonial era (1920-65) and finds no empirical grounds for these assumptions. On the contrary, Epprecht claims that even the most ostensibly 'conservative' women often adopted non-traditional, self-emancipatory behaviour. This article will be useful for both historians, political scientists and those working from the gender perspective.

Post-independence

220 **Clarion call! Struggle for a better Lesotho: a collection of speeches by His Majesty King Moshoeshoe II, 1976-1989.**

Edited by Mamello Morrison. Maseru: Mphatlalatsane Publishers, 1995. 258p.

A collection of speeches by the late King of Lesotho, Moshoeshoe II. This publication appears to have been planned during his time in exile in the early 1990s and, as such, was probably intended as a mechanism to raise his political profile. Whatever its intentions, this remains a interesting book that provides details of the King's public addresses, with explanatory commentary by local experts. Subjects covered include: religion and liberation; alternative strategies for sustainable development; international affairs; and dualism in Lesotho's legal system. It is available from Mphatlalatsane Publishers, PO Box 7066, Maseru 100, Lesotho.

221 **Foreign business and political unrest in Lesotho.**

Roger Tangri. *African Affairs*, no. 92 (1993), p. 223-38.

Discusses the underlying political and economic conditions which gave rise to the riots and worker agitation in Lesotho in 1991. Tangri argues that this unrest was partly rooted in the behaviour of foreign business itself, but also in corrupt government administration and political authoritarianism. He maintains that violence was linked to widespread disillusionment with military rule. Looking at the implications for the economy and politics, he finds that this unrest has acted as a deterrent to further investment from abroad and, thus, official industrial policy has been undermined.

222 **The future of 'traditional' hereditary chieftaincy in a democratic Southern Africa: the case of Lesotho.**

Sam Rugege. In: *Southern Africa after apartheid: prospects for the inner periphery in 1990s.* Edited by Sehoai Santho, Mafa Sejanamane. Harare: Southern Africa Political Economy Series (SAPES), 1991, p. 148-74. bibliog.

Rugege discusses the contemporary role of the chieftainship, arguing that, despite the fundamentally undemocratic nature of the institution and its poor record of performance, it has been retained as an integral part of the modern state in Lesotho. This is because of the dual functions the chieftaincy serves. It has a practical function of maintaining law and order and ensuring the performance of public services by the rural population. On the other hand, there is an ideological function, whereby the chieftaincy is depicted as the authentic 'traditional' authority. This has the effect of boosting the authority and legitimacy of the central state, which has lacked legitimacy in the past. Rugege argues that the chieftaincy in its present form would disappear under a democratic government. However, this latter argument fails to consider the multifaceted nature of political allegiances that could emerge under democracy.

223 **King or country: the Lesotho crisis of August 1994.**
P. Sekatle. *Indicator South Africa*, vol. 12, no. 1 (Summer 1994), p. 67-72.

This brief article argues that corruption and undemocratic actions led to a coup in 1994, in which the King Letsie III came into conflict with the democratically-elected government.

224 **Lesotho 1970: an African coup under the microscope.**
Bennett Makalo Khaketla. London: Hurst, 1971. 350p.

A detailed account of the political history of Lesotho during the period 1952-70, which was an era of important political developments. In 1952, many politically conscious Basotho joined a common independence movement, the Basotuland African Congress, which later changed its name to the Basotuland Congress Party (BCP) and became one of the two major political parties. Only in 1958 were political parties first formally allowed; in that year, a group of chiefs and commoners broke away from the BAC and formed the Basotuland National Congress (BNP), the other major party. In the pre-independence elections of 1965, the BNP won fifty per cent of parliamentary seats. Khaketla follows the progress of these two parties from independence to the 1970 state of emergency, which was imposed by the BNP, following elections in which the BCP won the majority of the vote. The author describes this event, and the civil unrest which followed, in detail.

225 **The Lesotho general election of 1970.**
W. J. A. Macartney. *Government & Opposition* (UK), vol. 8, no. 4 (1973), p. 473-94.

Covers the political history of the period 1965-70 and provides a detailed description of the January 1970 election, and the subsequent events. Macartney also cites the complete 1970 election results, which were suppressed at the time.

226 **Lesotho's political crisis since independence: the role of South Africa.**
Francis Makoa. In: *From destabilisation to regional cooperation in Southern Africa?* Edited by Mafa Sejanamane. Roma, Lesotho: National University of Lesotho, Institute for Southern African Studies, 1994, p. 151-67. bibliog.

This chapter highlights Lesotho's political crisis in the last decade and its underlying causes. Makoa identifies a prolonged period of political crisis in Lesotho since independence, which included an acute constitutional impasse. The period of military rule since the mid-1980s is examined, and the nature of political alignments during this period discussed. Makoa concludes that a combination of internal and external forces has led to impediments in the democratic process in Lesotho. However, this publication has been overtaken by events, as Lesotho now has a democratically-elected government.

227 **The military kingdom: a case for restructuring the system of government in Lesotho in the 1990s.**
Francis K. Makoa. In: *Southern Africa after apartheid: prospects for the inner periphery in 1990s.* Edited by Sehoai Santho, Mafa Sejanamane. Harare: Southern Africa Political Economy Series (SAPES), 1991, p. 175-85. bibliog.

Written prior to the actual event, this paper explores the challenges that a democratic South Africa could pose for Lesotho. The author argues that the demise of apartheid might lead to the collapse of the migratory labour system and thus the income that it generates. It is suggested that Lesotho could alleviate growing economic pressure by restructuring the government system, particularly the chieftaincy and the military. By doing this, financial resources presently used to support these institutions could be used for development purposes. However, the author does not fully consider the political imperatives that might lead to the continuation of these two institutions.

228 **The recent political crisis in Lesotho.**
Khabele Matlosa. *Africa Insight*, vol. 24, no. 4 (1994), p. 225-29.

The central thesis of this article is that Lesotho's transition to democracy is bedevilled by the historical role of the armed forces in politics. Matlosa argues that the post-democracy period of the 1990s has been hamstrung by forces whose interests are threatened by political liberalization.

229 **Some legal and political issues in respect of Lesotho's options in the context of a future democratic South Africa.**
Nqosa Leuta Mahao. In: *Southern Africa after apartheid: prospects for the inner periphery in 1990s.* Edited by Sehoai Santho, Mafa Sejanamane. Harare: Southern Africa Political Economy Series (SAPES), 1991, p. 194-208. bibliog.

Assesses the feasibility of acquiring territory conquered by South Africa in the last century. Sejanamane suggests that the application appears to be fraught with insurmountable hurdles. To accede to Lesotho's claims could encourage other land claims, which would effectively jeopardize the majority of South Africa's present land area. The author argues that an alternative is to merge the two countries.

A chief is a chief by the people.
See item no. 88.

Chieftainship and legitimacy: an anthropological study of executive law in Lesotho.
See item no. 231.

Constitution, Legal System and Human Rights

230 **Agricultural development in Lesotho: the legal framework and the executive.**
M. Huisman. Roma, Lesotho: National University of Lesotho, Department of Geography, 1983. 73p. (Urban and Regional Planning Research Reports, vol. 5).

This work investigates the links between the legal framework and agricultural development. The author discusses the land use objectives of the government, and reviews the laws surrounding land tenure, land use and marketing. Finally, the report evaluates the implementation of these laws and the degree to which development objectives have been met.

231 **Chieftainship and legitimacy: an anthropological study of executive law in Lesotho.**
Ian Hamnett. London: Routledge & Kegan Paul, 1975. 164p.

Discusses customary law, particularly those aspects which concern succession to chieftainship, private inheritance and land tenure.

232 **The common law in Lesotho.**
James E. Beardsley. *Journal of African Law*, vol. 14, no. 3 (Autumn 1970), p. 198-202.

A letter which discusses S. Poulter's article *The common law in Lesotho* (see item no. 233), with which Beardsley disagrees on several points. The relationship between Lesotho's legal system and that of the Republic of South Africa is discussed.

233 **The common law in Lesotho.**
Sebastian M. Poulter. *Journal of African Law*, vol. 13, no. 3 (Autumn 1969), p. 127-44.

Includes a discussion on how the Lesotho common law system is bound to that of the Republic of South Africa.

234 **Contemporary constitutional history of Lesotho.**
W. C. M. Maqutu. Mazenod, Lesotho: Mazenod Institute, 1990. 241p.

This book analyses the development of Lesotho's constitution after independence. The author explains how alterations to the constitution were related to changes in the balance of political forces. Section 4.2 deals with the transgression of human rights through the use of the Internal Security Act, while chapter five takes a more general view about the use of the law to prevent infringements of basic rights. Overall Maqutu takes a positive view of the human rights situation and argues that the rule of law has always won out. Despite the author's often difficult style, this book provides a good overview of the main political and legal events since independence and contains, in chapter seven, a useful summary of changes in land legislation.

235 **Contemporary family law of Lesotho.**
W. C. M. Maqutu. Roma, Lesotho: National University of Lesotho Publishing House, 1992. 389p. bibliog.

A detailed commentary on conflicts in the interpretation of family law. Maqutu argues that family law is in a confused state and that problems often surface in the practice of the law. Part one covers the historical roots of the system and the effects of the dual system on courts of family law. Part two deals in detail with customary marriage, as well as the position of women and children under Basotho custom. Part three looks at received family law and its implications for women and children. Although Maqutu's style is verbose, this is an essential text for up-to-date and detailed information on family law.

236 **Democracy in Lesotho: the electoral laws.**
M. P. Mamashela. *Lesotho Law Journal*, vol. 8, no. 2 (1993), p. 169-96.

A useful article on the nature of the electoral laws in Lesotho. The legal implications of the 1993 elections are discussed, as are political reforms in this area. Mamashela also analyses the electoral system in general.

237 **Family law and litigation in Basotho society.**
Sebastian M. Poulter. Oxford: Clarendon Press, 1976. 362p.

Based on an Oxford DPhil thesis, this book is a detailed and systematic account of customary family law. There is an introductory survey of the cultural, economic, social and institutional framework within which the law operates. The main part of the book concentrates on marriage, divorce, inheritance, and the status of widows, using the results of family litigation to analyse the guiding principles and rules, and their adaptation to change.

238 **Human rights and the migratory labour system.**
Chris Goldman. Roma, Lesotho: National University of Lesotho, Institute of Southern African Studies, 1988. 48p. bibliog. (Human and People's Rights Monograph Series, no. 3).

Examines the relationship between human rights and migrant labour in Southern Africa. In order to clarify the human rights issues, the situation of Lesotho is examined in detail. Of special importance is the role of family life in the spectrum of human rights: Goldman argues that the denial of a 'normal' family life is a major infringement of the rights of migrant workers. In addition, some attempt is made to consider the economic rights of a worker. Here, the author discusses the extent to which a worker fails to be fully compensated for his/her work, and although this section has not been developed as fully as it might have been, it does provide an interesting insight into the nature of human rights. This is a useful analysis and one that will be particularly helpful for those interested in the rights of workers in Lesotho.

239 **Human rights in Botswana, Lesotho and Swaziland: implications of adherence to international human rights treaties.**
Steven Neff. Roma, Lesotho: National University of Lesotho, Institute of Southern African Studies, 1986. 97p. bibliog. (Human and People's Rights Monograph Series, no. 2).

The author discusses the effect of the Banjul Charter on the legal systems of Lesotho, Botswana and Swaziland. The Charter was adopted by the Organization of African Unity in 1981 and reflects the first African initiative in the area. Neff's analysis shows that each of the countries he surveys falls short of the requirements of the Charter. He argues that it is not enough that a framework for human rights legislation exists and that it needs instead to be incorporated in 'living law'. This is a useful summary of human rights legislation.

240 **Human rights in Botswana, Lesotho and Swaziland: a survey.**
K. A. Maope. Roma, Lesotho: National University of Lesotho, Institute of Southern African Studies, 1986. 155p.

A useful survey of human rights in the countries of Botswana, Lesotho and Swaziland. Maope considers the implications for human rights of the legal and political systems in these countries. It is shown that human rights, broadly defined, are constrained by a number of legal and political rulings in these countries, including Lesotho. The author concludes that the status of human rights can only be understood within the context of local laws and practices.

241 **Law and natural-resource development: the case of water in Lesotho.**
F. O. Boadu. *Journal of Water Resources Planning and Management*, vol. 17, no. 6 (1991), p. 698-710.

This article discusses the evolution and structure of the Lesotho Water Resources Act of 1978. The Act was intended to promote equitable and efficient use of water. However, it has not been fully implemented due to lack of finances and personnel. Some proposals for effective implementation are provided.

242 **Legal dualism in Lesotho: a study of the choice of law question in family matters.**
Sebastian Poulter. Morija, Lesotho: Morija Sesuto Book Depot, 1981. 126p. bibliog.

Lesotho possesses two systems of family law. While customary law is applicable to the vast majority of the population, the common law system, imported during colonial times, exists side by side with it. This book examines and compares the different principals and rules of the two systems in the area of family law. It also considers the basis on which courts in Lesotho decide which of the two systems is appropriate for the resolution of a given debate. Poulter provided an update in 1986, citing additional cases: *Legal dualism in Lesotho: first supplement, up to date to 1st April 1986* (Morija, Lesotho: Morija Sesuto Book Depot, 1986. 24p.).

243 **The legal system of Lesotho.**
Vernon V. Palmer, Sebastian M. Poulter. Charlottesville, Virginia: The Michie Company, 1972. 574p. (Legal Systems of Africa Series).

The standard work on the legal system of Lesotho as it existed before the suspension of the Constitution following the 1970 elections. Part one (by S. M. Poulter) is devoted to the sources of law, namely the common law, customary law, and legislation, and includes a discussion on the applicability and validity of customary law. Part two (by V. V. Palmer) describes the 1959 and 1965 Constitutions, and (in much greater detail) the Independence Constitution of 1966, together with a considerable section on fundamental human rights. Part three (by S. M. Poulter) deals with the different types of courts, the judiciary and magistracy, and the legal profession. One of the appendices includes a substantial excerpt from the Independence Constitution.

244 **The place of the Laws of Lerotholi in the legal system of Lesotho.**
Sebastian M. Poulter. *African Affairs*, no. 283, vol. 71 (April 1972), p. 144-62. Reprinted in shortened version in *Lesotho Notes and Records*, vol. 10 (1973-74), p. 33-47.

Includes an account of the origin of the Basutoland National Council. Poulter describes and discusses the legal standing of the various editions of the Laws of Lerotholi. These were an overarching set of laws, intended to guide the governance of Basotuland. They were first approved in 1903; subsequent amendments were approved in 1919 and 1920, and a revised version was made widely available in 1922. Poulter makes considerable use of the Reports of Proceedings of the Basutoland National Council.

245 **Some anomalies in the marriage laws of Lesotho.**
Carol Harlow. *Journal of African Law* (UK), vol. 3 (Autumn 1966), p. 168-72.

Pages 173-77 contain reports on a decision of the Appeal Court in a specific case and discussions on some of the problems. The article itself includes discussion on the recognition of customary marriage and the question of bigamy. Harlow argues that there are ambiguities in the interpretation of the law; as a result, the offence of bigamy is rarely enforced. The author proposes that the marriage laws should be unified and overhauled, arguing that the present paucity of the law is due to the influence of South Africa, a country which has a 'cynical disregard for African family life'.

246 **Some notes on the concept of custom in Lesotho.**
Ian Hamnett. *Journal of African Law* (UK), vol. 15, no. 3 (1971), p. 266-73.

Describes customary law as applied in Lesotho courts by references to cases collected by the Judicial Commissioners.

247 **Sotho laws and customs: a handbook based on decided cases in Basutoland together with the Laws of Lerotholi.**
Patrick Duncan. Cape Town: Oxford University Press, 1960. 169p. bibliog.

A thorough study of Basotho law written as a companion to the Laws of Lerotholi. Duncan deals with customary law, cites many examples from judgements in Basotho courts, and describes social customs such as marriage ceremonies.

248 **Workers' collective rights under the Lesotho Labour Code.**
Sam Rugege. *Industrial Law Journal*, vol. 15, no. 5 (1994), p. 930-43.

The Lesotho Labour Code came into effect on 1 April 1993. Rugege assesses the characteristics of the Code and argues that there are a number of reasons to feel that it is a useful introduction. The Code streamlines previous legislation, improves health and safety regulations and generally introduces modern aspects of labour law. For example, the Code protects against sexual harassment and established a Labour Court, which came into operation in October 1994. Rugege discusses the effect of the Code on workers' rights and collective rights, such as the right to bargain and to strike. He feels that there has been considerable improvement over previous legislation; however, further improvements are needed to bring the law into conformity with developments in industrial nations in the region and elsewhere.

Law and population growth in Lesotho.
See item no. 96.

Legal constraints on women in development in Lesotho.
See item no. 163.

The legal situation of women in Lesotho.
See item no. 164.

Maintenance in Lesotho.
See item no. 166.

Struggling over scarce resources: women and maintenance in Southern Africa.
See item no. 169.

Maintenance payments for child-support in Southern Africa: using law to promote family planning.
See item no. 201.

Administration and Government

General

249 **Administration of planning in Lesotho. A history and assessment.**
D. Hirschmann. Manchester Papers on Development, 1981. 92p. (Working Paper, no. 2).

Studies government planning in Lesotho during the period 1965 to 1975. The evolution and character of planning is discussed and some conclusions are made about the nature of government planning machinery and possible reform. For a shorter analysis by the author, see also: 'Administration of planning in Lesotho: the second leg' (*Development and Change*, vol. 9, no. 3 [July 1978], p. 397-414).

250 **Decentralisation and development in Lesotho.**
E. R. M. Mapetla, S. W. Rembe. Maseru: Epic Printers, 1989. 84p. bibliog.

This book aims at reconciling the theory and practice of local administration, with the ultimate objective of formalizing proposals for a decentralized system of government in Lesotho. Chapter one explores forms of decentralization, while chapter two analyses the system of local administration in Lesotho. The final two chapters present recommendations for reform and future research activity. The general conclusion seems to be that decentralization has proceeded without a clear policy on objectives. As a result, attempts at decentralization have been piece-meal and haphazard, but the authors highlight a number of positive factors, such as a political commitment to decentralization and popular participation. These conclusions appear overly simplistic compared to other analyses that argue that the central government has been unwilling to relinquish bureaucratic power.

251 **Development administration and political control: the district administration in Lesotho.**

L. A. Picard. *Rural Africana*, vol. 18 (1984), p. 27-44.

This article presents an interesting and useful overview of the evolution of administrative initiatives in the early 1980s. The author argues that the decentralization policy of that period can be understood as a response to political imperatives. The ruling Basutoland National Party had begun to experience loss of political control in some rural areas, and decentralization was envisaged as a method of reducing opposition by stimulating rural development. Unfortunately, the timing of the article precludes an analysis of the success or failure of decentralization initiatives. This remains a valuable article, which can be used to assess the present forms of local administration in Lesotho.

252 **Experimenting with decentralisation through devolution in Lesotho: the Maseru City Council.**

R. C. Leduka. *Review of Southern African Studies*, vol. 1, no. 1 (January 1995), p. 1-28.

Discusses the nature of local administration in Lesotho. Local democracy in the form of elected local councils was instituted with the project to establish the Maseru City Council. However, it is argued that local democracy should not have preceded national democracy. The suppression of a national political forum led, in the author's view, to an inappropriate political environment for local democracy. Thus, the City Council took on a political character unrelated to local needs and this reduced its popular support. This is an interesting publication, presenting one of the few analyses of the success of the Maseru City Council, the first town council in Lesotho.

253 **Government and change in Lesotho, 1800-1966: a study of political institutions.**

L. B. B. J. Machobane. London: Macmillan Press, 1990. 374p. bibliog.

This study of the political institutions of Lesotho spans the colonial and independence periods. It also provides a description of pre-colonial government, a subject which has not often been investigated. Machobane discusses the introduction of new governmental institutions and regulations under colonial rule, with the eventual adoption of the 'Westminister' style of democracy. He argues that the lack of political understanding of the masses at independence can itself be ascribed to colonial rule, which attempted to stifle political thought. Although this book fails to consider the internal social and economic forces behind political change, it presents a useful discussion and description of trends in government and administration.

254 **Government and development in rural Lesotho.**

Roeland van de Geer, Malcolm Wallis. Morija, Lesotho: Morija Printing Works, 1984. 159p. bibliog.

A history of local administration in Lesotho. A number of case-studies are presented and the possibilities for decentralization are discussed. The nature of local organizations is investigated and the authors conclude that, at the time of writing, effective decentralization was unlikely. They argue that local government should have greater involvement in development policy formation. For an earlier publication by the same authors, see: *Government and development in rural Lesotho* (Roma, Lesotho: National University of Lesotho, Public Administration Research and Curriculum Development Project, 1982. 159p. bibliog.).

255 **Impeded democracy: chiefly hierarchy versus democratic institutions in village decision-making.**
A. Tiljander. Stockholm: University of Stockholm, Department of Social Anthropology, 1992. 28p. 1 map. bibliog. (Development Studies Unit Working Paper, no. 23).

This study is concerned with the nature and role of the chieftainship and Village Development Committes (VDCs). Using information from two villages in Mohale's Hoek, southern Lesotho, the paper discusses the socio-economic status of chiefs and VDC members and local attitudes to the role of women. Some research is also presented on attitudes to conservation. Results show a clear difference between the socio-economic position of village leaders and the majority of village people. Thus, the author argues that there should be greater consultation with ordinary people.

256 **It depends: planning and managing induced innovation in uncertain environments; a contingency approach to extension reforms in Lesotho.**
C. Ben Tyson. *Development Southern Africa*, vol. 10, no. 2 (May 1993), p. 199-209.

Discusses the role of planning and management in rural development programmes with reference to agricultural extension services in Lesotho. Tyson argues that several key features of the management system improved as the style of management became more decentralized and less authoritative.

257 **Making a fast buck: capital leakage and the public accounts of Lesotho.**
Paul Wellings. *African Affairs*, no. 82 (1983), p. 495-507.

A controversial account of financial mismanagement by the government of Lesotho. Wellings documents the misuse of donor money and inadequacies in the national accounts.

258 **Namibia, Botswana, Lesotho and Swaziland.**
L. H. Gann, Peter Duignan. In: *Politics and government in African states, 1960-1985*. Edited by Peter Duignan, Robert H. Jackson. London; Sydney: Croom Helm; Stanford, California: Hoover Institute Press, 1986, p. 345-76. bibliog.

A general overview of the political and administrative issues in four southern African countries. Despite cultural, linguistic and geographic differences, the authors argue that all four states have a common dependence on South Africa. Useful data is provided on social and economic characteristics, allowing a regional comparison of Lesotho's economy and society. Three pages are devoted to a joint analysis of the political systems of Lesotho and Swaziland. While this is rather brief, the reader is introduced to the main political events of the post-independence period in Lesotho, interpreted in a regional context. The authors discuss political and economic trends, ending with the military take-over of 1986.

259 **Public administration and community development: Lesotho's experience.**
Roeland van der Geer, Malcolm Wallis. Roma, Lesotho: National University of Lesotho, Institute of Southern African Studies, 1984. 24p. (Research Report, no. 7).

Examines Lesotho's experience with the community development approach, which attempts to promote rural development by maximizing popular participation. The nature of public administration is considered in terms of its effects on community development, with emphasis on the activities of the Ministry of Cooperatives and Rural Development. The paper finds, however, that there are only limited opportunities for participation at the local level and that the political environment is not conducive to such developments.

260 **The Ramabanta-Semonkong road project in Lesotho: a case study on community development and national planning.**
D. Hirschmann. *Humanitas*, vol. 9, no. 2 (1983), p. 135-40.

Hirschmann presents a case-study of a road project in Semonkong to illustrate the relationship between community development and central planning. The community had approached the Ministry of Planning to organize donor funds, but while the community had wanted to begin the road quickly using limited funds, the Ministry became involved in a protracted planning process for a far larger sum. This highlighted the divergence in methodology and expectations between the community and central government planners. Thus Hirschmann makes a more general point about the nature of national planning processes and the needs of the rural population.

261 **Report on a survey of primary producer cooperatives, village development councils and other organizations.**
Thuso Green. Maseru: Sechaba Consultants & Care International, Rural Enterprise Promotion Project, 1990. 66p.

Reports the results of a survey carried out in some Primary Producer Co-operatives (PPCs). The author examines the dynamics of cooperatives and assesses the potential for participation in future development. Green's findings show that a particular difficulty is the rewarding of individual cooperative members for work they have done, and tensions have sometimes been created between those members who are engaged in extra activities and those who are not. The PPCs investigated clearly do not function as cooperatives, and Green argues that this failure is related to the fact that many rural enterprise projects have been imposed on people by donors.

262 **Rural rehabilitation in the Basotho labour reserve.**
J. S. Crush, O. Namasasu. *Applied Geography*, vol. 5, no. 2 (1985), p. 83-98.

This paper attempts to explain the characteristics of development policies in Lesotho by reference to the operation of the migrant labour system. The authors argue that rural development policy can be understood as a response to the needs of the migrant labour system, because it maintains the viability of the labour reserve. Thus, development programmes, as a mechanism for rural rehabilitation, have also been the focus of rural resistance to the migrant labour system and political domination. Resistance to rural forestry programmes is offered as an example.

263 **A study of village development committees: the case of Lesotho.**
T. Thoahlane. Roma, Lesotho: National University of Lesotho, Institute for Southern African Studies, 1984. 64p. (Research Report, no. 8).

Village development committees (VDCs) were established as an alternative source of administration in the mid-1960s in Lesotho. Using fieldwork, Thoahlane investigates their structure and function and compares the role played by the chieftainship. Results find that VDCs provide a vital link between central Government and local communities. Thoahlane is generally positive about VDCs, but argues that membership guidelines and terms of reference for committees should be developed. However, other authors mentioned in this section have produced more ambiguous conclusions about the role of VDCs and their relationship with government structures and traditional authority.

Donor agencies

264 **The anti-politics machine: 'development', depolitization and bureaucratic power in Lesotho.**
James Ferguson. Cambridge, England: Cambridge University Press, 1990. 320p. bibliog.

An essential text on development projects and bureaucratic power in Lesotho, which has also become important reading on intra-household relations and attitudes towards livestock. Ferguson examines the nature of donor projects in Lesotho through the experience of an agricultural project in Thaba-Tseka. He argues convincingly that there is a divergence between the donor view of a 'less developed country' and the economic realities of Lesotho. In his discussion of the failures of the Thaba-Tseka project, it becomes clear that the central government was opposed to attempts to decentralize power to the local level. Ferguson's analysis of the project's livestock management schemes develops a compelling picture of the place of livestock in the village economy. Criticisms of this work have been levelled at its partial failure to analyse the origin of cultural attitudes or social stratification. However, it remains an important study on development in Lesotho.

265 **An evaluation of the Lesotho Red Cross Society.**
Jeanette Bloem, Sesomo Phalatsi. Maseru: Lesotho Red Cross Society, 1993. 63p.

The authors discover that Lesotho Red Cross is having operational difficulties due to both staff and finance problems. They argue that the organization has to consider reducing the burden of its activities, and problems are identified particularly in the nature of voluntarism on which it is dependent. Volunteers will only continue to offer help if there is some kind of reward, in terms of status, or material benefit. If support for voluntary activities is not forthcoming there will be a struggle to maintain impetus, therefore the Red Cross should seriously consider reducing the number and scope of its activities. Indeed, the report argues that it should take better note of its original objectives, as it has become involved in other activities such as tree-planting and soil conservation.

266 **An evaluation of the small-scale intensive agricultural production project (SSIAPP).**
Jeanette Bloem, Graham Howe. Maseru: Cole Consulting & Ministry of Agriculture, 1994. 49p.

Taking account of the very isolated nature of the area and climatically difficult growing conditions, the project described in this study is found to have had impressive results. Significant achievements have been made in the areas of gardening and nutrition, education and institution-building in the mountain districts.

267 **Identification of socio-economic constraints to project activities and an assessment of project impact.**
Thuso Green, David Hall. Maseru: Matelile Rural Development Project & Sechaba Consultants, 1991. 64p.

An evaluation of the donor-funded Matelile Rural Development project. The authors present issues pertinent to other rural development projects in Lesotho. They argue that projects should take a long-term approach to development and should ensure sustainability by refraining from inducements that a resource poor government will be unable to meet. More controversially, the report also suggests that donors should support individual initiatives as opposed to communal initiatives, as these have more chance of success. This report provides a good overview of the problems of development projects in Lesotho.

268 **Local initiatives: key to selfhelp in Lesotho.**
J. Madeley. *Development & Cooperation*, no. 4 (1989), p. 11-12.

Discusses the survival strategies of the rural poor in the southern Quthing District. Madeley finds that the poorest households engage in a number of non-farm activities during periods of crisis, with agriculture only contributing a small proportion of income. Examples are given of the assistance to local groups by the Local Initiatives Support Project, which aims to help local income-generating initiatives.

269 **Report on an evaluation of the Seforong Women's Integrated Rural Development Project.**
'Malejara Mothabeng, David Hall. Maseru: Unitarian Service Committee of Canada, 1989. 141p.

An evaluation of a donor-funded women's project, in which the authors conclude that the project has only had a limited success, and attribute its failure to poor design and lack of consultation. In addition, they found that the project had served the needs of the chieftains in the past and was presently under the influence of the male-dominated Village Development Council. This report makes interesting reading for those concerned with the problems of donor-funded development projects.

270 **Take out hunger: two case studies of rural development in Basutoland.**
Sandra Wallman. London: Athlone Press, 1969. 178p.

A detailed and careful analysis of the history of two development schemes, the Taung Reclamation Scheme, Mohale's Hoek District, and the 'Farmech' Mechanization Scheme, Mafeteng District. It discusses the reasons why one failed, while the other eventually has limited success. The book is particularly effective in portraying the feelings of the ordinary villager and the breakdown in communication between the planners of the scheme and the individuals affected. For a less detailed description, see: 'The Farmech Scheme: Basutoland (Lesotho)' (*African Affairs*, no. 267, vol. 67 [April 1968], p. 112-17).

International Relations

271 **Beggar your neighbour: apartheid power in Southern Africa.**
Joseph Hanlon. London: Catholic Institute for International Relations & James Currey; Bloomington, Indiana: Indiana University Press, 1986. 352p.

Discusses the political situation in the southern African region up to 1986. The role of regional organizations and political parties are considered. One chapter specifically deals with Lesotho's relations with South Africa, while others provide information on economic links.

272 **Dependency and the foreign policy options of small Southern African states.**
Mafa Sejanamane. In: *Southern Africa after apartheid: prospects for the inner periphery in 1990s*. Edited by Sehoai Santho, Mafa Sejanamane. Harare: Southern Africa Political Economy Series (SAPES), 1991, p. 15-25. bibliog.

In this discussion of foreign policy for small states, Sejanamane argues that two practical scenarios exist for the small state in southern Africa. The first is that these states maintain their political independence and their dependent economic status. However, for Lesotho and Swaziland, it is argued that this option has no meaning as both countries are integrated into South Africa far more than other countries in the region. Sejanamane suggests that this integration should be formalized and anticipates policy moves towards the granting of residence to miners and their families. Should this occur (as it, in fact, has done since the time of writing), he argues that the effect would be disastrous for these small states. Also see Sejanamane's PhD thesis: *Security and small states: the political economy of Lesotho's foreign policy – 1966-1985* (PhD thesis, Dalhousie University, Halifax, Canada, 1987).

273 **The diplomacy of isolation: South Africa's foreign policy making.**
Deon Geldenhuys. Johannesburg: Macmillan, 1984. 295p.

An overview of South Africa's foreign policy that contains many references to relations with Lesotho. Despite its dated nature, this book will remain useful to those interested in the history of international relations in the region.

274 **Lesotho and the inner periphery in the New South Africa.**
Richard F. Weisfelder. *Journal of Modern African Studies*, vol. 30, no. 4 (1992), p. 643-68.

Discusses the regional impact of changes in South Africa. The study seeks to identify factors that sustain international boundaries and thus prevent regional solutions. It is proposed that such isolationism could lead to dysfunctional political and economic outcomes for southern Africa. Weisfelder discusses a number of options open to Lesotho, and concludes that the most satisfactory would be federal integration of some kind with South Africa.

275 **Lesotho and the new South Africa: the question of reincorporation.**
Anthony Lemon. *Journal of Southern African Studies*, 20th Anniversary Special Issue (1994), 15p. bibliog.

The author questions the independent status of Lesotho given the advent of democracy in South Africa. A short history of Lesotho is offered and then the author considers the advantages and disadvantages of incorporation into South Africa. He argues that large sectors of the population of Lesotho would benefit from incorporation, including the rural poor, urban unemployed and professional workers. However, Lemon recognizes that the military and political élite would be disadvantaged by incorporation. For this reason, he concludes that the route Lesotho will take is unclear.

276 **Lesotho and the re-integration of South Africa.**
Roger Southall. In: *Southern Africa after apartheid: prospects for the inner periphery in 1990s.* Edited by Sehoai Santho, Mafa Sejanamane. Harare: Southern Africa Political Economy Series (SAPES), 1991, p. 209-27. bibliog.

Discusses the advantages and disadvantages of Lesotho's incorporation into South Africa. It is argued that incorporation requires the willingness of the socio-political élite in Lesotho to concede the privileges of international sovereignty, of which it has been the principal beneficiary. Southall proposes that South Africa would also need to be convinced that incorporation would be to its advantage. By opting to retain independence, Lesotho would stand in danger of becoming a 'de facto' bantustan at the very moment when the *de jure* bantustans have been re-incorporated.

277 **Lesotho's expensive border hoax.**
Daniel S. Prinsloo. *Focus*, no. 6 (March 1977), p. 1-14.

A discussion of Lesotho's claim for compensation after border disputes with the newly 'independent' Transkei. The government of Lesotho claimed that R82 million was lost as a result of the imposition of certain restrictions at the Transkeian borders and this article is a thinly veiled rejoinder by the South African government of the day. This is a useful paper for those interested in South Africa's relationship with

Lesotho during the 1970s, a period of tension and frequent border incursions. *Focus* is the journal of the Foreign Affairs Association, PO Box 26410, Pretoria, South Africa.

278 **Lesotho's security policy in post-apartheid Southern Africa.**
Mafa M. Sejanamane. In: *From destabilisation to regional cooperation in Southern Africa?* Edited by Mafa Sejanamane. Roma, Lesotho: National University of Lesotho, Institute for Southern African Studies, 1994, p. 168-88. bibliog.

This chapter has three aims: to outline the nature of South African foreign strategy in the past and its impact on security in Lesotho; to highlight the new challenges for Lesotho created by the dismantling of apartheid; and, finally, to forecast the ultimate direction of change in southern Africa. Readers new to this area will find the summary of South African foreign relations in the 1970s and 1980s useful. Sejanamane covers events such as the incursions into Lesotho for terrorist attacks, and argues that Lesotho has only two options in the future: incorporation or an advanced state of regional interdependence.

279 **Political economy of small states in southern Africa – dependency and development options – towards regionalism in the inner periphery.**
Sehoai Santho. In: *Southern Africa after apartheid: prospects for the inner periphery in 1990s.* Edited by Sehoai Santho, Mafa Sejanamane. Harare: Southern Africa Political Economy Series (SAPES), 1991, p. 2-14. bibliog.

Argues that given the characteristics of Lesotho, Botswana, Swaziland and Namibia, a strong case for regional economic, or even political, integration can be made. Santho suggests that the smallness of these countries precludes any basis for dynamic and sustainable development. Thus, their economic potentialities could be better realized within the framework of a regional economy, marked by gradual integration of production, distribution and exchange. The key question is whether the political forces in each of these countries will accept this vision of regionalism, as it will reduce political sovereignty. However, the economic underpinnings of this sovereignty are either already weak or are based on primary commodity export windfalls. In conclusion, the author analyses the ANC/COSATU (Congress of South African Trade Unions) recommendations for regional integration at the time of writing.

280 **The predicament of Lesotho's security in the 1990s.**
Nqosa L. Mahao. In: *From destabilisation to regional cooperation in Southern Africa?* Edited by Mafa Sejanamane. Roma, Lesotho: National University of Lesotho, Institute for Southern African Studies, 1994, p. 189-202. bibliog.

Mahao debates Lesotho's future relations with South Africa, first presenting a history of Lesotho's international relations. The prospects for incorporation are considered, and Mahao argues that many groups would benefit from such a move. While this paper does not advance much in the way of new insights, it will prove useful for those seeking an introduction to the issues involved.

281 **Regional cooperation and integration in Southern Africa: the case of the SADCC industrial sector.**
Oliver S. Saasa. In: *Southern Africa in the 1980s and beyond: Institute of Southern African Studies 1980-1990.* Edited by the Institute of Southern African Studies. Roma, Lesotho: University of Lesotho, Institute of Southern African Studies, 1993, p. 101-26. bibliog.

Lesotho is one of the southern African countries discussed in this assessment of regional cooperation. Some background information is presented on the nature of the former Southern Africa Development Coordinating Conference (SADCC) and data is given on manufacturing performance in several southern African countries. Transnational corporations are also discussed and it is in this section that the analysis of Lesotho appears particularly outdated, with the author referring to a diamond industry that has in fact been largely abandoned. Despite this, it is an interesting article that allows the reader to compare Lesotho's industrial performance with that of other countries in the region.

Economy

282 **Agricultural and economic development in Lesotho: analysis using a social accounting matrix.**

J. W. Carvalho, D. W. Holland. *Eastern Africa Economic Review*, vol. 5, no. 2 (1989), p. 104-20.

Uses a social accounting matrix (SAM) to analyse the role that agriculture plays in Lesotho's economy. The advantage of using a social accounting matrix is its ability to illustrate the linkages between agriculture and the rest of the domestic economy. This also shows that agricultural growth can have wider effects when these backward and forward linkages are strengthened. See item no. 283, for more detail on this use of a SAM for Lesotho.

283 **Agriculture and economic development in Lesotho: analysis using a social accounting matrix.**

Joe William Carvalho. PhD thesis, Washington State University, 1988. 168p.

A nation-wide social accounting matrix is developed for Lesotho in this thesis. Economic multipliers were found to be very small due to the domination of imports from South Africa. The economic linkages between domestic sectors were also found to be very weak. Carvalho argues that even under a best-case scenario, development projects are likely to have a small macroeconomic impact given Lesotho's economic structure.

284 **Another development for Lesotho? Alternative development strategies for the mountain kingdom.**

Foundation for Education with Production. Gabarone, Botswana: Institute of Southern African Studies, 1989. 217p.

The report of a seminar on 'Another Development for Lesotho' held in Maseru, Lesotho on 14-18 December 1987, sponsored by the Dag Hammarskjold Foundation of Uppsala, Sweden. This book contains summaries of papers and responses from Ministries in the military government of the time. The seminar was organized as part of the region-wide initiative to promote development that is need-orientated, self-reliant and more equitable. This is intended to contrast with past development, arguably geared to the needs of South Africa. The participation of government ministers has resulted in a publication that gives a useful summary of the stated Government policy of the late 1980s.

285 **The changing nature of economic dependence: economic problems in Lesotho.**
James H. Cobbe. *Journal of Modern African Studies*, vol. 21, no. 2 (1983), p. 293-310.

Examines the dependent nature of the Lesotho economy. After a short presentation of Lesotho's history, Cobbe attempts to quantify the extent of economic dependence using data on the number of migrant labourers and the size of migrant remittances. Cobbe also lays bare the contradictions between political rhetoric and economic reality, particularly around the futility of aid projects that hope to promote Lesotho's independence. Finally, the paper concludes with a call for greater domestic development.

286 **Consequences for Lesotho of changing South African labour demand.**
James H. Cobbe. *African Affairs*, vol. 85, no. 338 (January 1986), p. 23-48.

Cobbe explores the possibilities for the future of migrant labour based on the situation in the early 1980s. He constructs a number of scenarios around projected labour demand and then discusses the consequences of each. His analysis is relevant to the present day, although the political dimensions have changed. The general reader will be interested by his policy prescriptions and the overview of local employment, which remains largely accurate.

287 **Economic aspects of Lesotho's relations with South Africa.**
James H. Cobbe. *Journal of Modern African Studies*, vol. 26, no. 1 (March 1988), p. 71-89.

This article explores some of the issues surrounding the economic aspects of Lesotho's relations with South Africa, with particular focus on the causes of the 1986 military coup but also with a more general scope. The author argues that no fundamental economic change can be expected in the future; indeed, he suggests that prospects are bleak economically and ideally some degree of regionalism should occur with the advent of the post-apartheid South Africa.

288 **Lesotho: dilemmas of dependence in Southern Africa.**
John E. Bardill, James H. Cobbe. Boulder, Colorado: Westview Press, 1985. 224p. 3 maps. bibliog.

This is a well-balanced account of the political economy of Lesotho. As well as covering the modern period, it also contains information on the social and economic history of Lesotho. The only drawback of the book is that it has been overtaken by events since its publication, namely the institution of democratic rule and the decline in importance of migrant labour. Despite this, the book provides an excellent description of the context within which recent developments may be viewed.

289 **Lesotho: a strategy for survival after the Golden Seventies.**
John Gray, Neil Robertson, Michael Walton. *South African Labour Bulletin*, vol. 6, no. 4 (1980), p. 62-78.

Analyses the falling participation of households in labour migration to South Africa during the 1970s. The authors argue that a serious attempt should be made to develop the local economy and thus propose an economic strategy to increase domestic employment. This strategy rests on broadly-diffused agricultural development, the local manufacture of basic needs products and the use of more appropriate technologies in industry and agriculture. The paper provides some interesting statistics on the economy of the time, and readers will find that the economic analysis is still relevant today.

290 **Lesotho's economic policy and performance under the structural adjustment program: the external dependence.**
Lennart Petersson. Lund, Sweden: Institute for Economic Research, Lund University, 1990. 51p. bibliog.

The structural adjustment programme in Lesotho is discussed, using information on implementation and economic performance. Three basic components are considered: monetary policy and public debt; fiscal and public sector policy; and, finally, the need to reform incentives for the private sector. Petersson argues that the structural adjustment programme was needed because of the weakness of the economy arising from Lesotho's dependence on South Africa. The second part of the report discusses the nature of this economic dependence in detail, and Petersson suggests mechanisms by which this dependency may be reduced.

291 **Migration and development. Dependence on South Africa: a study of Lesotho.**
Gabrielle Winai Ström. Uppsala, Sweden: Scandinavian Institute of African Studies, 1986. 2nd ed. 171p. 1 map. bibliog.

First published in 1978 under the title *Development and dependence in Lesotho; the enclave of South Africa*. The internal signs and effects of dependence on an external economy are stressed in this study. These 'signs' are not limited to the economic sphere, as Ström also details the political effects of dependence. Overall, she makes a convincing argument that Lesotho is overwhelmingly a dependent economy, and the book contains a useful, if somewhat dated, discussion of political parties. Unfortunately, the subject of migration is not given the depth of analysis that would be expected from the title.

292 **Re-evaluating modernisation and dependency in Lesotho.**
George Pavlich. *Journal of Modern African Studies*, vol. 26, no. 4 (December 1988), p. 591-605.

Examines Lesotho's economic predicament in the light of the predictions of economic theory. Pavlich finds that neither of the main economic paradigms sufficiently addresses the position of Lesotho. He suggests that, if we are to understand poverty and development in Lesotho, we must re-evaluate the application of economic theory. In particular, we must enter the community and use local concepts if we wish to define the problem from the perspective of local inhabitants.

293 **South African mine wages in the seventies and their effects on Lesotho's economy.**
J. Eckert, R. A. Wykstra. Fort Collins, Colorado: Colorado State University, Department of Economics, Lesotho Agricultural Sector Analysis Program, 1980. 25p. bibliog. (Research Report, no. 7).

This paper analyses trends during the 1970s in wages for migrant miners and the effect of these on the economy. Real wages rose sharply during this period and the authors discuss the impact of this increase through an investigation of the characteristics of migrants and the nature of remittances. The linkages to domestic wage setting and agricultural production are also considered. Although this report is somewhat dated, it offers a useful analysis of the economic effects for Lesotho of increases in mine wages.

294 **Towards a political economy of adjustment in a labour-reserve economy: the case of Lesotho.**
Michael Neocosmos. In: *Social change and economic reform in Africa.* Edited by Peter Gibbon. Uppsala, Sweden: Nordiska Afrikainstitutet, 1993, p. 134-60. bibliog.

Provides an assessment of socio-economic and political relations in Lesotho, paying particular attention to rural areas. Although the discussion occurs in the context of the structural adjustment policy under way in Lesotho, the analysis of adjustment itself is weak. Despite this, Neocosmos provides an interesting appraisal of the political economy of Lesotho, and also presents data on the distribution of land and the prevalence of share-cropping. This is important reading for those intending to undertake research into social conditions and economic differentiation in Lesotho.

Finance and Banking

295 **Banking for development or underdevelopment: the case of Lesotho.**
Basil C. Muzorewa. *Lesotho Notes and Records*, vol. 10 (1973-74), p. 15-32.

Surveys the major financial institutions of Lesotho, and examines the extent to which they are agents of development or underdevelopment. Muzorewa argues that indigenous credit institutions are more likely to promote development.

296 **The banking system and the formation of savings in Lesotho.**
Marco Onado, Antonio Porteri. Milan, Italy: Cassa di Risparmio delle Provincie Lombarde, 1974. 140p.

Based on fieldwork carried out by the authors in 1972, this work outlines Lesotho's economy and then describes in detail Lesotho's financial institutions. A third part is concerned with strategies for the formation and mobilization of savings.

297 **Lesotho co-operative credit union movement.**
A. T. Lelala. *Education in Botswana, Lesotho and Swaziland*, no. 6 (Nov. 1973), p. 43-47.

This brief article describes the Lesotho cooperative credit union movement, including organizational details and historical notes.

298 **Monetary and exchange rate management in tiny, open underdeveloped economies.**
Peter J. Drake. *Savings and Development*, vol. 7, no. 1 (1983), p. 5-20.

Uses Botswana, Lesotho and Swaziland as case-studies in a study of monetary and exchange-rate management. Drake considers feasible exchange-rate and monetary régimes.

299 **Statutory regulation and supervision of banks and banking services in Lesotho.**

W. Kulundu-Bitonye. *Lesotho Law Journal*, vol. 8, no. 2 (1993), p. 19-58.

The author reports on the regulation and supervision of banks in Lesotho. An analysis is made of the Financial Institution Act (1973) which governs such regulation. This is a useful article for those interested in bank regulation and supervision.

300 **Quarterly Review.**

Maseru: Central Bank of Lesotho, 1982- . quarterly.

This is a quarterly survey of the main monetary and financial aggregates for Lesotho. Statistics are given on trends in exchange rates, interest rates and the money supply. A summary is provided on the government's budgetary operations and the financing of the budget deficit, and information is also offered on the main development-finance institutions and the commercial banks. In addition, an overview is provided on foreign trade and the balance of payments.

Trade

Internal

301 **Agricultural marketing development in Lesotho.**
Motsamai Mochebelele, None Mokitimi. In: *Southern Africa in the 1980s and beyond: Institute of Southern African Studies 1980-1990.* Edited by the Institute of Southern African Studies. Roma, Lesotho: University of Lesotho, Institute of Southern African Studies, 1993, p. 85-100. bibliog.

Seeks to articulate the roles and functions of the informal and formal marketing channels utilized by Basotho livestock owners. More specific analysis focuses on cattle marketing and dairy farming. Drawing extensively from the findings of the Agricultural Marketing Research Project of the Institute of Southern African Studies, the authors find that the utilization of informal marketing channels in Lesotho prevails over the formal markets in the livestock industry. The evidence indicates that eighty-two per cent of cattle, sixty-two per cent of sheep and ninety-two per cent of goats are sold through informal marketing arrangements. A similar trend is documented for milk marketing, where only thirty-one per cent of total milk production is channelled through formal outlets. The main reasons are the inadequacy of the marketing infrastructure and the lack of price incentives in the formal marketing channels.

302 **Agricultural marketing in Lesotho.**
Motsamai T. Mochebelele, None L. Mokitimi, M. T. Nggaleni, Gary G. Storey, Brent M. Swallow. Ottawa, Canada: International Development Research Centre, 1992. 153p. (Manuscript Report, no. IDRC-MR321e).

Provides the results from an IDRC project on Agricultural Marketing in Lesotho. The focus is on livestock, wool and mohair, dairy and vegetables. The report presents information on the evolution of agricultural markets, as well as on the trade links between Lesotho and South Africa. The importance of certain institutions is discussed, along with the role of education in institutional change. Detailed information is given on livestock marketing and vegetable production in Lesotho. Lesotho appears to be highly dependent on South Africa for vegetables and government efforts to reduce this dependency are analysed. Chapter five investigates the structure and development of Lesotho's dairy industry. In chapter six, wool and mohair marketing are examined. This report offers the reader a comprehensive analysis of marketing in Lesotho and will be useful for both researchers and agriculturalists.

303 **Agricultural marketing in Lesotho and price transmission to the village level: implications and options for policy.**
Brendan Bayley. Maseru: Drought Relief Implementation Group, 1994. 36p. 2 maps. bibliog. mimeo.

A rare analysis of village-level informal markets in Lesotho. This paper argues that there is a need for a review of agricultural policy objectives in the light of this investigation into village-level agricultural marketing. The analysis shows that net-consumers of agricultural commodities far outnumber net-producers, i.e. most households are dependent on the purchase of agricultural produce. Bayley makes several recommendations for change in the internal marketing of agricultural products. This is essential reading for those interested in village-level agricultural marketing.

304 **Cattle marketing in Lesotho.**
Brent M. Swallow, None Mokitimi, Ray F. Brokken. Roma, Lesotho: National University of Lesotho, Institute of Southern African Studies, 1986. (Research Report, no. 13); Maseru: Ministry of Agriculture, Farming Systems Research Division, 1986. 75p. bibliog.

Describes the evolution and current structure of the cattle marketing system in Lesotho. This report reviews the relevant literature and discusses the results of studies of livestock marketing. Given the picture that emerges of the cattle marketing system, implications for the development of marketing are laid out. The authors find the situation of overstocking paradoxically accompanied by an ownership pattern that leaves many households with an insufficient number of cattle for draught purposes, and by the absence of a large commercial beef sector.

305 **The current agricultural marketing situation and activities in Lesotho.**
Philip A. P. Cole, Clive Drew, Gerald Feaster. Maseru: USAID, Lapis Project, 1992. 138p. bibliog.

The authors provide an analysis of the marketing situation for fresh produce, paying particular attention to the market for fruits and vegetables. A description of the marketing activities of government, donors, vegetable production schemes, individual commercial vegetable farmers, and fresh produce traders is provided.

306 **The distribution system for fresh milk and mafi in Lesotho.**
Philip Cole, Thloriso Thelejane, Andrew Wakiro. Maseru: Lesotho National Dairy Board, Cole Consulting, 1994. 58p.

This study investigates the distribution system for fresh milk and *mafi* (sour milk). Details are provided on sales by district and the results of a small survey of traders are presented. These results support the conclusion that many traders, especially in and around Maseru, perceive the quality of fresh milk to be poor. However, these perceptions may not be grounded in the actual condition of this milk.

307 **The economics of milk production and marketing in Lesotho: survey results.**
Motsamai Mochebelele. Roma, Lesotho: University of Lesotho, Institute of Southern African Studies, 1990. 120p. bibliog. (Research Report, no. 28).

Highlights the common features that characterize dairy farmers in Lesotho, and discusses production costs and management patterns. This study offers the reader an analysis of the incentives to hold livestock, the central tenet being that farmers demonstrate rationality by adopting certain production patterns.

308 **The evolution of the wool and mohair marketing system in Lesotho: implications for policy and institutional reform.**
J. P. Hunter, N. L. Mokitimi. Addis Ababa: International Livestock Centre for Africa, 1989. 20p. bibliog. (African Livestock Policy Analysis Network Paper, no. 20).

An analysis of the wool and mohair marketing system in Lesotho. Wool and mohair have long been one of Lesotho's most important agricultural exports and this report discusses the historical evolution of the marketing system. The authors make a number of recommendations for change, and argue that marketing should predominantly be carried out by traders due to monopoly conditions in the market. Increased competition on the purchasing side would provide the appropriate environment for a reduction in excess profits.

309 **The market for fresh vegetables in Leribe and Butha-Buthe, 1993.**
Philip Cole, Tom Cunningham, Andrew Wakiro. Maseru: Ministry of Agriculture, Small-scale Irrigated Vegetable Project, 1995. 26p.

Similar to the earlier study of Maseru and Teyateyaneng (see item no. 310), this report is based on a survey of the larger vegetable traders in Maputsoe, Leribe and Butha-Buthe towns and the major villages of the two districts of Leribe and Butha-Buthe. Detailed information is collected on types of vegetables sold and turnover. The importance of imported vegetables appears to be far higher than official figures would suggest. The authors find that very limited quantities of domestic produce are purchased.

310 **The market for fresh vegetables in Maseru and Teyateyaneng, 1992.**
Philip Cole, Tom Cunningham, Andrew Wakiro. Maseru: Ministry of Agriculture, Small-scale Irrigated Vegetable Project, 1994. 34p.

Similar to a later study of Leribe and Butha-Buthe (see item no. 309), this report is based on a survey of the major vegetable traders in Maseru District and in Teyateyaneng town. Detailed information is collected on types of vegetables sold and turnover. Data was also collected on the importance of imported vegetables, which appears to be far higher than official figures would suggest.

311 **The market for imported fresh dairy products in the lowland districts of Lesotho.**
Philip A. P. Cole. Maseru: Ministry of Agriculture, Lesotho/Canada Dairy Development Project, 1991. 24p.

Cole discusses the results of a survey to identify the market in lowland Lesotho for imported dairy products. Information is offered on wholesale and retail purchases and prices, as well as supply methods. The markets for long-life milk and milk powder are identified as especially important. The growth in these products has led to a loss of market share by fresh milk.

312 **Marketing channels utilised by Basotho livestock owners.**
None L. Mokitimi. In: *Agricultural marketing and policy development in Lesotho*. Edited by None L. Mokitimi, Motsamai T. Mochebelele. Roma, Lesotho: University of Lesotho, Institute of Southern African Studies, 1993, p. 5-16. bibliog.

Examines the marketing channels utilized by Basotho livestock owners. A major portion of the paper is based on a summary of the research outlined in item no. 302; however, Mokitimi does provide some additional information. This is a short, well-written introduction to the topic.

313 **Purchasing patterns of milk and poultry in rural lowlands of Lesotho.**
J. R. Campbell, T. G. Jobo, L. S. Phakisi. *Agrekon*, vol. 29, no. 4 (1990), p. 335-40.

Using survey data from a rural lowland area of Lesotho, the authors investigate the purchasing patterns of milk and poultry. Most of the milk purchased was long-life, although fresh milk was preferred by respondents. Milk purchases appeared relatively insensitive to income or household size. Most of the poultry purchased was in the form of live chickens, and purchases seemed highly responsive to differences in income, particularly that from non-salaried sources, such as self-employment. Interestingly, responses concerning current purchases seemed reliable, while responses concerning future purchases appeared to be exaggerated.

External

314 **Does Lesotho have any future outside the Southern African Customs Union?**
D. T. Lekoetje. MA thesis, University of Manchester, England, 1987. 75p.

A political and historical analysis of the Southern African Customs Union (SACU). Lekoetje argues that the SACU changed from being a revenue collection instrument to a protective device after 1969, when South Africa began greater industrialization behind a wall of tariff barriers. However, the author is generally pessimistic about the future of Lesotho outside the SACU, although several suggestions are made for complementary trade arrangements. This thesis provides some useful information on Lesotho's trade patterns and trading arrangements.

315 **New sanctions against South Africa.**
Roger C. Riddell. *Development Policy Review*, vol. 6 (1983), p. 243-67.

In his discussion of the scope and effect of sanctions against South Africa, Riddell considers the position of Lesotho as one of the front-line states. He presents data on Lesotho's trade dependence on South Africa, which will still prove valuable to present-day researchers.

316 **Renegotiating dependency: the case of the Southern Africa customs union.**
Jon Walters. *Journal of Common Market Studies*, vol. XXVIII, no. 1 (September 1989), p. 29-52.

Extends the debate on the Southern African Customs Union (SACU) by clarifying the concepts underlying the agreement and by examining some key trade features of the actual workings of the customs union. Several proposals for modification are made by Walters, who pays particular attention to industrial protection and customs-revenue sharing.

317 **The Southern African Customs Union (SACU) and the post-apartheid South Africa: prospects for closer integration in the region.**
Setsomi G. Hoohlo. In: *Southern Africa after apartheid: prospects for the inner periphery in 1990s.* Edited by Sehoai Santho, Mafa Sejanamane. Harare: Southern Africa Political Economy Series (SAPES), 1991, p. 92-108. bibliog.

Hoohlo analyses the performance of Botswana, Lesotho and Swaziland under the Southern African Customs Union (SACU) and concludes that SACU membership has succeeded only in providing these states with relatively cheaper commodities. Polarization has been detrimental to these economies, particularly in the case of Lesotho. Given the nature of their geographic locations and their long-standing trading relationships, it is argued that no amount of financial concessions can compensate for this lack of industrial development. Thus, for their own benefit and that of a post-apartheid South Africa, they should incorporate their economies. Hoohlo provides data up to the late 1980s on trade, national output and taxation revenue.

Industry

General

318 **Core and periphery: a study of industrial development in the small countries of Southern Africa.**

Percy Selwyn. Brighton, England: Institute of Development Studies, University of Sussex, 1973. 232p. (Institute of Development Studies Discussion Paper, no. 36).

Reports on a survey of industries in Botswana, Lesotho and Swaziland during the 1960s. Also offered is an analysis and interpretation of the information obtained in the economic setting of the three countries, which are argued to be dependent on the South African economy. On the same topic, but in less detail, see also: *Industrial development in peripheral small countries* (Brighton, England: I. D. S., University of Sussex, 1973. 44p. [Institute of Development Studies Discussion Paper, no. 14]). See also, by the author: *Industries in the Southern African periphery: a study of industrial development in Botswana, Lesotho and Swaziland* (London: Croom Helm; Boulder, Colorado: Westview Press, 1975. 156p. map).

319 **Environmental responsibility under severe economic constraints: re-examining the Lesotho Highlands Water Project.**

A. Ciccolo. *Georgetown International Environmental Law Review*, vol. 4, no. 2 (1992), p. 447-67.

Ciccolo discusses the environmental impact assessment completed for the Lesotho Highlands Water Project, arguing that the development of such an impact assessment should ensure that the project does minimum environmental damage. In this way, the use of Lesotho's water resources can have the greatest socio-economic benefit. However, Ciccolo does not tackle the issues of the economic impact in sufficient detail. Other authors have been more critical of the economic benefits of the project for the local community.

320 **Lesotho Highlands Water Project.**
Trans-Caledon Tunnel Authority. Pretoria: Trans-Caledon Tunnel Authority, 1992. 2nd ed. 39p. 2 maps.

The Lesotho Highlands Water Project is one of the largest and most intricate construction projects in southern Africa. In 1992, it was expected to cost $US 5.2 billion over thirty years. This document offers information on the geology of the project, and its funding and design. This edition updates a publication of the same title produced in 1990.

321 **Lesotho Highlands Water Project: Environmental Action Plan. A synopsis of studies and proposed programmes.**
Lesotho Highlands Development Authority. Maseru: Lesotho Highlands Development Authority, 1990. 71p. 3 maps.

Provides a history of the project and presents an environmental action plan, which considers developmental issues as well as the potential environmental impact.

322 **Lesotho Highlands Water Project: Vol 2.**
Trans-Caledon Tunnel Authority. Pretoria: Trans-Caledon Tunnel Authority, 1993. 38p. 1 map.

Discusses the progress of the project. The characteristics of the local rock and the project's impact on it are examined. The nature of the environmental and social impacts are also considered, and it is shown that attempts have been made to reduce the adverse effects of the projects.

323 **Lesotho National Development Corporation: Annual Report.**
Maseru: Government Printer, 1971- . annual.

This illustrated report discusses the financial position of the corporation, outlining the latest developments and projects.

324 **Lesotho small and microenterprise strategy – phase II: subsectoral analysis.**
William Grant, Jeanne Downing, Steve Haggblade, John McKenzie, Harvey Schartup. Maseru: USAID, Growth and Equity through Microenterprise Investment and Institutions (GEMINI) Project, 1990. 111p. bibliog.

This document provides an overview of small and microenterprises (SMEs) in Lesotho. A detailed analysis is made of four sub-sectors: garment manufacture; weaving; construction; and leather goods. Data is given on the number of firms, employment and sales in each sub-sector, as well as estimates for potential growth and expansion. The authors also provide information on the number of women employed in the sub-sector and the use of local inputs into production. This is an essential document for those interested in the characteristics and potential of the SME sector in Lesotho.

325 **A look at the Lesotho Highlands Water Project.**
M. Murray. *Water, Sewage & Effluent* (South Africa), vol. 15, no. 3 (September 1995), p. 61-63.

Reports on the Lesotho Highlands Water Project (LHWP), the most important engineering project in Lesotho's recent history. The author focuses on the phased implementation of the project, giving details on the tunnelling and hydropower developments involved. This is a useful summary of the LHWP, which is one of the most influential domestic factors affecting Lesotho's economy.

326 **National transport study: first interim report on roads sector.**
Scott Wilson Kirkpatrick. Maseru: Ministry of Planning, Economic and Manpower Development, 1993. 137p.

An investigation of road type and traffic flow in Lesotho. This report offers estimates of the cost of strengthening and upgrading the road network and finds that there is a serious backlog of maintenance. It also predicts the need for future improvements.

327 **Resettlement and rural development aspects of the Lesotho Highlands Water Project.**
M. Tshabalala. Washington, DC: World Bank, Technical Paper no. 227 (1994), p. 59-70.

Provides an overview of the Lesotho Highlands Water project. The author presents information on the environmental impact assessment and basic social and economic information about the project area. The paper then covers the compensation and rural development programmes associated with the project and ends with a discussion of the resettlement programme.

328 **A state of dependence.**
David Crush, Jonathan S. Crush. *The Geographical Magazine,* vol. 55, no. 1 (January 1983), p. 24-29.

The authors provide an overview of Lesotho's tourist industry during the 1970s and early 1980s, finding that tourism is dominated by South African visitors. While this is an interesting analysis of the tourism industry, it should be remembered that by the 1990s Lesotho's tourism from South Africa was in long-term decline.

329 **A strategic review.**
Simon Gill. Maseru: Lesotho Cooperative College, and Cole Consulting, 1995. 54p. bibliog.

This report focuses on the activities of the Lesotho Cooperative College (LCC), including activities around the cooperative sector and the small and informal business sector. It contains information on other institutions that support cooperatives and small-scale enterprises, both in Lesotho and in the Free State Province of South Africa. This information will be useful to those interested in support to the small- and micro-sector, while the detailed information on the LCC will interest those involved in projects and development interventions.

330 **Towards a redefined role of the Lesotho Highlands Water Project in the post-apartheid Southern Africa.**

Tumelo Tsikoane. In: *Southern Africa after apartheid: prospects for the inner periphery in 1990s.* Edited by Sehoai Santho, Mafa Sejanamane. Harare: Southern Africa Political Economy Series (SAPES), 1991, p. 109-27. bibliog.

Discusses a redefined role for the Lesotho Highlands Water Project given the changing political environment in southern Africa. Tsikoane examines the role played by international finance in the inception of the scheme and argues that the vested interests of finance capital have been safeguarded at the expense of Lesotho's future economic expansion. This chapter provides a description of the project and its funding, and the author investigates the political underpinnings surrounding the signing of the treaty. This will be a helpful publication for those interested in both the past and the future of the Highlands Water Project.

Energy

331 **Energy demand and consumption patterns of Maseru peri-urban areas, with particular reference to low-income locations.**

L. M. Khalema. In: *African energy: issues in planning and practice.* Edited by African Energy Policy Research Network. London: Zed Books, 1990, p. 64-68.

Household energy demand and consumption are investigated in peri-urban, low-income areas of Maseru. The areas chosen had previously received a government subsidy towards electrification. Results find that the demand for power is 'suppressed' due to the rising costs of electricity and internal household wiring. The paper recommends that more cost-effective energy programmes should be developed and should be accompanied by campaigns to ensure the economical utilization of energy.

332 **Energy management in Lesotho.**

L. Mohapelao. In: *Energy management in Africa.* Edited by M. R. Bhagavan, S. Karekezi. London; Atlantic Highlands, New Jersey: Zed Books & African Energy Policy Research Network, 1992, p. 9-41. bibliog.

The current situation of energy management is analysed in this chapter, and policy recommendations are made on how to improve the use of energy in the transport sector. This study highlights the need for greater private investment in transport services, and argues for incentives and training schemes for mechanics and drivers.

333 **National survey of biomass and woodfuel activities in Lesotho.**
Thuso J. Green. Maseru: Sechaba Consultants & SADCC Energy Sector Technical and Administrative Unit (TAU), 1990. 42p. 1 map. bibliog.

Large increases in fuel demand have led to serious woodfuel shortages in Lesotho. Green finds that traditional sources of energy such as dung, crop residues and woodfuel continue to play dominant roles in the residential energy sector. It appears that many tree planting programmes have been hampered by a lack of trained and experienced staff, and that there is an urgent need to carry out a staffing plan. In addition, Green contends that the Forestry Division should pursue greater individual and community involvement. By encouraging a switch from crop and animal residues, increased amounts of woodfuel could contribute to soil conservation and agricultural production. This report contains a number of photographs of woodlots and other areas of tree cultivation.

334 **Renewable and conservation energy technology in the Kingdom of Lesotho: a socio-economic study of constraints to wider adoption by households and in residential buildings.**
John Gay, Thuso Green, David Hall. Maseru: Sechaba Consultants & Ministry of Water, Energy and Mining, Dept. of Energy, 1993. 127p. bibliog.

An evaluation of renewable and conservation energy technology in Lesotho. This report contains a history of such technology, including a section on traditional energy technology. The authors find that there are a number of constraints to the propagation of existing conservation energy technology, which must take account of a number of factors, among which are: cultural patterns; input availability; initial costs; clarity of technical information; and the amount of labour inputs. Few technologies presently being promoted in Lesotho meet these criteria. In addition, the authors feel that the government should withdraw from the process of dissemination and leave these activities to the private sector.

335 **Rural electrification in Lesotho.**
L. M. Khalema. In: *Rural electrification in Africa.* Edited by V. Ranganathan. London; Atlantic Highlands, New Jersey; Zed Books & African Energy Policy Research Network, 1992, p. 141-61. bibliog.

The author examines the provision and institutional aspects of rural electrification in Lesotho. Electricity consumption accounts for only one per cent of total energy consumption, which reflects the low rate of electrification. Khalema provides an overview of government electrification programmes, paying particular attention to small-scale hydro-power initiatives. A methodology is developed for assessing the effects of electrification on rural development, and the author presents the results of three surveys that found that electrification had a more significantly positive effect than other forms of energy.

336 **Rural energy and poverty in Kenya and Lesotho: all roads lead to ruin.**

B. Wisner. *IDS Bulletin*, vol. 18, no. 1 (1987), p. 23-29.

A comparison of fuelwood crises in Kenya and Lesotho, who both face fuelwood shortages, but for different reasons. In Kenya, privatization of land has led to this crisis. The author argues that, in Lesotho, the migrant labour system has had a detrimental effect on agricultural productivity and social relations, and it is these factors which have caused the fuelwood crisis. A critique of rural energy policies is provided, and it is argued that such policies have typically been informed by functionalist approaches, designed to restore equilibrium to an essentially stable pattern of livelihood systems.

Agriculture

General

337 **Agricultural development in Southern Africa: farm-household economics and the food crisis.**
Allan R. C. Low. London: James Currey; Portsmouth, New Hampshire: Heinemann; Cape Town: David Philip, 1986. 218p. 2 maps. bibliog.

Links declining per capita agricultural production in southern Africa to farm-household economics, specifically opportunities for labour migration. This book has become a classic publication on the links between labour migration and agricultural output. Although Swaziland is used as the major case-study, considerable space is devoted to the situation in Lesotho. Rural and agricultural policy are also discussed.

338 **Agricultural production and marketing policies and management of soil, water and forestry resources to promote increased productivity and improved nutrition in Lesotho.**
Lesotho Government. Maseru: Ministry of Agriculture, 1988. 11p.

A brief summary of government agricultural policy in Lesotho as it stood at the date of publication. This will still prove a useful document for those interested in the recent history of agricultural policy.

339 **Agroclimatic hazard perception, prediction, and risk-avoidance strategies in Lesotho.**
G. C. Wilken. Fort Collins, Colorado: Colorado State University, 1982. 73p. bibliog. (Natural Hazard Research Working Paper, vol. 44).

A survey of hazard perception, prediction and risk-avoidance strategies among farmers. Such strategies include the adaptation of crops and farming techniques in order to reduce risk. Risk perception on the part of farmers centred on crop damage and drought. The study found that farmers' prediction of risk was concentrated in the short to medium-term, rather than on longer term perceptions of agroclimatic hazard.

340 **Alternative structures for rural development in Lesotho.**
C. Goldman. Roma, Lesotho: National University of Lesotho, Faculty of Social Sciences, 1982. 23p. bibliog. (Staff Seminar Papers, vol. 33).

Places the blame for Lesotho's poverty on incorporation into the South African economy. Given poor employment prospects and high population growth, the author argues that agriculture is the only viable sector for the provision of employment and critically evaluates the agricultural policies of the government.

341 **Census of Agriculture Report.**
Maseru: Bureau of Statistics, 1950- . decennial.

Provides detailed tables on: households, population and holdings; land utilization; crops; livestock and poultry; employment in agriculture; farm population; agricultural power and machinery and general transport facilities; fertilizers and soil dressings; and association of agricultural holdings with other industries. The tables are generally divided by district or ecological zone (lowland, foothill, mountain or Orange River Valley).

342 **Gross and net margins of agricultural enterprises in the Mafeteng District.**
Graham Howe. Maseru: Ministry of Agriculture, Mafeteng Development Project, & Cole Consulting, 1995. 27p. bibliog.

This report is similar to item no. 343, which covers the Matelile Area. It presents data on the gross and net margins of both commercial and low-input farmers. Three types of production are studied: livestock, crops and forestry. This is one of the few publications that attempts to quantify the economics of farming in Lesotho.

343 **Gross margins for agricultural enterprises in the Matelile area.**
Philip Cole. Maseru: Ministry of Agriculture, Matelile Rural Development Project, & Cole Consulting, 1993. 58p. bibliog.

Presents data for both commercial and low-input farmers in the Matelile area (see item no. 342 for a similar report on Mafeteng farmers). Three types of production are considered: livestock, crops and forestry. This is useful for those interested in the economics of farming in Lesotho.

344 **Labour migration and agricultural change: observations in Lesotho 1970-1982.**
M. Huisman. Roma, Lesotho: National University of Lesotho, Department of Geography, Urban and Regional Planning Programme, 1983. 67p. (Research Report, no. 4).

Huisman discusses the links between agricultural change and labour migration. Agricultural change is envisaged as those processes operating at the level of the household, specifically farm size, crop and livestock production, and labour resources.

345 **Lesotho Agricultural Situation Analysis Report.**
Lesotho Government. Maseru: Ministry of Agriculture, Agricultural Planning, 1984- . irregular.

Provides an analysis of agricultural trends over the previous decade. Data is offered on the distribution of arable land, production and livestock ownership.

346 **Ministry of Agriculture, Co-operatives and Marketing: Annual Reports.**
Maseru: Ministry of Agriculture Co-operatives and Marketing, 1966- . annual.

This publication continues the Basutoland Government Department of Agriculture series which ends in 1963. The reports contain separate reports from the different divisions of the Ministry: Conservation Division; Crops Division; Livestock Division; the Lesotho Agricultural College; Marketing Section; Agricultural Planning Unit; Department of Co-operatives; Thaba-Bosiu Project; Agricultural Information Services; and Agricultural Education Section.

347 **A review of Lesotho's agricultural policies and strategies.**
Malijeng Ngqaleni. In: *Southern Africa after apartheid: prospects for the inner periphery in 1990s.* Edited by Sehoai Santho, Mafa Sejanamane. Harare: Southern Africa Political Economy Series (SAPES), 1991, p. 128-46. bibliog.

Presents historical trends in Basotho agriculture and in agricultural policy. Among important policy initiatives is the Food Self-Sufficiency Programme, which was motivated by Lesotho's dependence on imports and its vulnerability to political trade shocks during the 1970s and 1980s. However, these self-sufficiency programmes were unsuccessful because of the large cost incurred. Ngqaleni argues that the advantages of production on a large scale were not realized due to managerial diseconomies and the cooperative pooling of land. It proved also difficult to 'discipline' farmers. These failures also illustrate the risks of dryland cropping and the problems of inappropriate technology. The author argues that agricultural policy should instead be aimed at products for which Lesotho has comparative advantage, such as asparagus. In particular, agricultural policy should be reformulated as it has lost its previous, political rationale which was to reduce dependence on South Africa.

348 **A spatial analysis of agricultural intensity in a Basotho village of southern Africa.**
R. Stevens, Y. Lee. *Professional Geographer*, vol. 31, no. 2 (1979), p. 177-83.

Yield variations are analysed to determine the factors affecting cultivation intensity. Among the factors tested is the distance between the homestead and the field. Results show that distance cannot explain variations in yield, even when other physical factors are held constant. It appears that variables not included in the analysis, such as household characteristics, may provide better explanations.

349 **The state and development: an analysis of agricultural development in Lesotho.**
Deborah Johnston. *Journal of Southern African Studies*, vol. 22, no. 1 (1996), p. 119-38.

A general analysis of the nature of agricultural policy since the early 1970s. The author argues that government policy has reflected both the demands of donor agencies and the needs of a rural élite.

350 **Toward the year 2000: strategies for Lesotho's agriculture.**
J. B. Eckert. Maseru: LASA Research Report, Lesotho Agricultural Section Analysis Program, 1982. 327p. bibliog. (Research Report, no. 10).

Provides an evaluation of agricultural policy and some projections of future economic trends. Part one describes the agricultural sector and the overall economy, while part two offers a technical analysis of various agricultural sub-sectors: cropping, conservation, livestock and marketing. Part three makes summary recommendations on employment and trade. This publication has been instrumental in changing attitudes towards the role of agriculture in Lesotho, particularly in the policy shift from food self-sufficiency to employment creation.

Land

351 **Dynamics of land tenure and spontaneous changes in African agrarian systems.**
J. C. Riddell. *Journal of Rural Reconstruction*, vol. 25, no. 1 (1992), p. 39-52.

Lesotho is one of eight countries studied by Riddell, who investigates the extent to which land tenure systems obstruct agricultural development. However, the case-studies show a relatively high level of spontaneous land tenure changes, particularly through inheritance and sharecropping. This contradicts the strict view of unchanging and inactive 'traditional' tenure systems. Despite this, Riddell argues for greater land registration as this would clearly delineate land rights and thus facilitate transactions. On the same subject, see 'Dynamics of land tenure and spontaneous changes in African agrarian systems' (*Land Reform, Land Settlement and Cooperatives*, no. 1/2 [1988], p. 39-52).

352 **Land reform and agricultural development.**
P. Kishindo. *Journal of Rural Development*, vol. 13, no. 3 (1994), p. 319-26.

Evaluates the introduction of the 1979 Land Act, which sought to improve agricultural productivity by conferring greater security of tenure for landowners. It was envisaged that enhanced security would lead to higher output through greater investment in land improvement and agricultural machinery. However, the author finds that few farmers have registered their land for tenure upgrade as required by the Act. In addition, little improvement in agricultural output has occurred. Kishindo argues that land legislation is not sufficient to improve agricultural productivity and that greater effort must be made in the rural sector. The paper suggests that the control of soil erosion should be given greater priority and that land holdings should be consolidated into viable units.

353 **Land tenure and agricultural development in Lesotho.**
I. V. Mashinini. Roma, Lesotho: National University of Lesotho, Department of Geography, Urban and Regional Planning Programme, 1983. 46p. (Research Reports, no. 6).

Mashinini investigates the relationship between customary land tenure and agricultural development in Lesotho. Unlike other analyses, this study finds that the land tenure system is not an important constraint to agricultural development. More important factors are: the harsh ecological conditions; inferior farming and marketing methods; and labour migration to South Africa.

354 **Lesotho: land tenure and economic development.**
John C. Williams. Pretoria: Africa Institute, 1972. 52p. maps. bibliog. (Communications of the Africa Institute, no. 19).

Outlines the problems resulting from the traditional land tenure system of Lesotho and makes suggestions for reform. Three techniques for reforming land use are suggested: individual title; land tax; and production co-operatives. Improvements for the efficient allocation of livestock grazing privileges are also discussed.

355 **Transactions in cropland held under customary tenure in Lesotho.**
Steven W. Lawry. In: *Land in African agrarian systems.* Edited by Thomas J. Bassett, Donald E. Crummey. Madison, Wisconsin: The University of Wisconsin Press, 1993, p. 57-75. bibliog.

This chapter explores the issue of land tenure in Lesotho. Lawry describes how policy-makers, despite pressure from donors to sanction tenure reform, have ensured the pre-eminence of customary rules. However, the author explains that informal and formal borrowing mechanisms – including sharecropping and leasing - have given landless and commercial farmers access to land despite the customary system. Evidence is produced to show that the poorest households are often unable to make use of their land. This paper is useful not only for understanding the distribution of agricultural production, but also the extent of economic differentiation in rural Lesotho.

Forestry and woodlots

356 **Community forestry in Lesotho: the people's perspective.**
David Hall, Thuso Green. Maseru: Sechaba Consultants & Ministry of Agriculture, Community Forestry Programme, 1989. 233p. bibliog.

Provides information for the planning and development of effective forestry programmes by investigating community attitudes to tree cultivation. The authors find that the most significant variable affecting attitudes towards forestry was the ecological zone that interviewees lived in. Thus, people who live in the mountain areas, where the shortage of fuel wood is most severe, were the most interested in tree cultivation. Even so, tree cultivation for many was not a top priority, as most people were more concerned with meeting basic needs. However, this report finds that a community forestry approach is viable and can overcome negative attitudes. The study also contains detailed socio-economic data on the survey group and a glossary of Sesotho terms for selected flora.

357 **Community forestry sociological study report.**
Thope Matobo, Letlamoreng Mosenene. Maseru: Ministry of Agriculture, Forestry Division, 1989. 48p. bibliog.

An investigation of the current situation of community tree initiatives and people's perceptions about trees. This report presents socio-economic data on interviewees and finds that tree ownership is common. Fruit trees, especially peach, are favoured, but poplar and pine are also popular among those that have forest trees. This publication also offers a range of information on other, locally prevalent trees.

358 **Integrated community forestry and agricultural resource management project.**
Philip Cole, David Hughes, Mapalesa Mothokho. Maseru: CARE & Cole Consulting, 1991. 90p. bibliog.

An evaluation of a large forestry and agricultural project. Its usefulness comes from the generalizations made about forestry project success in Lesotho. This will be helpful for those researching into general farming issues, while the discussion of project activities helps in the evaluation of donors.

359 **The Lesotho woodlot project: progress, problems and prospects.**
P. I. Powell, P. A. Wellings. *Development Studies Southern Africa*, vol. 5, no. 3 (1983), p. 350-70.

This report on the progress of the Lesotho woodlot project is a useful indicator of the problems of forestry projects in Lesotho. Special attention is paid to training. The project is involved in a wide spectrum of forestry operations, including the acquisition of land and the felling of trees. Despite problems related to land tenure, the project has succeeded in establishing a number of woodlots and in training local people.

360 **Social forestry manual – an aid to rural development in Lesotho.**
Gavin Armstrong. Kalbaskraal, South Africa: Published by the Author, 1992. 117p. bibliog.

Based on the social forestry initiatives of the German-funded Matelile Rural Development Project in the Mafeteng district of Lesotho. Armstrong argues that the philosophical underpinning of and motivation behind the implementation of agroforestry projects is as important as the choice of trees and the nature of planting. The needs and priorities of the target group are likewise a factor which need to be taken into consideration at the outset to prevent failure and disillusionment. However, despite the intellectual importance Armstrong assigns to these issues, he gives little by way of practical examples. Considerable space is devoted to the design of agroforestry projects in Lesotho. This publication is available from: Gavin Armstrong, Camphill Village, PO Kalbaskraal 7302, South Africa.

Fieldcrops and horticulture

361 **An assessment of the interest and capacity of households to undertake irrigated vegetable production. Vol 1: Masianokeng, Ha Jimisi and Ha Motloheloa, Maseru District, Lesotho.**
David Hall. Maseru: Sechaba Consultants & Ministry of Agriculture, Small-scale Irrigated Vegetable Project, 1995. 38p.

This study has three basic objectives: to compile a baseline for future evaluations; to collect data on community attitudes; and to evaluate the capacity of households to undertake irrigated vegetable production. The results show that the socio-economic status of fieldowners in the survey area is higher than in other parts of rural Lesotho. Indeed, many households might be described as peri-urban. As well as discussing fieldowners' expectations of an irrigation scheme, the document offers an analysis of previous (failed) irrigation schemes and a short history of irrigation projects in Lesotho.

362 **The attitudes and socio-economic conditions of irrigation scheme members: the results of a survey conducted for the Small Scale Irrigated Vegetable Project.**
David Hall, Philip Cole. Maseru: Sechaba Consultants & Ministry of Agriculture, Small-scale Irrigated Vegetable Project, 1990. 108p. 1 map. bibliog.

Describes the attitudes of landholders involved in four irrigation schemes being implemented by the Small-scale Irrigated Vegetable Project in Leribe and Butha-Buthe districts. Although there are a number of variations in the success of these schemes, in general it is clear that where landholders have maintained the right to work their fields individually, they do so with great enthusiasm. In cases of individual production, such schemes are able to overcome many of the social conflicts inherent in communal schemes. Nevertheless, given the complexities of irrigated agriculture compared to traditional dryland farming, the report argues that there is clearly a need for considerable training for scheme members before they can be expected to manage their schemes by themselves. Baseline socio-economic data is presented for the interviewees.

363 **Attitudes of asparagus farmers in five areas in Maseru District.**
Thuso J. Green. Maseru: Sechaba Consultants & the Lesotho National Development Corporation, 1995. 41p.

Green finds that farmers are very interested in growing asparagus despite the very serious management problems that exist. These problems are exacerbated by the poor management of their cooperative and the inadequate services provided by Basotho Farm Produce. The report contends that farmers are not consulted enough, leading to their frustration. Monies are deducted from sales revenue without farmers being informed, payment systems are unclear, and the pricing of other inputs is not justified to farmers. In general, farmers are not sufficiently informed about most aspects of asparagus growing, management and trade, and the report argues that they need to be given greater involvement in decision making.

364 **Changes in the attitudes and socio-economic status of irrigation scheme members 1990-1992.**
David Hall. Maseru: Sechaba Consultants & Ministry of Agriculture, Small-scale Irrigated Vegetable Project, 1992. 23p.

This is a follow-up to an earlier survey (see item no. 362). The report presents data on changes in the socio-economic status of members since 1990, and also provides information on the attitudes of members, comparing earlier data where applicable. The author finds that while scheme members are successfully producing vegetables on an individual basis, the collective management of schemes has not been successful. Furthermore, management committees are not functioning as intended, and farmers are not keen to be involved in scheme management as it brings them into conflict with their own relatives and neighbours. Likewise, wider village conflicts affect the working of the scheme and can paralyse the decision-making process.

365 **Contract farming and outgrower schemes: asparagus production in Lesotho.**
Sam Rugege, Sehoai Santho. *Eastern Africa Economic Review* (Special issue 1989), p. 20-41.

This report provides a general overview of government agricultural policy and the contract farming system in Lesotho. It then goes on to discuss the situation of asparagus growers in detail, using the results of almost 300 outgrowers in Maseru District. The nature of the production, processing and marketing systems are discussed in detail. A gender analysis is also offered, which considers the position of women both as growers and workers. It is argued that the success of the project has been due not only to the nature of the farming system, but also to the existence of a guaranteed market in Europe and the availability of concessionary financing. The authors conclude that it is unlikely that the success of asparagus could be replicated with other crops.

366 **Contract farming and outgrower schemes in east and southern Africa.**

D. Glover. *Journal of Agricultural Economics*, vol. 41, no. 3 (September 1990), p. 303-15.

Presents the results of a three-year study of outgrower schemes, whereby small farmers are contracted to sell their output to larger public or private bodies for processing and marketing. Glover critically evaluates the elements that make for a successful project. Lesotho is one of six southern African countries he studies; however, he places particular emphasis on the Lesotho scheme, which he finds relatively successful. Those interested in agricultural innovation in Lesotho will find this a useful comparative paper.

367 **Household vegetable gardens in Africa: case studies from Mauritania and Lesotho.**

T. R. Frankenberger, M. P. Stone, S. Saenz-de-Tejada. *Arid Lands Newsletter*, vol. 29 (Fall/Winter 1989), p. 21-24.

An assessment of the factors that affect the success of vegetable garden projects. Case-studies are used for Mauritania and Lesotho. The Lesotho case-study shows that the cultivation of vegetables can displace other food crops; therefore care must be taken to ensure the complementarity of vegetable production with other crops.

368 **Land use on irrigation schemes: case studies from the 'Malere and Rasekila II schemes, Butha-Buthe district, Lesotho.**

David Hall. Maseru: Sechaba Consultants & Ministry of Agriculture, Small-scale Irrigated Vegetable Project, 1993. 21p.

Considers the factors that cause low productivity on irrigation schemes and proposes a number of steps that might be taken to facilitate land use agreements in the future. For maximum benefit from irrigation schemes, the author argues that land should be used as intensively as possible. However, he finds that, for a variety of reasons, not all scheme members were using land to the fullest and in a few cases some were not using land at all. A number of factors appear necessary for sustainable production: the absence of family emergencies; good production and sales; adequate and timely inputs; reasonable plot size compared to the availability of labour; reasonable soil; and access to other fields for cereal production.

369 **The Lesotho national fruit and vegetable production survey.**

Lesotho Government. Maseru: Ministry of Agriculture, 1992. 173p.

This report presents statistics on home-garden production of fruit and vegetables, and contains information on typical production practices and the constraints of home-gardeners. The report also looks at larger farmers and donor schemes. It argues that information on the socio-economic characteristics of households is important to understand their capacity to invest and, thus, helps determine effective agricultural policy.

370 **The low-input, sustainable agriculture (LISA) prescription: a bitter pill for farm-households in southern Africa.**
Allan R. C. Low. *Project-Appraisal*, vol. 8, no. 2 (1993), p. 97-101.

Low uses Lesotho as one of three case-studies of the failure of low-input sustainable agricultural production. He discusses hybrid maize and fertilizer adoption in Lesotho, and argues that farmers are more concerned with sustainable livelihoods than sustainable environments. Thus, projects should be designed with a clear understanding of the constraints and needs of farmers and the natural resource environment.

371 **Manure and fertilizer applications to three crops in Lesotho 1987-1991.**
Garry Massey, Motabang E. Pomela, Napo Ntlou, Lieketso Moremoholo. Maseru: Ministry of Agriculture, Agricultural Research Division and LAPIS, 1991. 44p. bibliog.

Reports findings on the yield responses of maize, sorghum and beans to fertilizer. The authors discover that there is a good response; however, Basotho farmers have, in the past, applied manure and received little or no results. It is argued that this is probably due to the small amount used, but this failure has discouraged greater use. Thus, it is recommended that manure be applied in far higher quantities, as one of a number of potential fertilizers. This is a useful publication on farming habits and attitudes to fertilizer.

372 **Pinto beans in Lesotho: the farmer's perspective.**
Jeanette Bloem. Maseru: Sechaba Consultants & Ministry of Agriculture, LAPIS project, 1992. 16p.

Reveals enthusiasm for pinto beans, as most farmers interviewed felt that pinto beans provide higher yields and prefer them for their drought-resistant properties. This report offers statistics on yields and farmer characteristics.

373 **Vegetable growing for home consumption and cash. Implementation manual.**
Dieter Lippman. Eschborn, Germany: German Agency for Technical Cooperation, [n.d.]. 101p.

A manual intended to promote vegetable production in Lesotho using appropriate technology. Written in a 'popular' style, it contains information and diagrams on the establishment of a vegetable garden.

Livestock

374 **Communal grazing and range management: the case of grazing associations in Lesotho.**
S. W. Lawry. Addis Ababa: International Livestock Centre for Africa, 1987. 10p. bibliog. (African Livestock Policy Analysis Network Paper, no. 13).

Documents the difficulties of range management in the remote mountain area of Sehlabathebe. Range management in this area was supported by a donor-funded project. The study finds that the grazing plan drawn up by project staff was unenforceable, and was worsened by the heterogeneity in livestock ownership within the target area. In addition, methods of livestock management did not change with the introduction of the rangeland programme and livestock farmers continued in 'traditional' low-input methods. Despite this lack of success in some areas, the project has embarked on a cooperative management strategy which encourages participation from local leadership in areas of policy development. This management strategy not only promises greater success but also provides a prescriptive model for other similar projects. For greater detail, see the author's doctoral thesis: *Private herds and common land: issues in the management of communal grazing land in Lesotho, Southern Africa* (PhD thesis, University of Wisconsin, Madison, 1988. 335p.).

375 **Dairy products: permit and levy study.**
Philip A. P. Cole, Tlhoriso Telejane, Mapule T. M. Makoro. Maseru: Lesotho National Dairy Board & Cole Consulting, 1992. 33p.

The system of import permits and levies for agricultural produce in Lesotho is described, as is the system for sales tax. In addition, the existing provisions for quality control of dairy products, both imported and domestically produced, are contrasted with the measures in force in South Africa. For comparison, the operation of dairy levy systems in South Africa and Swaziland are explained. Given this information, the authors recommend a system of permits to distribute dairy produce based on the maintenance of quality standards. For a more theoretical analysis, see: *Dairy price structuring study*, by Philip Cole (Maseru: Lesotho National Dairy Board, & Cole Consulting, 1992. 49p. bibliog.). See also: *Study on a dairy information system*, by Philip Cole (Maseru: Lesotho National Dairy Board, 1992. 46p. bibliog.).

376 **Livestock development and range utilization in Lesotho.**
Gary G. Storey. In: *Agricultural marketing and policy development in Lesotho*. Edited by None L. Mokitimi, Motsamai T. Mochebelele. Roma, Lesotho: University of Lesotho, Institute of Southern African Studies, 1993, p. 17-41. bibliog.

Basing his study on a survey of 537 livestock-owning households, the author concludes that economic considerations are very important to livestock owners, despite a low number of formal sales. This is an important survey, not only for an understanding of livestock ownership but also for an analysis of range degradation.

377 **Local participation, equity, and popular support in Lesotho's Range Management Area Programme.**
Neil E. Artz. *African Journal of Range and Forage Science*, vol. 10, no. 1 (1993), p. 54-62.

Range Management Area Programmes were set up to improve livestock productivity and the quality of grazing land in Lesotho. These programmes are based on the collective management of communal grazing areas and thus require a high degree of participation from local people. Success in achieving this aim is investigated in a study of two programme areas and local support for the programmes was found to be high. Issues around the equity effects of programmes were also investigated and results show that there was no perception of inequality of participation. Thus, the study finds that range management programmes have had considerable success. This contrasts with earlier range management projects that have experienced significant criticism. See item no. 264 for an in-depth critique of one such programme.

378 **The needs of dairy farmers: the farmer's perspective.**
John Gay, Thuso Green. Maseru: Sechaba Consultants & Lesotho National Dairy Board, 1992. 45p.

A study undertaken in the lowland and foothill districts of Lesotho. The authors present socio-economic data on dairy farmers, and information is also given on constraints, extension services and credit sources. The results show that cattle farming continues to be a male domain, and dairy farming households appear to be richer than other households. This report offers an interesting picture of the relative agricultural success of some households in rural Lesotho.

379 **Report on range and livestock management in four sub-areas of the Matelile Project area.**
John Gay, Thuso Green. Maseru: Sechaba Consultants & Matelile Rural Development Project, 1993. 65p. bibliog.

Provides information on range and livestock management in the Matelile area. The authors found that very few households kept animals for sale and that usually animals were used for ploughing purposes. In relation to the availability of range land, most villagers felt that there was enough grazing if people kept to restrictions and also maintained a system of grazing rotation. However, interviewees felt that chiefs and Village Development Councils had a negative effect on range management.

380 **A survey of the production, utilization and marketing of livestock and livestock products in Lesotho.**
Brent M. Swallow, 'Mabaitsi Motsamai, Limpho Sopeng, Ray F. Brokken, Gary G. Storey. Roma, Lesotho: National University of Lesotho, Institute of Southern African Studies, (Research Report, no. 17); Maseru: Ministry of Agriculture, Farming Systems Research Division, 1987. 276p. 2 maps. bibliog.

This work presents in-depth research into the livestock system in Lesotho, centred around a geographically-representative survey of livestock owners. The first part of the report briefly describes research issues, while the second part presents research results. These results are divided into sections dealing with different aspects of livestock-marketing and livestock-production. A translation is also provided of the questionnaire. Although rather narrowly economic in viewpoint, this document gives a good insight into livestock issues in Lesotho. For more detail, see: *Livestock development and range utilization in Lesotho*, by Brent M. Swallow, Ray F. Brokken, 'Mabaitsi Motsamai, Limpho Sopeng, Gary G. Storey (Roma, Lesotho: National University of Lesotho, Institute of Southern African Studies [Research Report, no. 18]; Maseru: Ministry of Agriculture, Farming Systems Research Division, 1987. 83p. bibliog.).

The persistence of women's invisibility in agriculture: theoretical and policy lessons from Lesotho and Sierra Leone.
See item no. 168.

Women, land and agriculture in Lesotho.
See item no. 173.

Human Resources and Employment

General

381 **The demand for and supply of labour in Lesotho: patterns and implications for socioeconomic development.**
A. O. Okore. In: *Southern Africa in the 1980s and beyond: Institute of Southern African Studies 1980-1990.* Edited by the Institute of Southern African Studies. Roma, Lesotho: University of Lesotho, Institute of Southern African Studies, 1993, p. 157-82. bibliog.

Discusses the labour situation in Lesotho, beginning with an analysis of the economic context. This chapter provides a considerable amount of data and, most usefully, attention is paid to skilled labour, usually an under-researched area. Okore argues that education should provide the greater technical and vocational skills in order to ease the problem of unemployment. While this is not a new argument, Okore provides an interesting analysis and significant technical support for this line of reasoning.

382 **Farm labour in Lesotho: scarcity or surplus?**
R. A. Wykstra. Fort Collins, Colorado: Colorado State University, 1978. 42p. (LASA Discussion Paper, no. 5).

Wykstra investigates the supply of labour, with particular reference to agricultural labour, and concludes that aggregate underemployment exists in agriculture, but that at particular periods labour scarcities emerge. Peak labour demands are not met and the author argues that a significant increase in available manpower is required. Thus, the paper refutes the general idea that Lesotho experiences a labour surplus. However, it is possible that the results of this paper are no longer valid, given the recent falls in employment in mining and high growth in the labour force. Despite this, it remains an interesting piece of work, which will be useful for research into labour markets.

383 **Female labour in the textile and clothing industry of Lesotho.**
Carolyn Baylies, Caroline Wright. *African Affairs*, no. 92 (1993), p. 577-91.

Argues that Lesotho's present industrialization strategy rests on cheap female labour. Contributory factors to this policy include the failure of successive agricultural projects and the need to absorb new entrants to the labour market at a time when recruitment to the South African mines is declining. The authors argue that a combination of social convention and economic convenience has led to the heavy reliance on women in the textile and clothing industry.

384 **The labour force of Lesotho.**
Lesotho Government. Maseru: Bureau of Statistics, 1990. 69p.

Based on a labour force survey carried out in 1985/86, this report presents statistical information on the characteristics of Lesotho's working age population. In particular, this survey has more accurate data on female employment compared to the population census, and will be useful for students seeking information on employment and unemployment.

385 **Lesotho's employment challenge: alternative scenarios, 1980-2000 AD.**
J. B. Eckert, R. Wykstra. Fort Collins, Colorado: Colorado State University, 1979. 25p. (LASA Discussion Paper, no. 7).

Discusses trends in the labour force until the end of the century. The authors make several assumptions in order to extrapolate their information into the future. Although this document was written in the late 1970s, the data and arguments remain pertinent to the discussion of unemployment in Lesotho today. This paper and the project from which it emerged have become influential in policy formulation.

386 **The political economy of the Southern African periphery: cottage industries, factories and female wage labour in Swaziland compared.**
B. J. Harris. Basingstoke, England: Macmillan Press; New York: St. Martin's Press, 1993. 295p. bibliog.

Swaziland has experienced growth in textile production based on the use of female labour. Harris situates these trends within a wider discussion of industrialization and poverty. Part three of the book (chapters seven to nine) provide comparative studies, with particular attention paid to Lesotho. Harris argues that a similar process of industrialization using cheap labour can be identified in the case of Lesotho. Other chapters will also be of interest to the student interested in Lesotho's economy, as patterns of industrialization and implications for the structure of labour markets are discussed for southern African as a whole. Harris also examines the possibility of alternative modes of industrial development in a regional context.

387 **Research on rural non farm employment in Lesotho: results of a baseline survey.**
M. P. Senaoana, S. D. Turner, G. J. van Apeldoorn. Maseru: National University of Lesotho, Institute of Southern African Studies, 1984. 81p. bibliog.

Using the results of interviews carried out in four villages in Maseru District, this report discusses the employment in the rural non-farm sector in Lesotho. Grass weaving, brewing, sewing and informal construction were the most common rural non-farm activities. Although wage employment in both South Africa and Lesotho remains a more significant form of employment, this type of informal, non-farm employment appeared particularly important for the poorest rural households, especially those headed by females. The authors discuss the constraints to non-farm employment and make recommendations for government policy support.

388 **Wage employment of rural Basotho women: a case study.**
Judith S. Gay. *South African Labour Bulletin*, vol. 6, no. 4 (1980), p. 40-53. bibliog.

Publications on labour in Lesotho have tended to focus on male migrant workers, while women are usually cast in the role of the female dependent. This paper aims to investigate women's position as entrepreneurs and wage workers, both domestically and as migrants. It is argued that female labour and income-generating activities are vital to the economic survival of many Basotho households. Female earnings are particularly crucial to those women who have no male wage earner to support them. Despite the fact that this study was published in 1980, its importance remains undiminished. Indeed, the sharp rise in male unemployment rates makes an investigation of female employment of greater interest to those studying living conditions in Lesotho.

Migrant labour

389 **Another blanket.**
Edited by Dan Matsobane, Toine Eggenhuizen. Horison, South Africa: Agency for Industrial Mission, 1976. 46p.

An account of the findings of twenty-three Lesotho theological students from Roma and Morija who investigated the migrant labour system in June 1976. Reports cover: the effect on families left behind in Lesotho; the indignities of the recruiting process (eight students actually became mine recruits) and of compound life and work; and the interaction between migrant workers and township dwellers. The work also contains an annex on the individual and national costs of migrant labour by James H. Cobbe: 'Notes on the social costs of migrant labour from Lesotho' (p. 36-38).

390 **The Bantustan brain gain: a study into the nature and causes of brain drain from independent Africa to the South African Bantustans.**
Kwesi K. Prah. Roma, Lesotho: National University of Lesotho, Institute of Southern African Studies, 1989. 74p. bibliog. (Southern African Studies Series, no. 5).

Lesotho is one of five countries included in this study of skilled labour emigration. Prah investigates the extent of the loss and discusses the cause of this outflow of labour. Data is included on the characteristics of a sample of migrants, which Prah uses to help explain why this migration occurs. It is an interesting study and, given that 'brain drain' is likely to increase as a problem for Lesotho, this study will remain useful for researchers and students alike.

391 **The changing labour demand in South Africa and prospects for re-absorption of returning migrants in Lesotho's economy.**
Khabele T. Matlosa. In: *Southern Africa after apartheid: prospects for the inner periphery in 1990s.* Edited by Sehoai Santho, Mafa Sejanamane. Harare: Southern Africa Political Economy Series (SAPES), 1991, p. 71-82. bibliog.

Highlights features of the reduction in foreign labour on South African mines and the Lesotho government's reaction to these processes. Matlosa discusses the South African National Union of Mineworkers' position on the migrant labour system and finally deals with prospects for a re-integration strategy for returning migrants. He argues that government responses so far have not reduced dependence on migrant labour, nor have they facilitated greater re-absorption of repatriated migrant miners.

392 **The effects of social, political and economic constraints on the black African's allocation of time: evidence from oscillating migrants in the Republic of South Africa.**
D. E. Ault, G. L. Rutman. *Oxford Economic Papers*, vol. 44, no. 1 (January 1992), p. 135-55.

Labour migrants from Lesotho are included in this study of migration, in which the authors consider the incentives to engage in minework. The report investigates the decision to migrate as well as the use of remittances. This will be useful for academic researchers interested in the economic analysis of labour migration from Lesotho.

393 **Emigration to South Africa's mines.**
Robert E. B. Lucas. *American Economic Review*, vol. 77, no. 3 (June 1987), p. 313-30.

Basing his study on data from Lesotho, Botswana, Malawi and Mozambique, Lucas attempts to quantify the economic effects of labour migration to South Africa's mines. In Lesotho, he finds that such migration diminishes domestic crop production in the short run but in the long run enhances cattle accumulation through invested remittances. He speculates that greater mine employment may increase local wages but does not attempt a statistical investigation for Lesotho. The data included in this paper is particularly useful for researchers concerned with the economic effects of labour migration. A detailed appendix, listing the data and itemizing sources, is available from the author upon request.

394 **Foreign workers in SA: comrades or competitors?**
Roger Southall. *South African Labour Bulletin*, vol. 18, no. 6 (December 1994), p. 68-73.

Concentrating on the case of workers from Lesotho, Southall considers the position of foreign workers and the labour market. This is an interesting paper which illustrates the ambiguity in attitudes towards foreign workers on the part of trade unionists and labour market analysts.

395 **The future of international labour migration in Southern Africa: focus on Lesotho.**
Khabele Matlosa. In: *Southern Africa in the 1980s and beyond: Institute of Southern African Studies 1980-1990*. Edited by the Institute of Southern African Studies. Roma, Lesotho: University of Lesotho, Institute of Southern African Studies, 1993, p. 183-207. bibliog.

Focuses on the prospects for the transformation of the regional economy from a labour reservoir to a more dynamic, labour-absorbing one. Lesotho is used as a case-study in the second part of the paper. Matlosa provides an array of data on the importance of migrant labour and its rate of decline in Lesotho. The paper concludes that Lesotho needs to create more viable employment alternatives domestically to absorb retrenched and prospective migrants, and a critique is offered of present employment-creation programmes.

396 **Future prospects for foreign migrants in a democratic South Africa.**
Fion de Vletter. In: *Southern Africa after apartheid: prospects for the inner periphery in 1990s*. Edited by Sehoai Santho, Mafa Sejanamane. Harare: Southern Africa Political Economy Series (SAPES), 1991, p. 28-51. bibliog.

Provides an overview of trends in migrant labour in South Africa, with data provided up to 1990. This is a useful paper for those who would like a summary of recent trends in migrant labour. De Vletter argues that reduced restrictions on residence and opportunities for black South Africans in post-apartheid South Africa will lead to the gradual marginalization of foreign mineworkers. Although foreign nationals now dominate higher skill categories, it is argued that mines will prefer to invest in nationals who have greater security of residence. Foreign workers with few satisfactory employment alternatives will accept poorer conditions than domestic workers and thus lead to a greater supply of labour to unskilled positions. While de Vletter does not consider the question of the granting of residence rights to some migrants (which has since occurred), this is a good summary of policy and trends in migrant miners.

397 **International migration and international trade.**
Sharon Stanton-Russell, Michael Teitelbaum. Washington, DC: World Bank, 1992. 84p. bibliog. (Discussion Paper, no. 160).

Lesotho is one of the labour-exporting countries considered in this international survey of migration. Although briefly covered, this report places migration flows from

Lesotho in a regional context and provides a host of data from the 1980s on the size and importance of remittances for the Basotho economy. It provides a good overview for those attempting to get a general picture of Lesotho's place in regional migration trends. Although it does not offer data on the recent falls in mine labour recruitment, it does anticipate this reduction in the demand for labour and discusses the possible consequences.

398 **Labour migration from Botswana, Lesotho, and Swaziland.**
W. Elkan. *Economic Development and Cultural Change*, vol. 28, no. 3 (1980), p. 583-96.

Presents information on labour migration to South Africa from Botswana, Lesotho and Swaziland, concentrating particularly on Lesotho. The author investigates the social and economic consequences of such migration, and attempts to explain changes in the flow of migrants over time. The author argues that despite the monetary benefits of labour migration, the degree of dependence on this source of income must also be regarded as a cost. This argument has particular relevance for the present day, when Lesotho is experiencing the difficulty of adjusting to lower rates of migrant employment.

399 **Labour migration in South Africa and agricultural development: some lessons from Lesotho.**
J. C. Plath, D. W. Holland, Joe W. Carvalho. *Journal of Developing Areas*, vol. 21, no. 2 (1987), p. 159-76.

The authors investigate the relationship between labour migration and agricultural development. The incentives for migration are illustrated by a comparison of the income earned by migrant workers and the income generated by agricultural production. However, in an important but controversial conclusion, the authors argue that agriculture could generate sufficient income with adequate land under rotations of traditional field crops with improved practices.

400 **Lesotho migration in post-apartheid South Africa: options and constraints.**
Leketekete V. Ketso. In: *Southern Africa after apartheid: prospects for the inner periphery in 1990s.* Edited by Sehoai Santho, Mafa Sejanamane. Harare: Southern Africa Political Economy Series (SAPES), 1991, p. 52-70. bibliog.

This short paper provides a sensible and well-balanced account of the demand for Basotho migrant labour in its discussion of prospects in post-apartheid South Africa. Ketso argues that while political considerations may reduce the demand for migrant labour, economic considerations indicate the desire for continued migration. To support this conclusion he considers the rationale for employing migrants and links this migration to the process of accumulation in South Africa. Due to the need for migrant labour, Ketso argues, there is a possibility of a special arrangement between Lesotho and South Africa. It also appears likely that clandestine migration may rise.

401 **Lesotho: the role of agriculture and migration.**
Leketekete V. Ketso. In: *Studies in the economic history of Southern Africa, Volume II: South Africa, Lesotho and Swaziland.* Edited by Z. A. Konczacki, J. L. Parpart, T. M. Shaw. London: Frank Cass, 1991, p. 240-59. bibliog.

Ketso discusses the impact of migration on agricultural production, presents an historical analysis of labour migration, and argues that labour migration has had two distinct phases. The first phase, covering the late 19th century until the 1960s, saw an expansion in the number of migrant workers. During the second phase, from the 1970s onwards, real wages have risen substantially. However, the proportion of men going to work on the mines has fallen, and it is argued that this, coupled with the shortage of alternative employment and poor agricultural prospects, has led to social differentiation and increased unemployment. Although the treatment of agriculture is rather brief, this is a helpful overview of trends in labour migration.

402 **Men without work: unemployed migrant labour in Lesotho.**
Caroline Wright. Durham, England: University of Durham, 1989. 62p. (Working Paper in Sociology, no. 22).

An exploration of unemployment among men in rural Lesotho. Wright provides the results of fieldwork carried out in the foothills of the Maloti mountains, and argues that the disruption of established employment patterns may challenge the existing relationship between the sexes.

403 **'Stabilization' and structural unemployment.**
Colin Murray. *South African Labour Bulletin*, vol. 6, no. 4 (1980), p. 58-61.

The trend towards greater stabilization in migrant mine employment is discussed. Murray investigates the effects on the rural population and argues that it is likely to create a pool of permanently unemployed men.

404 **Technology, ethnicity and ideology: Basotho miners and shaft-sinking on the South African gold mines.**
Jeff Guy, Motlatsi Thabane. *Journal of Southern African Studies*, vol. 14, no. 2 (January 1988), p. 257-79.

Examines ethnic stereotyping on the South African gold mines. This stereotyping is based on the belief that inherent tribal characteristics distinguish certain African workers from others. Basotho workers have a reputation for shaft-sinking and this book draws together general information with the results of an Oral History Project conducted at the National University of Lesotho in 1982. Central to the paper is the argument that the association of Basotho with shaft-sinking was not the prerogative of mine management, but that the Basotho themselves made similar associations and classifications. The authors argue that such stereotyping can be understood by the existence of tremendous labour oppression and the suppression of more formal types of worker organization. Thus, the propagation of ethnic ideas and the mobilization of workers around them was a source of protection, a qualified form of work satisfaction and above all a means of securing a greater income.

405 **Unemployment and casual labour in Maseru: the impact of changing employment strategies on migrant labourers in Lesotho.**
Motlatsi Thabane, Jeff Guy. Cape Town: Second Carnegie Inquiry into Poverty and Development in Southern Africa, 1984. 25p. bibliog.

A discussion of the attitudes towards unemployment of men seeking work on the South African mines. The authors argue that the failure of able-bodied men to obtain work contracts is potentially the most radical change in Lesotho's history since its loss of independence. This paper does not discuss the problems of defining the unemployed nor does it seek to quantify the phenomenon in detail. Instead, it presents the phenomenon of unemployment as it is perceived by work seekers themselves.

406 **Unemployment, migration and changing gender relations in Lesotho.**
Caroline Wright. PhD thesis, University of Leeds, England, 1993. 339p.

Explores the effects of growing unemployment on internal migration and urbanization. Encompassing an evaluation of much of the recent literature on Lesotho, this thesis provides a thoughtful analysis of the effects of unemployment. Particular attention is paid to changes in gender relations, and Wright identifies a new pattern of gender conflict arising from the potential for greater female economic autonomy. This thesis, however, refers only obliquely to issues of class differentiation, preferring to concentrate on the issue of gender disadvantage. It will be useful to readers interested in a detailed, well-grounded discussion of unemployment and urbanization.

The Labour Movement and Trade Unions

407 **The future of the migrant labour system: a NUM perspective.**
Kate Phillip. In: *Southern Africa after apartheid: prospects for the inner periphery in 1990s.* Edited by Sehoai Santho, Mafa Sejanamane. Harare: Southern Africa Political Economy Series (SAPES), 1991, p. 83-90.

A brief overview of the South African National Union of Mineworkers' policy on migrant labour. These policies centre around the abolition of the migrant labour system and the dismantling of workers' compounds.

408 **Industrial relations in Lesotho in the 1980s and the challenges for the 1990s.**
Jobere Molefi. In: *Southern Africa in the 1980s and beyond: Institute of Southern African Studies 1980-1990.* Edited by the Institute of Southern African Studies. Roma, Lesotho: University of Lesotho, Institute of Southern African Studies, 1993, p. 208-26. bibliog.

Attempts to assess industrial relations in Lesotho in the 1980s with a view to ascertaining the situation in the 1990s and beyond. After documenting the industrial conflicts of the 1980s, Molefi concludes that the return to democracy enhances the chances of future industrial stability. This is a useful publication on the experience of industrial relations in Lesotho, which will provide the reader with an introduction to legislation and the nature of past labour conflict.

409 **The labour market and trade unions at the South African periphery: Lesotho and Transkei.**
Roger Southall. *African Affairs,* vol. 93, no. 373 (October 1994), p. 565-86.

Southall considers the long-term, intractable decline of labour markets in Lesotho. He discusses the character of the government responses to labour militancy and addresses the limits and possibilities of trade unionism given Lesotho's labour surplus. Southall considers the impact of the return to civilian rule in Lesotho on the labour movement. While he welcomes the introduction of a new labour code by the democratic government, he remains undecided on whether the new code will restore investor confidence and produce a more predictable, representative and viable industrial relations régime.

410 **Migrancy and militancy: the case of the National Union of Mineworkers of South Africa.**

Jonathon Crush. *African Affairs*, vol. 88, no. 1 (1989), p. 5-23.

Illustrates the importance of Basotho mineworkers in the initial organization of the National Union of Mineworkers of South Africa. Crush shows that Basotho workers were among the first to join the union and often held important positions within the union hierarchy. This contrasts strongly with the widely held view that labour migrants are 'passive' workers and do not involve themselves in union organization.

Statistics

411 **Basotho women and their men: statistics on women and men in Lesotho, 1993.**

Lesotho Government. Maseru: Bureau of Statistics, 1993. 2nd ed. 74p. 1 map.

An update of a volume published in 1989. It contains a breakdown by gender for statistics on demography, health, education, employment, crime and decision making.

412 **Lesotho Statistical Yearbook.**

Maseru: Bureau of Statistics, 1989- . irregular.

Produces yearly and time-series data on socio-economic conditions in Lesotho. Statistics are produced on a comprehensive set of issues, including: climate; population; education; health; migrant labour; economic production; and financial issues. This publication replaces *Annual Statistical Bulletin* (Maseru: Bureau of Statistics, [1961- . annual]).

413 **Quarterly Statistical Bulletin.**

Maseru: Bureau of Statistics, 1976- . quarterly.

A series of publications with varying content, intended to give up-to-date information ahead of the *Lesotho Statistical Yearbook.*

Environment

General

414 **Acid precipitation in Lesotho.**

Gisela Prasad. In: *Southern Africa in the 1980s and beyond: Institute of Southern African Studies 1980-1990.* Edited by the Institute of Southern African Studies. Roma, Lesotho: University of Lesotho, Institute of Southern African Studies, 1993, p. 261-77. 1 map. bibliog.

A survey of the rainwater samples collected in Roma and Maseru during the 1991/92 rainy season indicated low pH values, i.e. acid rain. These findings have raised concern as industries in Lesotho are not thought to be emitting the type of pollutants that cause acid rain. Since the pollution apparently does not come from within Lesotho, the most likely source areas are in South Africa, particularly the Vaal Triangle. This paper attempts to assess the seriousness of the situation and recommends the continued testing of rainwater to help understand the phenomenon.

415 **Manpower vs machinery: a case study of conservation works in Lesotho.**

R. A. Wykstra, J. B. Eckert. Fort Collins, Colorado: Colorado State University, Department of Economics, Lesotho Agricultural Sector Analysis Program, 1980. 24p. bibliog. (Research Report, no. 6).

Given the need for employment creation, this paper argues that labour-intensive conservation work has greater viability than capital-intensive work. Data from these two types of work is compared and information is calculated in terms of rates of return. This is a useful publication for those interested in the economics of conservation work. The authors offer an appendix showing details from the analysis.

416 **National environmental planning and sustainable development: theory and applications in the Lesotho context.**
I. V. Mashinini. *NUL Journal of Research*, vol. 4 (1994), p. 87-109.

An assessment of the National Environmental Action Plan (NEAP) approach in the context of Lesotho. A NEAP outlines various environmental problems and then assigns policy options for their solution. Mashinini argues that there has been a lack of participation in the development of the NEAP for Lesotho, with the involvement of chiefs used as a proxy for true grass-roots participation. Furthermore, environmental policies have often been devised by donor agencies and this has led to another diversion from the grass-roots approach. Given the development of this top-down approach, Mashinini argues that it is unsurprising that environmental policies have been techno-centred rather than people-centred. Such techno-centred approaches are, in the author's opinion, often expensive endeavours that do not yield positive results.

417 **A preliminary list of the ecological sites of Lesotho.**
Lesotho Government. Maseru: Ministry of Agriculture, Division of Range Management, Land Conservation and Range Development Project, 1984. 36p.

Ecological sites are areas with particular plant communities and environmental factors. This document defines 850 such ecological sites in Lesotho.

418 **The Southern African environment: profiles of the SADC countries.**
S. Moyo, P. O'Keefe, M. Sill. London: Earthscan Publications, 1993. 354p.

A comprehensive environmental profile of the countries of the Southern African Development Community, including Lesotho. The profile gives information on physical and human geography, ecology, agriculture, economy, population and political structure of the country. Within this, it investigates environmental conditions and the institutional context for resolving environmental problems.

419 **Vanishing bogs of the mountain kingdom.**
R. H. Meakins, J. D. Duckett. *Veld & Flora*, vol. 79, no. 2 (June 1993), p. 49-51.

Discusses the critical state of mountain bogs in Lesotho. Erosion is destroying these bogs, and this has important implications for water-flow and water-filtering in the mountain areas.

Land degradation and soil erosion

420 **Case study: benefit-cost analysis of soil conservation in Maphutseng, Lesotho.**

J. Bojo. In: *The economics of dryland management.* Edited by J. A. Dixon, D. E. James, P. B. Sherman. London: Earthscan Publications, 1989, p. 250-88. bibliog.

The author presents a cost-benefit analysis of a soil conservation project. Calculations are made for actual and projected benefits until the year 2004. The benefits centre on the increased production value of maize, sorghum, fodder and fuel arising from the adoption of soil conservation measures. It is estimated that net benefits will be negative until 1990 and positive thereafter.

421 **A comprehensive approach to village-based conservation development.**

David Hall. Maseru: Sechaba Consultants & Ministry of Agriculture, Soil and Water Conservation Project, 1990. 82p. 1 map. bibliog.

A study of the attitudes towards conservation. The author finds that the time-span of conservation projects has a direct effect on their sustainability, and he argues that projects need to be continued into the long-term to have maximum effect on people's attitudes and practices. He also claims that the use of unsustainable financial inducements used to guarantee community involvement is detrimental in the long run. While he advocates the involvement of the community, he finds that not all villages have organizations suitable for soil conservation activities.

422 **The economics of land degradation: theory and applications to Lesotho.**

J. Bojo. Stockholm: Stockholm School of Economics, Economics Research Institute, 1991. 352p. bibliog.

Land degradation has long been of concern in Lesotho and this book places its analysis in an economic context. The author presents a general economic picture of Lesotho and then attempts to estimate the degree to which soil erosion has affected national output. It is argued that, in an attempt to reduce degradation, the government should promote a redefinition of property rights. The author also offers a cost-benefit analysis of the Farm Improvement with Soil Conservation (FISC) programme, and gives a general critique of cost-benefit methods. This is an interesting study of the economic issues surrounding soil conservation in Lesotho. However, it is arguable that a greater socio-political analysis should be made of the forces influencing land use.

423 **From knowledge to practice: village based resource management with special attention to soil conservation.**

Sechaba Consultants. Maseru: Sechaba Consultants & Ministry of Agriculture, Soil and Water Conservation (SOWACO) Project, 1993. 51p. bibliog.

Provides the results of a study carried out for SOWACO, located in the southern district of Mohales Hoek. This report investigates the role of village-level organizations in the management of community resources. The authors find that knowledge of soil erosion and methods to control it is widespread. However, most interviewees preferred curative efforts to handle erosion and did not see the importance of preventative efforts, such as grazing control. Only a very small proportion of people had attempted to combat erosion on their own fields, and this seemed to be due to a lack of resources. However, the situation may have been worsened by the earlier practice of paying individuals for erosion activities.

424 **Land degradation and class struggle in rural Lesotho.**
Kwesi K. Prah. In: *Ecology and politics: environmental stress and security in Africa.* Edited by A. H. Ornas, M. A. M. Salih. Uppsala, Sweden: Scandinavian Institute of African Studies, 1989, p. 117-30. bibliog.

This paper links land degradation to rural power relations, asserting that the present land tenure system has preserved the power of traditional landlords. Class conflict has ensued between small producers and traditional landlords who use the state apparatus to ensure access to capital resources. The author argues that the dominant classes are not concerned with conservation, resulting in land degradation and a conflict of interest between the landless and landlords. This is a interesting article that will prove thought-provoking for those involved in both agriculture and conservation.

425 **Local level institutional development for sustainable land use.**
R. J. Bakema. Amsterdam: Royal Tropical Institute (RTI), 1994. 63p. bibliog. (Bulletin of the Royal Tropical Institute, no. 331).

This article is concerned with the relationship between environmental management and the development of decision-making bodies at the local level. The first section presents approaches used to involve local people in natural resource management using examples from West Africa. The second section studies range management in Lesotho in its attempt to develop community-based approaches to regulate land use. This paper will be useful for research into range management, conservation and community participation.

426 **Production through conservation: a strategy towards village-based participatory rural development.**
G. Shone, J. E. Carlsson, P. Evans, Y. Khativada, L. Lundgren. *IRD Currents*, no. 7 (1994), p. 4-8.

A description of a Swedish aid project in Lesotho. The project was aimed at soil conservation, and the article is particularly concerned with the approach of production through conservation (PTC). This is a participatory approach, intended to build the capacity of the rural people to plan and implement their development activities. The article charts the development of local capacity in the project, and the relationship between participants and government ministries.

427 **Soil conservation: administrative and extension approaches in Lesotho.**
D. Turner. *Agricultural Administration*, vol. 9, no. 2 (1982), p. 147-62.

Reviews soil conservation work in Lesotho. While the population is found to understand the problem of soil erosion, rural inhabitants appear unwilling to make investments for prevention. The author argues that this is due to the large cost and time requirements of such work, as well as the long-term nature of its benefits. However, local participation is essential for conservation work. Thus, the approach to extension is crucial and conservation needs to be linked to other agricultural initiatives.

428 **Soil erosion in the Kingdom of Lesotho: origin and colonial response, 1830s-1950s.**
Kate B. Showers. *Journal of Southern African Studies*, vol. 15, no. 2 (January 1989), p. 263-86.

In this article, Showers contradicts the widely-held view that Lesotho suffers from exceptional, population-induced soil erosion. She argues that the bareness of the landscape and the high rates of soil erosion are partially natural features, in existence long before dense human habitation. This contrasts with the view that soil degradation is caused by population density and land management practices, an assumption on which a number of soil conservation projects have been based. Showers argues that such conservation projects have failed because of this lack of understanding of soil erosion and the failure to appreciate Basotho soil management practices. Showers has also co-authored a paper on the use of oral evidence in the assessment of long-term environmental change in Lesotho: 'Oral evidence in historical environmental impact assessment: soil conservation in Lesotho in the 1930s and 1940s' (*Journal of Southern African Studies*, vol. 18, no. 2 [June 1992], p. 276-96).

Education

General

429 **Adult literacy in Lesotho. Parts 1 and 2.**
Linda Ziegahn, E. Sakoane. Maseru: Lesotho Distance Teaching Centre, 1985. 148p.

A two-part study into adult and child literacy in Sesotho. Almost two thirds of the adult population were found to have satisfactory reading and writing skills, although certain groups fared worse than others. These include people in the foothills and mountains, certain occupational groups and men in general. Given these results, the authors suggest that universal primary education should be encouraged, with particular help given to those groups that have been identified as least literate. A number of more detailed changes in policy and planning are also recommended. Part two of the report compares the results on adult literacy with those of an earlier survey of literacy among children. In this section, the 'experiencial' aspect of literacy is illustrated by the superior performance of adults given similar education.

430 **Annual Report of the Ministry of Education and Culture.**
Maseru: Ministry of Education and Culture, 1966- . irregular.

Contains educational statistics and a survey of educational development. This publication, whose title has varied, continues the series published pre-independence, under the Basutoland Government Education Department: *Annual Report of the Director of Education.*

431 **Education for frustration.**
J. Makibinyane Mohapeloa. *Education in Botswana, Lesotho and Swaziland*, no. 7 (March 1974), p. 36-46; also in *West African Journal of Education*, vol. 17, no. 1 (Feb. 1973), p. 127-42.

The author discusses the relevance of primary and secondary education for Lesotho's development needs.

432 **The education sector survey: report of the taskforce.**
Lesotho Government. Maseru: Ministry of Education, 1982. 75p.

This is an invaluable review of the state of education in Lesotho. Information is presented on both the formal and informal sectors, including a discussion of costs, access and quality. Section three discusses trends in the demand for education, using enrolment data as illustration. Although the report was prepared in the early 1980s, it remains a useful guide to the characteristics and conflicts of the education system in Lesotho.

433 **Educational policy guidelines.**
Lesotho Government. Maseru: Ministry of Education, 1981. 11p.

An overview of guidelines for educational policies issued by the Ministry of Education. Educational goals are set out in this document.

434 **The educational system, wage and salary structure, and income distribution: Lesotho as a case study, circa 1975.**
James H. Cobbe. *Journal of Developing Areas*, vol. 17, no. 2 (1983), p. 227-42.

Discusses the educational system in Lesotho within the wider socio-economic structure. The link between educational attainment and labour market experience, in terms of employment and wages, is investigated. The costs of education are also measured. Given these factors, Cobbe argues that formal education has been an important factor in the evolution of social classes in Lesotho. Although this study dates from the mid-1970s, it remains an important assessment of the wider social effects of the education system in Lesotho.

435 **Literacy and cultural identity in Lesotho.**
M. Lebusa. Morija, Lesotho: Lesotho Alliance of Women, 1983. 44p.

Traditional, formal and non-formal educational systems are described. The author argues that the independence struggle in Lesotho had an important impact on Basotho cultural identity by developing a strong nationalistic spirit. The author discusses the possibilities for curriculum reform in the educational system.

School system, teaching and teacher training

436 **Action research and reflection-in-action: a case study of teachers' research into development studies teaching in Lesotho.**
J. S. Stuart. *Caribbean Journal of Education*, vol. 15, no. 1/2 (1988), p. 119-44.

An investigation into teaching methods and classroom strategy for the teaching of development studies.

437 **Classroom action-research: case studies in development studies teaching in Lesotho classrooms.**
J. S. Stuart, P. Makhetha, M. Musi. Maseru: Lesotho Ads, 1985. 137p. bibliog.

Presents case-studies of teaching in Lesotho. The authors provide extracts from lessons, teachers' comments and student scripts in order to develop the discussion around classroom teaching. This book will be useful for researchers and education practitioners.

438 **Classroom action research: materials for use by teachers in developing self-reflection and appraisal skills.**
J. P. Lefoka. Roma, Lesotho: National University of Lesotho, Institute of Education, 1992. 20p. bibliog.

Designed as a reference book for teachers and teacher trainers in Lesotho, this work brings together papers on classroom research and teaching materials. This publication will prove useful for in-depth education research on teacher attitudes and techniques in Lesotho. For a more academic discussion on the same initiative, see: *Development of self-reflection skills among primary school teachers in Lesotho: a narrative report*, by C. M. Chabane (Roma, Lesotho: National University of Lesotho, Institute of Education, 1991. 20p.).

439 **Educational selection procedures and policies in Lesotho: an overview.**
E. M. Sebatane. *Boleswa Educational Research Journal*, no. 5 (1987), p. 12-22.

An overview of the selection procedures for entry into secondary schools and higher education institutions in Lesotho.

440 **Practical studies curriculum in Lesotho: some reflections.**
A. L. Monyooe. *South African Journal of Education*, vol. 12, no. 4 (November 1992), p. 414-17.

Monyooe investigates the introduction of agricultural studies as part of the primary curriculum, making certain recommendations about the extent of the introduction, financing and links to other educational facilities.

441 **Primary agricultural curriculum in Lesotho – a demarcation of imperatives.**
L. A. Monyooe. *International Journal of Education Development*, vol. 14, no. 4 (1994), p. 351-60.

Discusses the agricultural curriculum in primary schools and argues that the development of an appropriate curriculum requires radical changes in approach. The author concludes that a comprehensive reform of education is needed in order to respond to the problem of Lesotho's dependency on South Africa.

442 **Primary school enrolment in Lesotho.**
Michael Ward. *Education in Botswana, Lesotho and Swaziland*, no. 9 (January 1975), p. 44-50.

This article discusses the anomalously high enrolment ratios in Lesotho primary schools in the 1970s and the possible reasons for them.

443 **Teacher education and the teaching profession in Lesotho: the state of the art.**
M. Sebatane. Roma, Lesotho: National University of Lesotho, Institute of Education, 1993. 103p.

The report of a conference held in 1993, this publication concentrates on the quality and efficiency of teacher education and the teaching profession. Among the other issues discussed are the role of teacher organizations, the morale of teachers, and conditions of employment. This is a useful publication for those interested in the nature of teacher education, the attitudes of teachers and the characteristics of the teaching profession in Lesotho.

444 **Teacher learning strategies in Lesotho primary school classrooms.**
C. M. Chabane, J. P. Lefoka, E. M. Sebatane. Roma, Lesotho: National University of Lesotho, Institute of Education, 1989. 190p.

The authors present a study intended to elicit information on classroom teaching and learning strategies used in primary schools in Lesotho. The design of the survey and data collection methods are also presented in detail. Information is provided on the actions of teachers and pupils, and the use of teaching materials is discussed. A very similar paper has been published elsewhere: *Teacher learning strategies in Lesotho: an empirical perspective on primary school classrooms* by E. M. Sebatane, C. M. Chabane, J. P. Lefoka (Roma, Lesotho: National University of Lesotho, Institute of Education; Ottawa: International Development Research Centre, 1992. 171p. bibliog.).

University education

445 **Academic activities: some useful indicators.**
A. M. Maruping, T. J. Makatjane. Roma, Lesotho: National University of Lesotho, 1983/84. 35p.

Presents a number of statistics on the size and nature of courses taught at the National University. This is an update of an earlier publication: *The student academic workload: are students overloaded?* by A. M. Maruping (Roma, Lesotho: National University of Lesotho, [n.d.]). This publication contains more recent data and covers a wider range than the earlier work. Data is presented on enrolment, student workload and performance. The size of the teaching staff and University expenditure are also considered. This is a useful publication for those interested in quantifying the activities of the University.

446 **For the light in the night.**
Edited by Patrick Mohlalefi-Bereng. Roma, Lesotho: Division of Extra-Mural Services, National University of Lesotho, 1976. 32p.

An account of the past and present of the National University of Lesotho, including recollections of its forerunners: the University of Botswana, Lesotho and Swaziland; and Pius XIII College.

Vocational, adult and non-formal education

447 **Basic education and agricultural extension: costs, effects and alternatives.**
H. Perraton. Washington, DC: International Bank for Reconstruction and Development, 1983. 285p. 1 map. (World Bank Staff Working Paper, vol. 564).

Lesotho is one of the three case-studies in this volume on agricultural extension, basic education and the mass media. The discussion on Lesotho centres on the use of mass media for education and extension by the Lesotho Distance Teaching Centre.

448 **Continuing Education Programmes for socioeconomic development in Nigeria: an antidote for mass student failure in COSC in Lesotho.**
Dele Braimoh, O. Anthony Adeola, V. Mantina Mohasi. *Journal of Social Development in Africa*, vol. 10, no. 1 (1995), p. 37-52.

There have been very high rates of failure in the Cambridge Overseas School Certificate examinations (the school leaving examinations) in Lesotho. Moreover, there is little opportunity for adults in Lesotho to improve on academic deficiency. This paper analyses the extent to which a Continuing Education Programme (CEP) could assist by integrating adults through the provision of functional and vocational education. This is considered particularly important given the return of largely illiterate adult miners to Lesotho. The *modus operandi* of the CEP in Nigeria is used to present issues and signposts for the implementation of this policy in Lesotho. Recommendations are made as to the modalities of conducting CEPs for institutions that presently organize non-formal education programmes. This is a short but interesting paper, useful for those researching non-formal education in Lesotho.

449 **Information sources as a factor of adults' occupational choice in selected non-formal educational institutions in Maseru.**
Dele Braimoh, M. M. Moshoeshoe-Chadzingwa. *NUL Journal of Research*, vol. 4 (1994), p. 111-32.

Investigates the reasons for choice of occupation by adults at vocational institutions in Maseru. The survey finds that a large proportion of respondents have little or no knowledge of the occupation they have entered into. Thus, the authors conclude that the provision of occupation information is grossly inadequate in Lesotho.

450 **National study of non-formal education in Lesotho: first report to the Lesotho Distance Teaching Centre, February 1982.**
E. V. Adams. Maseru: Lesotho Distance Teaching Centre, 1982. 84p.

Adams describes non-formal education programmes in Lesotho, identifies problem areas, and finds that approximately 240 non-formal education programmes existed in the early 1980s, with further growth predicted. Most programmes are concerned with education for economic growth or with domestic activities. The report suggests that there is a need for greater staff training and for further development of educational materials. The author also recommends that more attention should be given to functional literacy. This report provides a good overview of non-formal education in Lesotho, which should be useful for education planners and researchers.

451 **The role of adult education in development at the Institute of Extra Mural Studies of the National University of Lesotho, Africa.**
D. Russell. *Fort Hare Papers* (Fort Hare, South Africa), vol. 8, no. 1 (1985), p. 38-41.

Discusses the aims of the Institute for Extra Mural Studies and gives an overview of its educational principles.

452 **Structuring agricultural education in Lesotho.**
K. Oenema, W. van den Bor. In: *South-North partnership in strengthening higher education in agriculture.* Edited by W. van den Bor, J. C. M. Shute, G. A. B. Moore. Wageningen, Netherlands: Centre for Agricultural Publishing and Documentation, 1989, p. 178-97. bibliog.

This chapter discusses the establishment of a faculty of agriculture, and considers the nature of such a faculty and the courses which could be offered. Some indication is made of the training needs and financing. The present system of agricultural education is analysed.

Research and Development

453 **A baseline survey of 52 farmers involved in demonstrations on intensive intercropping farming systems in the Makhaleng extension area of Mohale's Hoek district.**
Thuso J. Green. Maseru: Sechaba Consultants & Ministry of Agriculture, Soil and Water Conservation Project, 1994. 31p.

Discusses the impact of demonstrations of intensive intercropping using a survey of farmers. Green finds a clear improvement in welfare from the new system, which generates extra income that is mainly used for paying school fees. The additional income also appears to be used to purchase household items, such as carpets and radios, and the researcher observes an improvement in quality of food.

454 **Five years of practical maize demonstration work in Lesotho lowlands and foothills.**
G. Massey, E. Pomela, T. Malataliana, P. Alotsi. Maseru: Ministry Agriculture, Agricultural Research Division, 1992. 54p. 1 map.

Using five years of data on farmers in lowlands and foothills, this report shows that maize hybrid varieties lead to increased yields at lower incremental costs. However, these findings are very sensitive to rainfall patterns and the time of planting.

455 **Information and development research: the case of ISAS.**
M. M. Chadzingwa, G. K. Khapwale. In: *Southern Africa in the 1980s and beyond: Institute of Southern African Studies 1980-1990.* Edited by the Institute of Southern African Studies. Roma, Lesotho: University of Lesotho, Institute of Southern African Studies, 1993, p. 11-22. bibliog.

This paper attempts to show the link between information and development research using the case of the Institute of Southern African Studies (ISAS), National University of Lesotho. The argument is that there is a symbolic link between the two elements, as information is a crucial resource for research. The information and research activities of ISAS are described in brief, with particular attention paid to publishing and the compilation of 'grey' literature, i.e. literature from government departments, parastatals, international organizations and non-governmental organizations. This overview will prove useful for those wishing to embark on a course of research in Lesotho or those who wish to learn about the activities of ISAS.

456 **Lesotho Highlands Water Project: research opportunities beyond the year 2000.**
M. Maema, S. Turner, T. Putsoane. In: *Southern Africa in the 1980s and beyond: Institute of Southern African Studies 1980-1990.* Edited by the Institute of Southern African Studies. Roma, Lesotho: University of Lesotho, Institute of Southern African Studies, 1993, p. 257-60.

A short paper on the research possibilities inherent in work on the Lesotho Highlands Water Project (LHWP). The LHWP is a multi-purpose water control and development project which will be constructed in phases during the period 1990-2020. Phase I is presently under way and involves the construction of a number of dams and tunnels that will collect water in Lesotho and then pump it under gravity to South Africa. It is argued that there are many opportunities for research to support later phases of the project and a number of potential research areas are outlined.

457 **Report on the evaluation of attitudes of farmers to demonstrations of the 1990/91 season.**
Thuso Green. Maseru: Sechaba Consultants & Ministry of Agriculture, Semonkong Rural Development Project, 1992. 36p.

Finds that farmers have positive attitudes towards demonstrations. Indeed, the farmers interviewed seem to have exaggerated the positive effects of demonstration practices, and the author suggests that the fact that farmers were offered free inputs may have affected participation. In addition, despite having been involved with demonstrations, farmers do not want to 'go it on their own'. Green argues that a solution is to give farmers greater involvement with project staff.

458 **A study on adoption of improved crop technologies promoted by the Local Initiatives Support Project.**
Judy S. Gay, Thuso Green. Maseru: Sechaba Consultants & Department of Agriculture, Local Initiatives Support Project, 1991. 38p.

Based on a survey of five villages, this report assesses the success of new technologies promoted by a low-input agricultural project. This low-input package required the use of new, appropriate technology and new working practices. The authors find that the acceptance of this package was affected by household status, with households headed by females being particularly constrained by resources. An interesting addition to the discussion is an analysis of the gender division of agricultural tasks. This shows that gender roles remain relatively fixed, although there is evidence of a small increase in male involvement in some previously 'female' work activities.

459 **Vegetables for all seasons: a grow-hole user's guide.**
Lesotho Government. Maseru: Ministry of Interior, Chieftainship Affairs and Rural Development, Appropriate Technology Section, [n.d.]. 52p.

A grow-hole is a cold-frame, or box, with a lid that can be opened or closed. It protects vegetables from cold and frost and so lengthens the growing season. This publication is aimed at explaining the use of grow-holes and promoting their development.

Literature

Literary criticism

460 **The form, content and technique of traditional literature in Southern Sotho.**
Samson Mbizo Guma. Pretoria: J. L. van Schaik, 1967. 216p.

Originally a University of South Africa doctoral thesis. The chapters are devoted to: analyses of myths and legends; riddles; proverbs and idioms; songs (including initiation songs); and praise poems. An appendix reproduces six Sesotho legends together with English translations.

461 **Four African literatures: Xhosa, Sotho, Zulu, Amnaric.**
Albert S. Gérard. Berkeley, California: University of California Press, 1971. 458p. maps. bibliog.

Despite minor errors caused by the author's unfamiliarity with country and language, this is the most detailed critical survey of Sesotho literature yet published. The principal works and their earlier critics are discussed at length and biographical sketches of the authors are provided.

462 **The heroic ideal in three Sotho novellas of labour migration.**
Robert Shanafelt. *African Studies* (South Africa), vol. 47, no. 1 (1988), p. 47-62.

Discusses the work of three writers of Sesotho prose. The author concentrates on three books: *Arola: Naheng ea Maburu* by Albert Nqheku (1942); *O sentse linako* by Simon Majara (1956); and *Moiketse* by Mallane Libakeng. All of this work was written before Lesotho's independence in 1966, but Shanafelt has not chosen the first generation of Sotho writers. The author argues that each novella is comprised of a unique blend of traditional narrative forms, Christian morality and Sotho ideals. However, they share a common conceptualization of heroism and the importance of heroic ideas in the face of the harsh realities of contemporary life.

463 **Literature of Lesotho.**
Albert S. Gérard. *Africa Report* (USA), vol. 11, no. 7 (1966), p. 68-70.

A critical survey of the literature of Lesotho. The author states that Lesotho was 'the first country on the continent to develop a modern literature', and that no other ethnic grouping in Sub-Saharan Africa has produced a larger number of vernacular authors and works. The article also refers to critical reviews of the authors' works.

464 **Thomas Mofolo and the emergence of written Sesotho prose.**
Daniel P. Kunene. Johannesburg: Ravan Press, 1989. 251p. bibliog.

Analyses the writing of Thomas Mofolo, discussing motivation and prose style. Mofolo is Lesotho's most famous writer, particularly well-known for his 1925 novel, *Chaka*, an historical novel which probes the life of the Zulu king. Mofolo's first novel, *Moeti oa Bochabela* (The pilgrim of the east, 1907), uses fictional characters to discuss the movement towards personal enlightenment. His second novel, *Pitseng* (At the pot, 1910), deals with the search for love of two fictional characters. Mofolo, who died in 1948, is regarded as an important influence on Sesotho prose. In this publication, Kunene discusses the context of his work and the reactions of contemporaries. His analysis also considers the conflict between the Christian influence in Mofolo's work, which arose from his upbringing by Christianized parents and in missionary schools, and his desire to depict Basotho customs and concerns. This will be a useful discussion for researchers into Mofolo's work, and, more generally, into Sesotho prose.

Poetry

465 **The germination of Southern Sotho poetry.**
Alosi Johannes Mafaleng Moloi. *Limi* (South Africa), no. 8 (1969), p. 28-58. bibliog.

A thorough and sensitive evaluation of the techniques of Sesotho poetry.

466 **Heroic poetry of the Basotho.**
Daniel P. Kunene. Oxford: Clarendon Press, 1971. 203p.

This book provides both an analysis and a description of Sesotho praise poetry. Particular attention is given to 'eulogies', in which the hero is praised through a host of associative references. There is also a description of the praise poets' cultural background and its influence on the use of symbol and metaphor. Throughout the book praise poetry is quoted from Z. D. Mangoaela's *Lithoko tsa Marena a Basotho*, each passage being accompanied by a translation. There are also discussions of praise poetry occurring: in Thomas Mofolo's *Chaka* and *Moeti oa Bochabela;* in J. J. Machobane's *Mphatlalatsane;* and in E. L. Segoete's *Raphepeng*. The poems of J. M. Mohapeloa and B. M. Khaketla, each describing a train, are discussed, and the views of both authors on Sesotho poetry are mentioned (and disagreed with). The work of the poetess Makhokolotso A. Mokhomo in her *Sebabatso* is examined in some detail and described as one of the most outstanding contributions to Sesotho poetry. The final chapter analyses in some detail a praise poem of Lerotholi Mojela.

467 **Lithoko: Sotho praise-poems.**
Mosebi Damane, Peter B. Sanders. Oxford: Clarendon Press, 1974. 289p. map. bibliog.

Includes an introduction covering the historical, social and cultural background to praise poems. Chapters also discuss the place of praise poems in Basotho life, and provide a structural analysis of the poems themselves. The praise poems of principal chiefs follow, each preceded by a historical note on the subject of the poem. The English translations are accompanied by extensive annotations. Sesotho texts are provided only for one poem on King Moshoeshoe I and one on King Moshoeshoe II.

468 **Poets of Lesotho: first steps of a brief incursion into Sesotho literature.**
Mofolo Bulane. *New African* (UK), vol. 6, no. 2 (Oct. 1967), p. 19-23.

This article concentrates on praise poems and on the works of D. C. T. Bereng, K. Ntsane, B. M. Khaketla and Azael Makara. It contains English translations of several poems.

469 **Sefela sa Liate Kometsi: human rights and civil justice.**
C. F. Swanepoel. *South African Journal of African Languages*, vol. 14, no. 4 (November 1994), p. 177-80.

The author analyses the oral poetry of Liate Kometsi, a migrant worker from Lesotho. This poetry reflects the difficulty of migrant workers.

470 **The structure and philosophy of Sotho indigenous poetry.**
Mosebi Damane. *Lesotho: Basutoland Notes and Records*, vol. 4 (1963-64), p. 41-49.

A study of praise poetry, comparing it to the epic poetry of Greece. The structure of the *lithoko* is discussed at some length.

471 **Then and now: the praise poem in Southern Sotho.**
Mofolo Bulane. *New African* (UK), vol. 7, no. 1 (1968), p. 40-43.

Discusses the praise poem as a form of protest literature, accompanied by translations of some poems.

The Arts

Rock art

472 **Art on the rocks of Southern Africa.**
D. N. Lee, H. C. Woodhouse. Cape Town: Purnell, 1970. 166p.

Includes commentary on seventeen photographs and drawings from Lesotho rock painting sites in Butha-Buthe, Maseru, Quthing and Qacha's Nek Districts.

473 **The bushman art of Southern Africa.**
H. C. Woodhouse. London: Macdonald General Books, 1980. 125p.

This extensive study of bushman art includes several paintings from the Setsoasi and Tsoelike valleys in Lesotho. The analysis of the paintings is non-academic in nature, although it does discuss themes of the paintings in terms of folklore, lifestyle and the environment of the bushman.

474 **Rock-painting sites in the upper Senqu Valley, Lesotho.**
Lucas G. A. Smits. *South African Archaeological Bulletin*, vol. 28 (1973), p. 32-38. bibliog.

Describes and reproduces illustrations of rock paintings at Sehonghong, Qutu, 'Melikane, and Khooanyane. Some of these are mentioned in the 1874 article by Orpen ('A glimpse into the mythology of the Maluti Bushmen' [*Cape Monthly Magazine*, vol. 9 (July 1874), p. 1-13. illus.]), and Orpen's Mangolong site is discovered to have been at Sehonghong. The Libesoaneng site is interpreted convincingly as depicting a San 'eland dance'.

475 **The rock paintings of Lesotho, their contents and characteristics.**
Lucas G. A. Smits. *South African Archaeological Bulletin*, special issue, no. 2 (May 1971), p. 14-19.

This paper summarizes the kinds of paintings that occur in Lesotho. The main characteristics are analysed together with techniques employed, and the author comments upon the light the paintings throw upon the artists and their way of life. The author has recorded more than 10,000 paintings in 100 sites in Lesotho.

Visual art and design

476 **House decoration in Southern Africa.**
G. F. Rohrmann. *African Arts* (USA), vol. 7, no. 3 (Spring 1974), p. 18-21.

Describes and illustrates house decoration including *litema* and mosaic patterns from Lesotho.

477 **Mural art of the Bantu.**
James Walton. *South African Panorama*, vol. 10, no. 4 (April 1965), p. 30-37.

A well-illustrated description of the various patterns used on walls of houses and enclosures, which includes examples from Lesotho, Transvaal and the Orange Free State. For a similar, but slightly shorter article, see 'Mural art of the Bantu' (*Bantu* [South Africa], vol. 12, no. 11 [Nov. 1965], p. 396-400).

478 **Visual art in the Southern African Development Community: the argument for a regional school of art and design.**
Southern African Development Community. Harare: National Gallery of Zimbabwe, 1994. 121p.

A proposition for a regional art school, which includes a short summary (p. 25-28) of the history of formal visual art in Lesotho. Although limited to formal arts and crafts, it is an up-to-date analysis of art in Lesotho. The paper decries the dearth of art teaching and the dominance of expatriates in the arts and crafts scene in Lesotho. However, the analysis lacks a discussion of the market for art, which would been an interesting addition to the work. Also, the potentially important effect of art and crafts on employment has not been discussed.

Architecture

479 **African village.**
James Walton. Pretoria: Van Schaik, 1956. 203p.

A comparative study of African villages, hut types, artefacts, etc., with considerable reference to the Basotho. The book contains many drawings and 113 photographs of which 33 were taken in Lesotho. See also: 'Corbelled stone huts in Southern Africa' (*Man* [England], vol. 51 [1951], p. 45-58).

480 **The Basotho hut: from late Iron Age to the present.**
J. Dreyer. *South African Journal of Ethnology*, vol. 16, no. 3 (September 1993), p. 79-86.

A study of the domed grass hut. This type of hut has been used by the Basotho to varying extent from the pre-*lifaqane* period. Using a variety of sources, Dreyer discusses the distribution and use of these huts.

481 **Historic buildings of Basutoland. Presidential address to the Basutoland Scientific Association.**
James Walton. Morija, Lesotho: Basutoland Scientific Association, 1957. 15p. bibliog.

Contains descriptions of historic missions, military and government buildings, particularly those at Hlotse, Maseru and Morija.

482 **Homesteads and villages of South Africa.**
James Walton. Pretoria: Van Schaik, 1965. 144p.

This work is primarily of interest for its accounts and photographs of Griqua houses in Mohale's Hoek and Quthing and of early mission houses.

483 **The silent language of stone.**
Dana Costa, photographs by Pierre Des Ormeaux, Dana Costa. Maseru: Epic Printers, 1990. 79p. 1 map.

In the face of a tremendous growth in new office development, this book aims to increase the appreciation of older sandstone buildings in an attempt to prevent their destruction. The history and significance of certain buildings is explained through the use of photographs. The author argues that the preservation of old buildings could stimulate local industry, through an increase in the demand for locally available sandstone rather than the imported materials used for modern buildings. His late Majesty King Moshoeshoe II has written a foreword, supporting the book's objectives.

484 **Sotho cattle kraals.**
James Walton. *South African Archaeological Bulletin*, no. 52, vol. 13 (Dec. 1958), p. 133-43.

Basotho cattle kraals are built of stone and the methods used are similar to those employed by earlier related peoples such as the Lihoja. The cattle kraal was not merely a cattle fold but a vital element in the life of the people, the burial place of the chiefs, the meeting place of the men, and the *Lekhotla* or court. The article includes several good photographs which show the various methods of building cattle kraals.

485 **South African peasant architecture: Southern Sotho folk building.**
James Walton. *Southern African Architectural Record*, vol. 34 (1949), p. 3-12; vol. 35 (1950), p. 30-39. Also in *African Studies* (South Africa), vol. 7, no. 4 (1948), p. 137-45.

Provides excellent illustrations of wall-designs and various types of houses, and shows how more complex types of houses evolved from the simplest.

Crafts

486 **Art and craft of Southern Africa: treasures in transition.**
Rhoda Levinsohn, edited by Barbara La Vine, photographs by Dr Morris Levinsohn. Craighall, South Africa: Delta Books, 1984. 144p. 5 maps. bibliog.

Discusses arts and crafts from Lesotho, Botswana and South Africa. Considerable emphasis is given to Basotho crafts and the book is illustrated with a large number of photographs. Levinsohn concentrates on basketry, pottery, dress and ornaments.

487 **Bantu pottery of Southern Africa.**
A. C. Lawton. *Annals of the South African Museum*, vol. 49. no. 1 (1967), p. 1-440.

An extremely detailed description of pottery in southern Africa, aimed at the specialist researcher. After a general discussion of techniques and decoration, the author differentiates pottery-making by ethnic group and geographic area. Twenty-nine pages are devoted to the southern Sotho, of which sixteen cover Lesotho. Details are given for individual Basotho clans. At the time of the study, pottery-making was widespread, especially amongst women; however, this is likely to have changed with the introduction of 'western' storage methods. A number of black-and-white photographs and illustrations are provided, as well as one photograph in colour.

488 **Bantu shields.**
Geoffrey Tylden. *South Africa Archaeological Bulletin*, no. 2, vol. 1 (March 1946), p. 33-37.

This brief article includes drawings of the various shapes of Basotho and Batlokoa shields. There is also a useful set of references.

489 **The dagga pipes of Southern Africa.**
James Walton. *Researches of the Nasionale Museum, Bloemfontein*, vol. 1, no. 4 (Dec. 1953), p. 85-113.

Describes and illustrates *dagga* (marijuana) pipes, including some from Lesotho.

490 **Lesotho tapestry weaving.**
Rhoda Levinsohn. *African Arts* (USA), vol. 9, no. 4 (July 1976), p. 52-55.

Levinsohn describes mohair weaving technicalities, and the work of the Royal Lesotho Tapestry Weavers, the Thabong Weavers, and the Blue Mountain Tapestries. While many of these particular tapestry companies have since folded, there remains an important tapestry industry in Lesotho.

491 **Pestles, mullers and querns from the Orange Free State and Basutoland.**

James Walton. *South African Archaeological Bulletin*, no. 30, vol. 8 (1953), p. 32-39.

Illustrates and describes early and contemporary querns. Two-handed quern-stones are thought to have occurred after the arrival of maize. The dates of the penetration of maize cultivation into southern Africa are considered. Correspondence arising from this article appears in several issues of the same journal: no. 32, vol. 8, p. 110-11; no. 33, vol. 9, p. 35; and no. 35, vol. 9, p. 102.

492 **Pottery guide: Lesotho.**

R. Olsson. Geneva, Switzerland: International Labour Office, Thabana li Mele Project Report, 1977. 60p.

A technical guide for craftsmen involved in the Thabana Li Mele handicraft project in Lesotho. This project attempts to maintain local pottery styles, while using Western pottery techniques.

493 **Weaving guide, Lesotho.**

B. K. White. Geneva, Switzerland: International Labour Office, Thabana li Mele Project Report, 1980. 124p. bibliog.

A guide for weavers and those involved in handicraft projects. This document intends to promote weaving activities in Lesotho in order to provide employment as well as stimulate local craft making. A glossary of technical terms in Sesotho is included.

Music

494 **Eloquent knowledge: Lesotho migrants songs and the anthropology of experience.**

David B. Coplan. *American Ethnologist,* vol. 14, no. 3 (1987), p. 413-33.

An analysis of the songs of labour migrants from Lesotho, in which Coplan analyses the poetic and social content of this music. By the same author, see also: 'The power of oral poetry: narrative songs of the Basotho migrants' (*Research in African Literatures* [Spring 1987], p. 1-35); and 'Musical understanding: the ethnoaesthetics of migrant workers' poetic song in Lesotho' (*Ethnomusicology*, vol. 32, no. 3 [1988], p. 337-68).

495 **The ethnomusicology of the Basotho.**

Sindile Moitse. Roma, Lesotho: National University of Lesotho, Institute of Southern African Studies, 1994. 128p. bibliog.

A comprehensive study of Basotho music. This publication analyses music in the context of Basotho culture and ritual, and contains several photographs of instruments. Among the topics discussed is the role of music in divination, initiation and birth.

496 **An introduction to the music of the Basotho.**
Robin E. Wells. Morija, Lesotho: Morija Museum and Archives, 1994. 338p. 1 map. bibliog.

A study of the musical styles of Lesotho, both past and present. Consequently a semi-historical approach has been adopted, and this also underlies the dominant theme of the book, namely, that musical transformation reflects changes in social experience. Although the author was unable to record certain types of music, in particular music that is socially prohibited to men, this book provides a comprehensive analysis of Basotho music.

497 **Report on research in Lesotho.**
Robin E. Wells. *African Music*, vol. 7, no. 2 (1992), p. 126-27.

A brief report on an investigation of indigenous music in Lesotho, with particular emphasis on the nature of musical change. This research is presented in detail in item no. 496.

Theatre

498 **Let my people play!: participatory theatre plays.**
Masitha Hoeane. Roma, Lesotho: National University of Lesotho, Institute of Southern African Studies, 1994. 158p.

Presents two plays by the author, with a critique by P. Shava. The context of the plays and the importance of participatory theatre are explained.

499 **Marotholi: theatre for another development.**
Elvira Ganter, Don Edkins. Maseru: Christian Council of Lesotho, The Village Technology Information Service, 1989. 2nd ed. 93p.

This publication portrays the work of the Marotholi Travelling Theatre, using photographs and short commentaries. The players aim to motivate rural communities into self-help initiatives, using theatre to facilitate discussion around development. The text is presented in both English and German, and there is a short foreword by the late King Moshoeshoe II on Marotholi's work. Although the English translations are sometimes poor, this book has attractively captured the environment in which the theatre group works.

500 **When people play people: development communication through theatre.**
Zakes Mda. Johannesburg: Witwatersrand University Press; Atlantic Highlands, New Jersey; London: Zed Books, 1993. 250p. 1 map. bibliog.

The author is a well-known South African poet and playwright and has been involved in theatre-for-development projects in Lesotho. The book examines the experiences of extension workers in the use of theatre-for-development and explores the author's own attempts to develop a new model of theatrical communication. Through his book, Mda aims to correct the imbalance between the developed and less developed countries in terms of their contributions to the field of communications.

Culture, Customs and Folklore

Folklore

501 **Basuto folk-lore.**
R. Sharpe. *Basutoland Witness*, vol. 6, no. 1 (January-March 1952), p. 18-22.

A brief description of the folklore of Lesotho. Sharpe discusses local fables and legends, showing the rich history of folklore in Lesotho.

502 **Basutoland: its legends and customs.**
Minnie Martin. London: Nichols, 1903. 174p. Reprinted, New York: Negro Universities Press, 1969.

Contains many legends and a history of Lesotho up to the time of writing, as well as sections on clothing and birth, marriage and death customs. For a similar collection of legends by the same author, see also: *The Sun Chief: legends of Basutoland* (Durban, South Africa: Knox, 1943. 89p.).

503 **Myths and legends of Botswana, Lesotho and Swaziland.**
Jan Knappert. Leiden, Netherlands: E. J. Brill, 1985. 254p. 1 map.

A compilation of southern African folk-tales and myths. This book contains a number of tales from Lesotho and the author also presents a history and short grammar of Sesotho.

504 **Tales from the Basotho.**
Minnie Postma, translated by Susie McDermid. Austin, Texas: American Folklore Society, 1974. 178p.

Brings together twenty-three folk-tales, accompanied by an index of motifs, tale types and comparable African folk-tales.

505 **The treasury of Ba-Suto lore being original Se-Suto texts, with a literal English translation and notes, Vol. I.**

Edited and translated by Edouard Jacottet. Morija, Lesotho: Sesuto Book Depot; London: Kegan Paul, Trench, Trubner & Co., 1908. 288p.

This work contains forty-two folk-tales in English and Sesotho, with explanatory footnotes, some of the footnotes comparing the tales with other folklore traditions. Some tales are from Azariele Sekese, who was a well known writer; others are taken from Basotho storytellers, the names of some of whom appear in the introduction. The book is one of the few Sesotho 'Loebs', with English and Sesotho on opposite pages. It was originally intended, as the preface explains, as part of an ambitious series of 'from eight to ten volumes'. As a result of financial difficulties, this seems to have been the only volume published in the planned format.

Culture, customs and dress

506 **The Bantu-speaking peoples of Southern Africa.**

Edited by W. D. Hammond-Tooke. London: Routledge & Kegan Paul, 1974. 526p.

A complete revision of Issac Schapera's *The Bantu speaking tribes of Southern Africa: an ethnographical survey* (Cape Town: Maskew Miller, 1937. 453p. map). This volume includes comparative material on the Basotho, and two chapters by the editor cover traditional religion. The most important of the remaining chapters are listed separately by author elsewhere in this bibliography.

507 **The Basuto: a social study of traditional and modern Lesotho.**

Edmond Hugh Ashton. London: Oxford University Press for International African Institute, 1967. 2nd ed. 355p. bibliog.

A detailed study dealing with most aspects of village life in Lesotho: customs; beliefs; agriculture; modern and traditional law; land tenure; trade; political organization; and medicine. The second edition (1967) differs from the first (1952) mainly in a new twenty-one page introduction and a supplementary bibliography. The original fieldwork was carried out in the 1930s, mainly among the Batlokoa of Mokhotlong District.

508 **The bovine mystique – power, property and livestock in rural Lesotho.**

James Ferguson. *Man*, vol. 20, no. 4 (1985), p. 647-74.

Ferguson attempts to unravel the factors that encourage the holding of livestock in Lesotho. In doing so, he offers a critique of the two dominant explanations for African livestock holding: one based on economic rationality; and the other on cultural motivation. He argues that cattle holding can be explained by some combination of these arguments. The article addresses issues relevant not only to livestock but also to the nature of rural power. However, Ferguson has been criticized for failing to take account of class-based social differentiation in rural Lesotho.

509 **High bridewealth, migrant labour and the position of women in Lesotho.**

Colin Murray. *Journal of African Law*, vol. 21, no. 1 (1977), p. 79-96.

Murray draws links between migrant labour and changes in the payment of bridewealth. He argues that the position of women is related to changes in these factors.

510 **Lesotho's heritage in jeopardy: report of the chairman of the Protection & Preservation Commission for the years 1980-1 and 1981-2 together with a survey of its past work and present challenges.**

Maseru: Protection and Preservation Commission, 1983. 47p. bibliog.

Aware of its inadequacy in meeting the challenges posed by the threats to Lesotho's heritage, the Commission has published this report on its needs and the needs of Lesotho. This book is a discussion of the condition of Lesotho's heritage, with chapters on fauna, flora, palaeontology, archaeology, rock paintings and historic buildings.

511 **Material culture.**

Margaret Shaw. In: *The Bantu-speaking peoples of Southern Africa.* Edited by W. D. Hammond-Tooke. London: Routledge & Kegan Paul, 1974, p. 85-134.

A discussion of the customs, crafts and life-style of the southern Sotho. Shaw covers in detail settlement types, housing, furnishing, attitudes, crops, animal husbandry, food and drink, clothing, ornamentation and cosmetics. Shorter descriptions are presented on: transport; hunting; ritual; recreation; war and weapons; the calendar of work; and trade. However, inadequate analysis is given to some issues, particularly in the case of the shorter sections, where description replaces analysis proper. In addition, Shaw has not explicitly placed her comments within an historical context, which is a drawback as Sotho culture has never remained static. An interesting comparison may be made with Eldredge's work (item no. 71), which stresses the degree of dynamism and change with the Sotho, even before colonial contact.

512 **The mountain Bushmen of Basutoland.**

Marion W. How. Pretoria: Van Schaik, 1962. 63p.

A lively and well-informed account which takes the story up to the last remaining San in Lesotho. It contains information on their customs, history and rock-painting techniques.

513 **The old clothing of the Basotho.**

Justinus Sechefo. Mazenod, Lesotho: The Catholic Centre, [c. 1958]. 30p. mimeo.

The title inside the cover is *Material clothing of the Basuto.* The author lived from 1867-1941, and the book was apparently produced posthumously without any editing. It is useful for its detailed descriptions of the kinds of traditional clothing worn by men and women, and for descriptions of the tools and work involved in preparing skins. Appendices include information on the different kinds of traditional cooking vessels and foodstuffs. The historical notes are written in a dramatic, if verbose, style, for example: 'Owing to superfluous troubles more or less caused by Chaka's supremacy of despotism those days were feudal and restless' (p. 6).

514 **Polygyny as myth: towards understanding extramarital relations in Lesotho.**
Andrew D. Spiegel. In: *Tradition and transition in Southern Africa.* Edited by Andrew D. Spiegel, P. A. McAllister. Johannesburg: Witwatersrand University Press, 1991, p. 145-66. bibliog.

Discusses infidelity in Lesotho and its rationalization in 'folk' explanations. Spiegel links these explanations to people's uses of notions about the past, as he argues that people frequently draw on images of the past to understand their experience of the present. In this way, the results of the migrant labour system are given local meaning. This is an interesting analysis of the relationship of modern 'custom' to traditional practices, and constitutes an essential paper for readers wishing to understand the changing nature of custom in Lesotho.

515 **Report on the effects of Sesotho culture, traditions and attitudes on agricultural development in Lesotho.**
Sheila K. Woods. Eschborn, Germany: German Agency for Technical Cooperation, 1988. 122p. bibliog.

This detailed report presents information on the cultural perceptions that affect agriculture. Topics include attitudes towards land tenure, livestock and field crops. In addition, a chapter is offered on group cooperation and participation, in which it is argued that the Basotho are by nature individualistic within the context of the extended family and Sesotho culture. Thus, many projects which have been dependent on cooperation and participation for success have encountered difficulties. Woods also discusses the problems of cross-cultural communication in development projects.

516 **Sex, smoking and the shades: a Sotho symbolic idiom.**
Colin Murray. In: *Religion and social change in Southern Africa: anthropological essays in honour of Monica Wilson.* Edited by Michael G. Whisson, Martin West. Cape Town: David Philip, 1975, p. 58-77.

Discusses three meanings of the work *koae*, as exemplified in the title. In this context, 'shades' refers to the supernatural world. Murray suggests that the possible ambiguities in Sesotho speech result in a metaphorical equivalence between smoking and the sexual act. The chapter also includes references to traditional doctors and techniques of divination.

517 **Some aspects of circumcision in Basutoland.**
Samuel Mbizo Guma. *African Studies* (South Africa), vol. 24, no. 3-4 (1965), p. 241-49.

This article describes the entire initiation procedure as practised in Lesotho. The information was obtained by the author from old men of the nation.

518 **Some economic and technological factors behind the adoption of the blanket as Basotho dress.**

Motlasi Thabane. *Review of Southern African Studies*, vol. 1, no. 1 (January 1995), p. 29-48.

A well-researched paper providing insights into an important symbol in contemporary culture. Imported woollen blankets are a common item of clothing in Lesotho, and the blanket has achieved the status of 'customary' dress. There are a number of different explanations for this phenomenon. 'Cultural' explanations consider the extent to which the blanket is traditional, national wear. 'Anthropological' analyses consider the symbolic role of the blanket, linked to attitudes to sex and fertility. Thabane argues that both analyses have limitations; the 'cultural' analysis fails to acknowledge that the blanket has not always been worn, while 'symbolism' theories are criticized as being irresponsible, pseduo-scientific scholarship. The paper instead presents an historical perspective, charting the rise in popularity of the blanket. Thabane highlights two factors in this trend: English industrialization; and technical and design innovations.

519 **Sotho fertility symbolism.**

Colin Murray. *African Studies*, vol. 39, no. 1 (1980), p. 65-76.

Argues that the Basotho reveal in their symbols and ritual practices a predominant concern with the vagaries of the weather and the vicissitudes of the seasonal cycle. Murray claims that customary prohibitions concerned with the regulation of sex relations and the human life cycle may be interpreted as ritual devices to control those factors which are in fact outside human control. Murray supports this assertion with many examples from his fieldwork in Lesotho. This is a useful paper for those interested in ritual belief and practices.

520 **The Southern Sotho (Ethnographic survey of Africa, Southern Africa, Part II).**

Vernon George John Sheddick. London: International African Institute, 1953. 88p. 1 map. bibliog.

A useful summary of the economy, social organization, chieftainship, land tenure, religious beliefs and traditional medicine of the Basotho. A concluding section deals with minority groups including the Makhoakhoa, Bakholokoe, Batlokoa, Baphuthi, Amahlophe, Amahlubi and Amavundle. The folded map in the endpapers shows the distribution of these people in and around Lesotho at the time of writing.

Some medicinal, magic and edible plants of Lesotho.
See item no. 48.

Medicine, magic and sorcery among the Southern Sotho.
See item no. 191.

Ritual and medicines: indigenous healing in South Africa.
See item no. 192.

Sotho medicine.
See item no. 193.

Suto (Basuto) medicines.
See item no. 194.

Sport and Recreation

521 **Attractions of Lesotho's first National Park.**
African Wildlife (South Africa), vol. 24, no. 3 (Sept. 1970), p. 254.

Describes Sehlabathebe National Park, located in Qacha's Nek District.

522 **A backpackers guide to Lesotho.**
Russell Suchet. Underberg, South Africa: Published by the author, 1994. 44p. 1 map.

A detailed description of scenic routes for hikers and backpackers. Suchet provides information on public transport, lodges, and places to buy supplies. There is also a section on pony trekking. For those who plan to drive, Suchet offers a brief assessment of road quality and petrol stops. This is an excellent handbook for hikers and all travellers who wish to see the rural areas of Lesotho; it is available from Russell Suchet, Sani Lodge, PO Box 485, Underberg 4590, South Africa.

523 **Climbs in the Malutis: mountains in Basutoland.**
R. P. E. Morgan. *Journal of the Mountain Club of South Africa*, no. 55 (1952), p. 86-87.

A short account, intended for the mountain climber, of the mountains of Lesotho and its immediate surroundings but excluding the Drakensberg escarpment.

524 **A guide to Morija.**
Stephen J. Gill. Morija, Lesotho: Morija Museum and Archives, 1995. 36p. bibliog.

A guide to the Morija area in Lesotho's southern lowlands. Morija includes many places of historic interest and the guide provides a detailed discussion of the importance of particular sites. Photographs are also included to support these descriptions. The guide includes a number of other local trails and offers information on local flora and fauna. This is a comprehensive publication, which also provides detailed and well-researched historical information.

525 **List of climbs in the Natal Drakensberg.**
P. Liebenberg. *Journal of the Mountain Club of South Africa*, no. 55 (1952), p. 73-77.

The climbs described in this article are graded according to standard and the year of the first known ascent, for which the names of the original party are given. A number of the peaks included are either partly or wholly within the boundaries of Lesotho.

526 **Southern Basutoland.**
Desmond Watkins. *Journal of the Mountain Club of South Africa*, no. 56 (1953), p. 64-67.

The first part of the article describes briefly an expedition with archaeological, canoeing and climbing interests along the Senqu Valley between Qacha's Nek and Sekake's. Climbs of the Middle Sister (first recorded climb) and Makomereng mountains are recorded. The rest of the article is concerned with the Natal Drakensberg.

Museums and Archives

527 **Morija museum and archives.**
Morija Museum. Morija, Lesotho: Published by the author, [n.d.]. 10p. 1 map.

Morija Museum is Lesotho's only museum and this guide provides a bi-lingual commentary to the exhibits. The museum also houses an archive, which was begun by one of the first missionaries, and which includes materials on the early period of missionary contact. As missionaries assisted in the formation of the nation, this collection is of value to those interested in Lesotho's history. The archives also contain photographs, maps and all early printed material from Lesotho, including government reports. This guide is available from: The Curator, Morija Museum and Archives, PO Box 12, Morija 190, Lesotho.

Mass Media and Books

Newspapers

528 **Leselinyana la Lesotho.** (The Little Light of Lesotho.)
Morija, Lesotho: Lesotho Evangelical Church, November 1863- . irregular.

A Sesotho newspaper founded by Adolphe Mabille, and from 1874 the mission newspaper of the P. E. M. S. (Société des Missions Evangéliques de Paris). As the longest continuously running newspaper in Lesotho, *Leselinyana* is both a chronicle of the times and a valuable historical source, the more so since it frequently includes articles on earlier history. In recent years *Leselinyana* has combined church news with coverage of Lesotho's social, economic and particularly its political problems. In the past, *Leselinyana* has often taken a critical view of government policies.

529 **Lesotho Today.**
Maseru: Department of Information and Broadcasting, 2 April 1977- . weekly.

An English-language newspaper produced by the Government. Information is presented on local news, with an irregular supplement, *Shoeshoe*, on women's issues.

530 **Moeletsi oa Basotho.** (The Basotho Advisor.)
Mazenod, Lesotho: Catholic Church, January 1933- . weekly.

A Sesotho newspaper, usually at least eight pages, which acts as the Catholic counterpart to *Leselinyana* (q.v.). Regular coverage includes court cases, education, commerce and items of general interest.

Printing and publishing

531 **111 years: Morija printing works; printed on the occasion of the Unesco International Book Year, 1972 for the book exhibition in Maseru, 24-29 November 1972.**

J. Zurcher. Morija, Lesotho: Sesuto Book Depot, 1972. 12p.

Provides the history of printing in Lesotho from 1835 until 1972. The press of the Paris Mission had a chequered history and was on several occasions moved from one mission station to another in times of war before finally settling at Morija.

532 **The Morija Sesuto Book Depot.**

L. Christeller. *Basutoland Witness*, vol. 5, no. 3 (July-Sept. 1951), p. 38-39.

The history of the best-known printing works in Lesotho.

533 **The press at Morija, Basutoland.**

Hans Schmoller. *South African Libraries*, vol. 25, no. 1 (1957), p. 5-11.

An account of the history of the Press, including the early work done at Beersheba and Bethesda. The article is of particular interest as the author worked on the staff of the Morija Press and he gives information about the technical side, the machines used and the attempt to produce excellent quality printing.

Periodicals

534 **African Affairs.**

London: Royal African Society, 1901- . quarterly.

Contains many references to Lesotho, especially during the colonial period when the annual reports were often summarized in the journal.

535 **African Studies.**

Johannesburg: University of the Witwatersrand, 1942- . quarterly.

This publication supersedes *Bantu Studies*, and regularly contains material on Lesotho. In particular, there is good coverage of the history and customs of the Basotho, and the journal provides a good forum for discussions on the social anthropology and social history of the region.

536 **Journal of Modern African Studies: a Quarterly Survey of Politics, Economics and Related Topics in Contemporary Africa.**

New York: Cambridge University Press, 1943- . quarterly.

Includes coverage of Lesotho with some frequency. A range of social science topics are discussed, including politics, economic dependency and development.

537 **Journal of Southern African Studies.**

Oxford; Cambridge, Massachusetts; Cammeray, Australia: Carfarx, 1974- . quarterly.

The journal frequently contains articles on the economy, society and political situation of Lesotho.

538 **Lesotho Law Journal.**

Roma, Lesotho: National University of Lesotho, 1985- . irregular.

Contains articles on law and legal interpretation. Most articles are specific to Lesotho and southern Africa and particular attention is paid to links between law and development.

539 **Mohlomi: Journal of Southern African Historical Studies.**
Roma, Lesotho: National University of Lesotho, Department of History, 1976- . irregular.

Approximately half of the articles contain material which is relevant to Lesotho, and these are listed separately in this bibliography.

540 **NUL Journal of Research.**
Roma, Lesotho: National University of Lesotho, 1991- . annual.

Contains short articles on the on-going research of the university in a number of fields.

541 **Public Lecture Series.**
Roma, Lesotho: National University of Lesotho, 1992- . irregular.

This series includes public lectures by staff of the University on a wide variety of topics. However, publication appears to be irregular.

542 **Review of Southern African Studies.**
Roma, Lesotho: National University of Lesotho, Institute of Southern African Studies, 1995- . twice yearly (January, June).

This is a review of the publications of staff members and visitors to the Institute of Southern African Studies. It contains many topical papers on the region, covering the range of social sciences, including economics, politics and sociology.

543 **The Teacher-Researcher.**
Roma, Lesotho: National University of Lesotho, 1991- . irregular.

Comprises research reports on teaching in Lesotho and writings by teachers on classroom experiences.

Encyclopaedias and Directories

544 **Directory of national sources of environmental information in Lesotho.**

E. M. Nthunya, A. M. Mathaha. Roma, Lesotho: National University of Lesotho, Institute of Education, 1992. 47p.

Originally compiled for inclusion in the United Nations Environmental Programme, this directory lists thirty-five national information sources. Each entry gives the name of the organization, contact person, nature of the sources, subjects covered and the extent of access. It is expected that the directory will be regularly updated.

545 **Encyclopaedia of Southern Africa.**

Eric Rosenthal. London: Warne, 1973. 6th ed. 662p.

Provides very brief entries about towns in Lesotho, and includes tables showing heights of mountain peaks in southern Africa, and dates of battles. It does unfortunately contain some inaccuracies.

546 **Guide to Lesotho secondary/high schools and technical/vocational training institutions.**

E. M. Nthunya. Roma, Lesotho: National University of Lesotho, Institute of Education, 1990. 97p.

Nthunya provides summary information about individual schools and vocational institutions in Lesotho. The guide is designed for use by pupils and their parents, but can also provide base-line information for researchers in the field of education. The information is arranged alphabetically.

547 **Lesotho: Investors Guide.**

Lesotho Government. Maseru: Lesotho National Development Corporation, [n.d].

A guide to companies and products made in Lesotho during the 1980s.

548 **Portfolio of black business in Southern Africa.**
Portfolio Business Publications. Johannesburg: Portfolio Business Publications, 1995. 176p.

Contains a list of contacts for black business in Lesotho. These are made up of predominantly black-business associations and coordinating bodies, development agencies, financial institutions, small business units, and advice centres.

549 **PRODDER's development directory 1992/93.**
D. Barnard. Johannesburg: Human Sciences Research Council, Programme for Development Research (PRODDER), 1993. 614p.

The directory is divided into two parts. The first part consists of introductory chapters covering the development scenario in southern Africa. The second part lists development-related organizations in eight southern African countries, including Lesotho. These organizations include government departments, parastatals, research institutions, NGOs and donor agencies.

Bibliographies

550 **Agricultural development in SADCC countries. A bibliography: Volume 3, Lesotho.**
Centre for Technical Cooperation in Agriculture. Wageningen, Netherlands: Centre for Technical Cooperation in Agriculture, 1991. 69p.

Derived from international agricultural databases, this is part of a series on the SADCC countries. The bibliography covers publications which have appeared since the 1960s, and up to the late 1980s. References are organized by publication date and author and subject indices are provided.

551 **Bibliography for planning and development in Lesotho: a partially annotated bibliography of holdings and references developed for the Lesotho Agricultural Sector Analysis Program.**
G. C. Wilken, C. J. Amiet. Fort Collins, Colorado: Colorado State University, Department of Economics, Lesotho Agricultural Sector Analysis Program, 1977. 200p. (Research Report, no. 1).

This bibliography includes a wide selection of material. Among the subjects covered are planning, development, agriculture and the environment, and general texts on politics, culture and economics are also included. Only some of the entries include annotations, but the locations of publications are indicated.

552 **Bibliography of creative African writing.**
Janheinz Jahn, Claus Peter Pressler. New York: Kraus Thompson, 1971. 446p. Reprinted, Millwood, New York: Kraus Reprint, 1973.

Lists the outstanding literary works in Sesotho with translations of the titles into English, French and German. The work also provides criticisms and translations but is by no means a complete survey of the literature.

553 **The black press in South Africa and Lesotho: a descriptive bibliographic guide to African, coloured and Indian newspapers, newsletters and magazines 1836-1976.**
Les Switzer, Donna Switzer. Boston, Massachusetts: G. K. Hall, 1979. 307p.

This publication includes Lesotho as part of a survey on the black press in South Africa, and is aimed at both journalists and those interested in popular culture. Information is presented on language and frequency of publication, as well as the holding libraries in southern Africa. A brief history of black publications is offered, as is a bibliography of secondary sources relating to black publishing. There is also an index of all known serial publications at that time. However, the guide does not include southern African publications (including those that were written in exile) held outside South Africa and Lesotho. Nor does it include information on photo-story magazines, popular in both South Africa and Lesotho among black people, but which are generally published by white-owned companies.

554 **Education in Lesotho: a bibliography.**
C. M. Qobo. Maseru: Lesotho Educational Research Association, 1991. 60p.

Covers the period 1960 to 1990. This bibliography is designed as a tool for readers interested in education, reseachers, planners and policy-makers. Publication details and a short description are presented for each entry.

555 **The French and the Kingdom of Lesotho: a bibliographical study.**
David P. Ambrose. Bordeaux, France: Domaine Universitaire, Centre d'Etudes d'Afrique Noire, Institut d'Etudes Politiques de Bordeaux, 1989. 23p. (Bibliographies du C. E. A. N., no. 1).

Ambrose discusses the early contact between the Basotho and French missionaries and the subsequent importance of French writing for analysis of the early history of Lesotho, as French missionaries were the first to provide written accounts of the people and geography of Lesotho. This bibliography confines itself to books, theses and to known unpublished manuscripts of book length. To qualify for inclusion, the Lesotho-related content was required to be at least half of the total. Although smaller missionary pamphlets and periodicals are not included, Ambrose does give some description of writing about Lesotho in these. Information is provided on the context of each publication and an indication of whether it has been translated is given. This is a useful work not only for those interested in Lesotho and French relations but also for those researching into the early history of Lesotho.

556 **Human rights and refugees in Africa: an annotated bibliography.**
Kesete Belay. Roma, Lesotho: National University of Lesotho, Institute of Southern African Studies, 1993. 139p. (Human and People's Rights Monograph Series, no. 11).

This bibliography has a section covering human rights publications on Lesotho. The author presents information on publication details and offers a short description of each work.

557 **Irrigation in Lesotho: bibliography.**
Philip Cole, Hugh Scott. Maseru: Ministry of Agriculture, Small-scale Irrigated Vegetable Project, 1991. 40p.

Provides a tool for irrigation planners, practitioners and researchers. With a few exceptions, the literature included has been developed for Lesotho; therefore this bibliography does not include manuals limited to non-Lesotho specific, technical issues. As well as general publication details, the authors offer information on where the works can be found in Lesotho, and short annotations on the content of the publications.

558 **Lesotho: a comprehensive bibliography.**
David Ambrose, Shelagh Willet. Oxford; Santa Barbara: Clio Press, 1980. 499p. 1 map.

A comprehensive bibliography of Lesotho, covering all main subject areas. Particular attention has been paid to historical material and colonial government reports. The authors provide annotations of varying lengths and full publication details.

559 **Lesotho's land tenure: an analysis and annotated bibliography.**
J. B. Eckert. Maseru: Lesotho Agricultural Sector Analysis Project, 1980. 54p. (Special Report, no. 2).

Provides an analysis of land tenure issues and presents annotated references on publications concerning land. These references are divided into four sections: land tenure in Lesotho; legal framework; relevant data; and references on southern Africa. Selected excerpts from the Laws of Lerotholi, which first codified land tenure, are included in an appendix.

560 **Library and information science: an annotated bibliography of theses and dissertations on Botswana, Lesotho and Swaziland.**
Thokozile Nkabinde. Roma, Lesotho: Institute of Southern African Studies, 1989. 72p. (Research Report, no. 21).

This bibliography provides an annotated list of theses and dissertations in archive, library and information studies on Botswana, Lesotho and Swaziland. Also included are undergraduate diploma projects. Researchers in this field will find it a useful tool and it also gives information on other more narrowly academic bibliographies.

561 **The small and the new in Southern Africa: the foreign relations of Botswana, Lesotho, Namibia and Swaziland since their independence: a select and annotated bibliography.**
Lydia Eve Andor. Johannesburg: South African Institute of International Affairs, 1993. 526p. (Bibliographic Series, no. 25).

A bibliography with particular emphasis on foreign relations. The author includes literature on foreign relations, international agreements and regional cooperation. A number of entries refer to more than one country. A significant number of entries apply to Lesotho, while many more are relevant to an understanding of regional relations. Each entry includes details of publication and a description of the contents.

562 **Women in development in Southern Africa: an annotated bibliography. Vol. II: Lesotho.**
M. M. Chadzingwa. Wageningen, Netherlands; Brussels: CTA Technical Centre for Agricultural and Rural Co-operation; Gaborone: Southern African Centre for Cooperation in Agricultural Research, 1991. 46p.

Published as part of a four-volume bibliography of women in southern Africa. In determining the selection of items for the bibliography, attention was also paid to the regional focus of the overall series. Thus, among the 157 volumes, there are a number of publications that also refer to Botswana, Malawi and Zambia. The work is also available directly from the Southern African Centre for Cooperation in Agricultural Research, Private Bag 00108, Gaborone, Botswana.

563 **Women in Southern Africa: a bibliography.**
Louise Torr, Heather Hughes, Judith Shier, Chantelle Wyley. Durban, South Africa: University of Natal Publications, 1991. 2nd ed. 181p.

A bibliography of literature on women in southern Africa which contains a number of references to publications on women in Lesotho. It deals with a wide range of subject material, including publications on marriage, employment and migrant labour, politics and the law. Full publication details are cited; however, no descriptions of the content of the works have been provided.

Indexes

There follow three separate indexes: authors (personal and corporate); titles; and subjects. Title entries are italicized and refer either to the main titles, or to many of the other works cited in the annotations. The numbers refer to bibliographical entry rather than page numbers. Individual index entries are arranged in alphabetical sequence.

Index of Authors

A

Acocks, J. P. H. 50
Adams, E. V. 450
Adams, M. 148
Adeola, O. A. 448
African Wildlife 521
Alotsi, P. 454
Ambrose, D. P. 1, 13, 58, 99, 555, 558
Amiet, C. J. 551
Anderson, J. H. 155
Andor, L. E. 561
Arbousset, T. 24
Armstrong, A. K. 164, 169, 201
Armstrong, G. 360
Artz, N. E. 377
Ashton, E. H. 156, 191, 216, 507
Ault, D. E. 392

B

Balfour, A. B. 27
Bam, E. E. 196
Banoub, S. N. 183
Bardill, J. E. 288
Barkly, F. 86
Barnard, D. 549
Bassett, T. J. 355
Bawden, M. C. 10
Bayley, B. 303
Baylies, C. 383
Beardsley, J. E. 232
Beaudoin, Y. 116
Belay, K. 557
Bereng, D. C. T. 468
Bernstein, H. 215
Berthoud, A. 115
Bezençon, L. 126
Bhagavan, M. R. 332
Blackett, I. C. 200
Blair, A. 199, 203
Bloem, J. 181, 265-66, 372
Boadu, F. O. 241
Bojo, J. 420, 422
Boleme, S. 41
Bond, K. 30
Bonner, P. L. 78
Boonstraand, L. D. 16
Braimoh, D. 448-49
Brandwijk, M. G. 194
Breytenbach, W. J. 211
Brokken, R. F. 304, 380
Bulane, M. 468, 471
Burman, S. B. 74, 76, 214

C

Campbell, B. K. 215
Campbell, J. R. 313
Carlsson, J. E. 426
Carroll, D. M. 10
Carter, P. L. 53
Carvalho, J. W. 282-83, 399
Casalis, E. 87, 93
Casella, G. 180
Cathcart, G. 89
Catholic Church 530
Central Bank of Lesotho 300
Centre for Technical Cooperation in Agriculture 550
Chabane, C. M. 438, 444
Chadzingwa, M. M. 455, 562
Christeller, L. 532
Ciccolo, A. 319
Cobbe, J. H. 133, 139, 285-88, 389, 434
Cole, P. 143, 305-06, 309-11, 343, 358, 362, 375, 557
Connelly, M. 106
Coplan, D. B. 111, 494
Costa, D. 483
Cousens, S. N. 176
Crummey, D. E. 355
Crush, D. 328
Crush, J. S. 262, 328, 410
Cunningham, T. 309-10

D

Damane, M. 467, 470
Damane, S. 193
Daniels, D. L. 176
De Vletter, F. 396
Dixon, J. A. 420
Doke, C. M. 114
Downing, J. 324
Drake, P. J. 298
Drew, C. 305
Dreyer, J. 480
Du Plessis, J. 122
Duckett, J. D. 419
Duignan, P. 258
Duncan, P. 247
Dunlevey, J. N. 17
Dyer, R. A. 44

E

Eckert, J. B. 12, 153, 293, 350, 385, 415, 559
Edgar, R. 218
Edkins, D. 499
Edwards, W. B. 16
Eldredge, E. A. 66, 71, 73
Elkan, W. 398
Ellenberger, D. F. 63
Ellenberger, V. 117
Epprecht, M. 119, 219
Esrey, S. A. 180
Evans, P. 426
Everist, R. 19

F

Feachem, R. G. 176
Feaster, G. 305
Ferguson, J. 129, 264, 508
Foundation for Education with Production 284
Frankenberger, T. R. 367
Freeman, J. J. 26

G

Galbraith, J. S. 69
Gann, L. H. 258
Ganter, E. 499
Gay, John 136-37, 157, 179, 334, 378-79
Gay, Judy S. 144, 159-60, 171, 388, 458
Geldenhuys, D. 273
Gérard, A. S. 461, 463
Germond, P. 124
Gibbon, P. 294
Gill, D. 136, 148, 157, 190, 197, 206
Gill, Simon 329
Gill, Stephen J. 5, 63, 524
Ginn, P. 33-34, 37
Glover, D. 366
Goldman, C. 238, 340
Gordan, E. 158
Grant, W. 324
Gray, J. 289
Green, T. 136, 146, 157, 261, 267, 333-34, 356, 363, 378-79, 453, 457-58
Grohn, Y. 154
Groves, C. P. 125
Guma, S. M. 460, 517
Gustafsson, B. 134
Guy, J. 404-05

H

Habicht, J. P. 154, 180
Haggblade, S. 324
Haliburton, G. M. 121
Hall, D. 136-37, 146-48, 157, 182, 185, 197, 204-05, 209, 267, 269, 334, 356, 361-62, 364, 368, 421
Hamilton, C. 94
Hammond-Tooke, W. D. 192, 506, 511
Hamnett, I. 231, 246
Hanlon, J. 271
Harlow, C. 245
Harris, B. J. 386
Heap, M. 184
Henry, H. G. 83
Himmelgreen, D. A. 195
Hirschmann, D. 249, 260
Hoeane, M. 498
Holland, D. W. 282, 399
Hoohlo, S. G. 317
Houlton, J. 23
How, M. W. 512
Howe, G. 266, 342
Hudson, W. K. 18, 79
Hughes, D. 358
Hughes, H. 563
Huisman, M. 230, 344
Hunter, J. P. 308
Hynes, P. H. 188

J

Jackson, R. H. 258
Jacot-Guillarmod, A. 39-40, 43, 47
Jacot-Guillarmod, C. F. 31
Jacottet, E. 109, 112-13, 505
Jahn, J. 552
Jamal, V. 127
James, D. E. 420
Jingoes, S. J. 88
Jobo, T. G. 313
Jochelson, K. 187
Johnson Riley, P. 161
Johnston, D. Z. 349
Jubb, R. A. 32

K

Kaburise, J. B. K. 96
Kane-Berman, J. S. 389
Kanno, N. 188
Kanono, L. M. 164
Karekezi, S. 332
Katona, E. 105
Keegan, T. 85
Kennan, T. B. 16
Ketso, L. V. 400-01
Khabele, M. K. 170
Khaketla, B. M. 224, 466, 468
Khalema, L. M. 331, 335
Khapwale, G. K. 455
Khativada, Y. 426
Kiker, G. A. 8
Kimane, I. 208
Kimble, J. 72, 81, 84, 215
Kirkpatrick, S. W. 326
Kishindo, P. 173, 352
Knappert, J. 503

Konczacki, Z. A. 401
Krogman, N. T. 161
Kulundu-Bitonye, W. 299
Kunene, D. P. 464, 466
Kunz, R. P. 8

L

Lagden, G. 59
Latham, M. C. 180
Lawry, S. W. 355, 374
Lawton, A. C. 487
Learman, R. T. 151
Lebusa, M. 435
Leduka, R. C. 252
Lee, D. N. 472
Lee, Y. 348
Leeman, B. 212
Lefoka, J. P. 438, 444
Legassick, M. 64
Leger, J. 187
Leistner, O. A. 46
Lekoetje, D. T. 314
Lelala, A. T. 297
Lemon, A. 275
Lesotho Government 7, 9, 98, 145, 174, 186, 207, 338, 341, 345, 369, 384, 411-13, 417, 430, 433, 459, 529, 547
Lesotho Highlands Development Authority 321
Lesotho National Development Corporation 318
Letuka, P. 166
Levinsohn, R. 486, 490
Liebenberg, D. P. 525
Lippman, D. 373
Low, A. R. C. 337, 370
Lucas, R. E. B. 393
Lundgren, L. 426
Lye, W. F. 22, 62
Lynn, T. 110

M

Mabille, A. 528
Macartney, W. J. A. 225
Macgregor, J. C. 63
Machobane, J. J. 466
Machobane, L. B. B. J. 118, 253
Maclean, G. 31
Madeley, J. 268
Maema, M. 456
Maggs, T. M. O. C. 52
Mahao, N. L. 229, 280
Makara, A. 468
Makatjane, T. J. 445
Makhaola, M. 152
Makhetha, P. 437
Makoa, F. K. 226-27
Makoae, L. N. 176
Makonnen, N. 134
Makoro, M. T. M. 375
Malahleha, G. 185
Malataliana, T. 454
Malie, J. G. 80
Maloka, T. 123
Mamashela, M. P. 166, 236
Mangoaela, Z. D. 109
Maope, K. A. 240
Mapetla, E. R. M. 250
Maqutu, W. C. M. 234-35
Marks, S. 81
Marres, P. J. T. 135
Marshall, R. D. 35
Martin, M. 502
Maruping, A. M. 445
Mary, T. 120
Mashinini, I. V. 353, 416
Massey, G. 371, 454
Mathaha, A. M. 544
Matlosa, K. 228, 391, 395
Matobo, T. 152, 357
Matsobane, D. 389
May, E. D. 45
Mayer, P. 141
Mbatha, L. 166
McAllister, P. A. 514
McClain, W. 96
McIlleron, G. 33-34, 37
McKenzie, J. 324
Mda, Z. 500
Meakins, R. H. 419
Meijs, L. 15
Mhlanga, M. 136
Milazi, D. 96
Ministry of Agriculture 150
Mitchell, A. A. 17
Mitchell, P. J. 51, 54-57
Mochebelele, M. 301-02, 307, 312, 376
Mochochoko, P. 166
Mofolo, T. 466
Mohale, M. 166
Mohapelao, L. 332
Mohapeloa, J. M. 75, 431, 466
Mohapi, M. 136
Mohasi, V. M. 448
Mohlalefi-Bereng, P. 446
Moitse, S. 495
Mojela, L. 466
Mokhehle, N. 92
Mokitimi, N. 301-02, 304, 308, 312, 376
Molefi, J. 408
Moloi, A. J. M. 465
Moloi, F. L. 170
Monaphathi, T. E. 164
Monyooe, A. L. 440-41
Moodie, T. D. 202
Moore, G. A. B. 452
Moremoholo, L. 371
Morgan, R. P. E. 523
Morija Museum 527
Morojele, C. M. H. 77
Morris, C. D. 41
Morrison, M. 220
Mosenene, L. 357
Moshoeshoe-Chadzingwa, M. M. 449
Moteetee, M. 178
Mothabeng, M. 269
Mothibe, T. 213
Mothibeli, M. 187
Mothokho, M. 358
Motsamai, M. 380
Mouton, P. 36
Moyo, S. 418
Mphi, M. 198
Mugambwa, J. 96
Muntemba, S. 170
Murray, C. 60, 62, 128, 130, 132, 403, 509, 516, 519
Murray, J. 19
Murray, J. P. 31
Murray, M. 325
Musi, M. 437
Muzorewa, B. C. 295

N

Namasasu, O. 262
Ndatshe, V. 202
Neff, S. 239
Nelson, N. 158
Neocosmos, M. 294
Ngqaleni, M. 302, 347
Nkabinde, T. 560
Nthunya, E. M. 544, 546
Ntimo-Makara, M. T. 162
Ntlou, N. 371
Ntsane, K. 468

O

O'Keefe, P. 418
Oberholzer, A. 2
Oenema, K. 452
Okore, A. O. 381
Olsson, R. 492
Onado, M. 296
Ornas, A. H. 424
Orpen, J. M. 67

P

Palmer, E. 49
Palmer, V. V. 243
Paroz, R. A. 107
Parpart, J. L. 401
Pavlich, G. 292
Perraton, H. 447
Perry, J. W. B. 13
Peters, C. 100
Petersson, L. 290
Phakisi, L. S. 313
Phalatsi, S. 265
Phillip, K. 407
Phillips, E. P. 42
Picard, L. A. 251
Pinstrupandersen, P. 154
Pitman, N. 49
Plath, J. C. 399
Pomela, E. 454
Pomela, M. E. 371
Porteri, A. 296
Portfolio Business Publications 548
Postma, M. 504
Pottier, J. P. 149
Poulter, S. 96, 233, 237, 242-44
Powell, P. I. 359
Poynton, J. C. 28
Prah, K. K. 390, 424
Prasad, G. 414
Pressler, C. P. 552
Prinsloo, D. S. 277
Protection and Preservation Commision 510
Putsoane, T. 456

Q

Qobo, C. M. 554
Qunta, C. N. 172

R

Ramluckan, V. R. 17
Ranganathan, V. 335
Redd, S. 178
Rembe, S. W. 250
Reynolds, G. W. 38
Riddell, J. C. 351
Robertson, N. 289
Rohrmann, G. F. 476
Romerodaza, N. 195
Rosenthal, E. 545
Roy, P. 131
Ruel, M. T. 154
Rugege, S. 222, 248, 365
Russell, D. 451
Rutman, G. L. 392

S

Saasa, O. S. 281
Saenz-de-Tejada, S. 367
Safilios-Rothschild, C. 168
Sakoane, E. 429
Salih, M. A. M. 424
Sanders, P. B. 91, 467
Santho, S. 213, 222, 227, 229, 272, 276, 279, 317, 330, 347, 365, 391, 396, 400, 407
Schapera, I. 506
Schartup, H. 324
Schmoller, H. 533
Schulze, R. E. 8
Schwager, C. 3
Schwager, D. 3
Scott, H. 557
Sebatane, E. M. 439, 443-44
Sebatane, L. A. 170
Sechaba Consultants 4, 101-04, 423
Sechefo, J. 513
Seeiso, S. M. 163-64
Segoete, E. L. 466
Sejanamane, M. M. 213, 222, 226-27, 229, 272, 276, 278-80, 317, 330, 347, 391, 396, 400, 407
Sekatle, P. 223
Selwyn, P. 318
Sembajwe, I. 97
Senaoana, M. P. 387
Shanafelt, R. 462
Sharpe, M. R. L. 108
Sharpe, R. 501
Shaw, M. 511
Sheddick, V. G. J. 82
Sherman, P. B. 420
Shier, J. 563
Shone, G. 426
Showers, K. B. 167, 428
Shute, J. C. M. 452
Sibuyi, B. 202
Sisler, D. G. 180
Smit, P. 11
Smith, R. 464
Smits, L. G. A. 474-75
Sopeng, L. 380
Southern African Development Community 478
Southhall, R. 276, 394, 409
Spiegel, A. D. 141, 514
Standford, W. P. 31
Stanton-Russell, S. 397
Staples, R. R. 18, 79
Steinberg, J. M. 55
Sterkenburg, J. J. 149
Stern, J. 20
Stevens, R. 348
Stevens, R. P. 83
Stewart, J. 164
Stockley, G. M. 16

Stone, M. P. 367
Storey, G. G. 302, 376, 380
Strom, G. W. 291
Stuart, J. S. 436-37
Suchet, R. 522
Swallow, B. M. 302, 304, 380
Swanepoel, C. F. 469
Switzer, D. 553
Switzer, L. 553

T

Tainton, N. M. 41
Tangri, R. 221
Tau, M. N. 48
Teitelbaum, M. 397
Telejane, T. 375
Thabane, M. 142, 404-05, 518
Theal, G. M. 65
Thelejane, T. 306
Thelejane, T. S. 29
Thoahlane, T. 263
Thompson, L. 64, 68, 95
Tiljander, A. 255
Torr, L. 563
Trans-Caledon Tunnel Authority 320, 322
Trollip, J. 140
Trollope, A. 70
Tshabalala, M. 327
Tsikoane, T. 330
Tsotsi, M. N. 164
Turco, M. 21
Turner, S. 456
Turner, S. D. 138, 387, 427
Tylden, G. 61, 488
Tyson, C. B. 256

V

Van Apeldoorn, G. J. 138, 387
Van den Bor, W. 452
Van der Geer, R. 254, 259
Van der Wiel, A. C. A. 135
Van Geldermalsen, A. A. 175
Van Wyk, J. H. 36
Venter, F. A. 18
Vogel, J. C. 53-54

W

Wakiro, A. 306, 309-10
Waldman, R. 178
Walker, C. 74, 78
Wallis, M. 177, 254, 259
Wallman, S. 270
Walters, J. 316
Walton, J. 477, 479, 481-82, 484-85, 489, 491
Walton, M. 288
Ward, M. 442
Watkins, D. 526
Watt, J. M. 194
Weeks, J. 127
Weisfelder, R. F. 210, 274
Wellings, P. A. 189, 359
Wells, R. E. 496-97
West, M. 516
Whisson, M. G. 516
White, B. K. 493
Widdicombe, J. 90
Wilken, G. C. 6, 339, 551
Willet, S. 558
Williams, J. C. 354
Winterbottom, J. M. 31
Wisner, B. 336
Woodhouse, H. C. 472-73
Woods, S. K. 515
Wright, C. 402, 406
Wykstra, R. A. 293, 382, 385, 415
Wyley, C. 563

Y

Yates, R. 56

Z

Ziegahn, L. 429
Zurcher, J. 531

Index of Titles

111 years: Morija printing works; printed on the occasion of the Unesco International Book Year, 1972 for the book exhibition in Maseru, 24-29 November 1972 531
1960 agricultural census, Basutoland 77
1986/87 household budget survey in Lesotho: methodological report 145

A

Academic activities: some useful indicators 445
Acid precipitation in Lesotho 414
Action research and reflection-in-action: a case study of teachers' research into development studies teaching in Lesotho 436
Administration of planning in Lesotho. A history and assessment 249
Administration of planning in Lesotho: the second leg 249
Adult literacy in Lesotho. Parts 1 and 2 429
Africa misunderstood: or whatever happened to the rural-urban gap? 127
African Affairs 534
African energy: issues in planning and practice 331
African societies in South Africa: historical studies 64, 68
African Studies 535
African village 479
African women in the development process 158
Agricultural and economic development in Lesotho: analysis using a social accounting matrix 282
Agricultural development in Lesotho: the legal framework and the executive 230
Agricultural development in SADCC countries. A bibliography: Volume 3, Lesotho 550
Agricultural development in Southern Africa: farm-household economics and the food crisis 337
Agricultural marketing and policy development in Lesotho 312, 376
Agricultural marketing development in Lesotho 301
Agricultural marketing in Lesotho 302
Agricultural marketing in Lesotho and price transmission to the village level: implications and options for policy 303
Agricultural production and marketing policies and management of soil, water and forestry resources to promote increased productivity and improved nutrition in Lesotho 338
Agriculture and economic development in Lesotho: analysis using a social accounting matrix 283
Agroclimatic hazard perception, prediction, and risk-avoidance strategies in Lesotho 339
Agroclimatology of Lesotho 6
Aloes of South Africa 38
Alternative structures for rural development in Lesotho 340
Among Boers and Basutos and with Barkly's Horse: the story of our life on the frontier 86
Amphibia of Southern Africa 28
Analysis of the impact of labour migration on the lives of women in Lesotho 158
Andrew Smith's journal of his expedition into the interior of South Africa, 1834-1836: an authentic narrative of travels and discoveries, the manners and customs of the native tribes, and the physical nature of the country 22
Animals of Lesotho: snakes of Lesotho 29
Annual Report for the Ministry of Health and Social Welfare 174
Annual Report of the Director of Education 430
Annual Report of the Ministry of Education and Culture 430

Annual Statistical Bulletin 412
Another blanket 389
Another development for Lesotho? Alternative development strategies for the mountain kingdom 284
Anti-politics machine: 'development', depolitization and bureaucratic power in Lesotho 264
Archaeology of Tloutle rock-shelter, Maseru District, Lesotho 51
Art and craft of Southern Africa: treasures in transition 486
Art on the rocks of Southern Africa 472
Assault, a burden for a rural hospital in Lesotho 175
Assessment of the interest and capacity of households to undertake irrigated vegetable production. Vol 1: Masianokeng, Ha Jimisi and Ha Motloheloa, Maseru District, Lesotho 361
Atlas for Lesotho 13
Attitudes and socio-economic conditions of irrigation scheme members: the results of a survey conducted for the Small Scale Irrigated Vegetable Project 362
Attitudes of asparagus farmers in five areas in Maseru District 363
Attractions of Lesotho's first National Park 521

B

Backpackers guide to Lesotho 522
Banking for development or underdevelopment: the case of Lesotho 295
Banking system and the formation of savings in Lesotho 296
Bantu pottery of Southern Africa 487
Bantu shields 488
Bantu-speaking peoples of Southern Africa 506, 511
Bantu speaking tribes of Southern Africa: an ethnographical survey 506
Bantustan brain gain: a study into the nature and causes of brain drain from independent Africa to the South African Bantustans 390
Baseline survey of 52 farmers involved in demonstrations on intensive intercropping farming systems in the Makhaleng extension area of Mohale's Hoek district 453
Basic education and agricultural extension: costs, effects and alternatives 447
Basotho children's early development of speech 106
Basotho hut: from late Iron Age to the present 480
Basotho nation-state: what legacy for the future? 210
Basotho women and their men: statistics on women and men in Lesotho, 1993 411
Basotho women migrants: a case study 159
Basotho women's options: a study of marital careers in rural Lesotho 160
Basuto folk-lore 501
Basuto: a social study of traditional and modern Lesotho 507
Basutoland: its legends and customs 502
Basutoland records 65
Basutos; the mountaineers and their country; being a narrative of events relating to the tribe from its formation early in the nineteenth century to the present day 59
Basutos or, twenty-three years in South Africa 87
Beggar your neighbour: apartheid power in Southern Africa 271
Bibliography for planning and development in Lesotho: a partially annotated bibliography of holdings and references developed for the Lesotho Agricultural Sector Analysis Program 551
Bibliography of creative African writing 552
Birds of Lesotho: a guide to distribution past and present 30
Birth of a church: the Church of Basutoland 115
Black press in South Africa and Lesotho: a descriptive bibliographic guide to African, coloured and Indian newspapers, newsletters and magazines 1836-1976 553
Black villagers in an industrial society 141
Blessed Joseph Gérard O. M. I., apostle to the Basotho (1831-1914): letters to the Superiors General and other oblates; spiritual writings 116

Bogs and sponges of the Basutoland mountains 39
Botanical exploration in Basutoland 40
Bovine mystique – power, property and livestock in rural Lesotho 508
Bushman art of Southern Africa 473
Butha-Buthe District 1

C

Case study: benefit-cost analysis of soil conservation in Maphutseng, Lesotho 420
Case-control study of the impact of improved sanitation on diarrhoea morbidity in Lesotho 176
Catalogue of the birds of Basutoland 31
Cattle marketing in Lesotho 304
Census of agriculture report 341
Century of mission work in Basutoland (1833-1933) 117
Changes in the attitudes and socio-economic status of irrigation scheme members 1990-1992 364
Changes in body-weight in Basotho women: seasonal coping in households with different socioeconomic conditions 195
Changing nature of economic dependence: economic problems in Lesotho 285
Changing labour demand in South Africa and prospects for re-absorption of returning migrants in Lesotho's economy 391
Chief is a chief by the people 88
Chiefdom politics and alien law: Basutoland under Cape rule, 1871-1884 214
Chieftainship and legitimacy: an anthropological study of executive law in Lesotho 231
Child rearing in Lesotho: some aspects of child rearing in the Teyateyaneng area 196
Christianization and the African response among the Barolong and the Basotho, 1820-1890 118
Clarion call! Struggle for a better Lesotho: a collection of speeches by His Majesty King Moshoeshoe II, 1976-1989 220
Class, gender and the household: the development cycle in Southern Africa 128
Classification of the eastern alpine vegetation of Lesotho 41
Classroom action-research: case studies in development studies teaching in Lesotho classrooms 437
Classroom action research: materials for use by teachers in developing self-reflection and appraisal skills 438
Climatological Bulletin 7
Climbs in the Malutis: mountains in Basutoland 523
'Clinging to the chiefs': some contradictions of colonial rule in Basutoland, c 1890-1930 215
Common law in Lesotho 232-33
Communal grazing and range management: the case of grazing associations in Lesotho 374
Community forestry in Lesotho: the people's perspective 356
Community forestry sociological study report 357
Comprehensive approach to village-based conservation development 421
Consequences for Lesotho of changing South African labour demand 286
Contemporary constitutional history of Lesotho 234
Contemporary family law of Lesotho 235
Continuing Education Programmes for socioeconomic development in Nigeria: an antidote for mass student failure in COSC in Lesotho 448
Contract farming and outgrower schemes: asparagus production in Lesotho 365
Contract farming and outgrower schemes in east and southern Africa 366
Contradictions of accumulation in Africa: studies in economy and state 215
Contribution to the flora of the Leribe Plateau and environs with a discussion of the floras of Basutoland, the Kalahari and the South-Eastern regions 42

Corbelled stone huts in Southern Africa 479
Core and periphery: a study of industrial development in the small countries of Southern Africa 318
Correspondence of Lieut.-General the hon. Sir George Cathcart, K. C. B., relative to his military operations in Kaffraria until the termination of the Kafir War, and to his measures for the future maintenance of peace on that frontier and the protection and welfare of the people of South Africa 89
Crocodiles and commoners in Lesotho: continuity and change in the rule-making system of Lesotho 211
Cultural topography of wealth: commodity paths and the structure of property in rural Lesotho 129
Current agricultural marketing situation and activities in Lesotho 305

D

Dagga pipes of Southern Africa 489
Dairy price structuring study 375
Dairy products: permit and levy study 375
Dating of industrial assemblages from stratified sites in Eastern Lesotho 53
Decentralisation and development in Lesotho 250
Decentralization and primary health care in Lesotho 177
Demand for and supply of labour in Lesotho: patterns and implications for socioeconomic development 381
Democracy and indirect rule 216
Democracy in Lesotho: the electoral laws 236
Dependency and the foreign policy options of small Southern African states 272
'Desirable or undesirable Basotho women?' Liquor, prostitution and the migration of Basotho women to the Rand, 1920-1945 78
Development administration and political control: the district administration in Lesotho 251
Development and dependence in Lesotho; the enclave of South Africa 291
Development of self-reflection skills among primary school teachers in Lesotho: a narrative report 438
Diagnosis and management of acute respiratory infections in Lesotho 178
Diplomacy of isolation: South Africa's foreign policy making 273
Directory of national sources of environmental information in Lesotho 544
Disease in Lesotho: perception and prevalence 179
Distribution system for fresh milk and mafi in Lesotho 306
Does Lesotho have any future outside the Southern African Customs Union? 314
Dolerite dykes in Basutoland with special reference to the geomorphological effects of the dykes and their economic significance 15
Domesticity and piety in colonial Lesotho: the private politics of Basotho women's Pious Associations 119
Drinking water source, diarrhoeal morbidity, and child growth in villages with both traditional and improved water supplies in rural Lesotho, southern Africa 180
Drought relief and local organisations: report on the capacity of non-governmental organisations, Private Health Association of Lesotho and churches to participate in a drought relief operation 148
Dynamics of land tenure and spontaneous changes in African agrarian systems 351

E

Ecological survey of the mountain area of Basutoland 18, 79
Ecology and politics: environmental stress and security in Africa 424
Economic aspects of Lesotho's relations with South Africa 287

Economic history of Lesotho in the nineteenth century 66
Economics of dryland management 420
Economics of independence 80
Economics of land degradation: theory and applications to Lesotho 422
Economics of milk production and marketing in Lesotho: survey results 307
Education for frustration 431
Education in Lesotho: a bibliography 554
Education sector survey: report of the taskforce 432
Educational policy guidelines 433
Educational selection procedures and policies in Lesotho: an overview 439
Educational system, wage and salary structure, and income distribution: Lesotho as a case study, circa 1975 434
Effects of migrant labour: a review of the evidence from Lesotho 130
Effects of social, political and economic constraints on the black African's allocation of time: evidence from oscillating migrants in the Republic of South Africa 392
Elements of Southern Sotho 107
Eloquent knowledge: Lesotho migrants songs and the anthropology of experience 494
Emigration to South Africa's mines 393
Encyclopaedia of Southern Africa 545
Enhancing the diversified strategies of the rural poor in Lesotho 131
Energy demand and consumption patterns of Maseru peri-urban areas, with particular reference to low-income locations 331
Energy management in Africa 332
Energy management in Lesotho 332
Environmental responsibility under severe economic constraints: re-examining the Lesotho Highlands Water Project 319
Ethnomusicology of the Basotho 495
Evaluation of the Community Alcohol Rehabilitation Programme of Scott Hospital 197
Evaluation of the Lesotho Planned Parenthood Association community based distribution 181
Evaluation of the Lesotho Red Cross Society 265
Evaluation of the Scott Hospital Community Based Distribution Family Planning Programme 182
Evaluation of the small-scale intensive agricultural production project (SSIAPP) 266
Everyday Sesotho grammar 108
Everyday Sesotho reader 108
Evolution of the wool and mohair marketing system in Lesotho: implications for policy and institutional reform 308
Experimenting with decentralisation through devolution in Lesotho: the Maseru City Council 252

F

Factors influencing food production in Lesotho and Swaziland 149
Families divided: the impact of migrant labour in Lesotho 132
Family law and litigation in Basotho society 237
Farm labour in Lesotho: scarcity or surplus? 382
Farmech Scheme: Basutoland (Lesotho) 270
Father Patrick Maekane M. B. K. 120
Female alcoholism problems in Lesotho 198
Female labour in the textile and clothing industry of Lesotho 383
Fighting a two-pronged attack: the changing legal status of women in Cape-ruled Basutoland, 1872-1884 74
Fish of the Orange River 32
Five years of practical maize demonstration work in Lesotho lowlands and foothills 454
Flora of Lesotho (Basutoland) 43
Flora of Southern Africa: the genera of Southern African flowering plants. Vol. 1: Dicotyledons. Vol. 2: Gymnosperms and Monocotyledons 44

Food and Nutrition Information Bulletin 150
Food and nutrition planning – the Lesotho approach 151
Food systems in Central & Southern Africa 149
For the light in the night 446
Foreign business and political unrest in Lesotho 221
Foreign workers in SA: comrades or competitors? 394
Forest Arboretum of trees and shrubs of Lesotho: notes on the establishment of species represented, together with field records of their present occurrence and growth potential in Lesotho 45
Form, content and technique of traditional literature in Southern Sotho 460
Four African literatures: Xhosa, Sotho, Zulu, Amnaric 461
Fourteen years in Basutoland 90
French and the Kingdom of Lesotho: a bibliographical study 555
From destabilisation to regional cooperation in Southern Africa? 226, 278, 280
From granary to labour reserve: an analysis of Lesotho's economic predicament 60
From granary to labour reserve: an economic history of Lesotho 60
From knowledge to practice: village based resource management with special attention to soil conservation 423
Future of international labour migration in Southern Africa: focus on Lesotho 395
Future of the migrant labour system: a NUM perspective 407
Future of 'traditional' hereditary chieftaincy in a democratic Southern Africa: the case of Lesotho 222
Future prospects for foreign migrants in a democratic South Africa 396

G

Garden birds of Southern Africa 33
Gender-related factors influencing the viability of irrigation projects in Lesotho 161
Germination of Southern Sotho poetry 465
Getting the best value for money in health care 183
Global climate change and agricultural productivity in Southern Africa 8
Government and change in Lesotho, 1800-1966: a study of political institutions 253
Government and development in rural Lesotho 254
Government by proxy: ten years of Cape Colony rule in Lesotho, 1871-1881 75
Grammar of the Sesuto language 109
Grasses of southern Africa: an identification manual with keys, descriptions, classification and automated identification and information retrieval from computerized data 46
Gross and net margins of agricultural enterprises in the Mafeteng District 342
Gross margins for agricultural enterprises in the Matelile area 343
Guide to Lesotho 1
Guide to Lesotho secondary/high schools and technical/vocational training institutions 546
Guide to Morija 524

H

Ha Khotso rock paintings and the Mountain Road 1
Health and disease in south-eastern Lesotho: a social anthropological perspective of two villages 184
Health and family planning services in Lesotho: the people's perspective 185
Health in Lesotho 186
Heroic ideal in three Sotho novellas of labour migration 462
Heroic poetry of the Basotho 466
High bridewealth, migrant labour and the position of women in Lesotho 509
High Commission Territories in South Africa: Pt. II Basutoland 23
Historic buildings of Basutoland. Presidential address to the Basutoland Scientific Association 481

History of the Basuto: ancient and modern 63
History of the Basutus of South Africa 67
History of Christian missions in Lesotho 121
History of Christian missions in South Africa 122
Home gardens nutrition program: 1989/90 baseline survey 152
Homesteads and villages of South Africa 482
House decoration in Southern Africa 476
Household data for the Matelile ward, Mafeteng district: a compilation of secondary data 143
Household income and expenditure in rural Lesotho: a village-level case study 144
Household vegetable gardens in Africa: case studies from Mauritania and Lesotho 367
How the Church of Basutoland came into being 115
Human immunodeficiency virus and migrant labour in South Africa 187
Human rights and the migratory labour system 238
Human rights and refugees in Africa: an annotated bibliography 556
Human rights in Botswana, Lesotho and Swaziland: implications of adherence to international human rights treaties 239
Human rights in Botswana, Lesotho and Swaziland: a survey 240

I

Identification of socio-economic constraints to project activities and an assessment of project impact 267
Impeded democracy: chiefly hierarchy versus democratic institutions in village decision-making 255
Implications of the sociocultural environment for women and their assumption of management positions: the case of Lesotho 162
In the Lesuto: a sketch of African mission life 90
Incomes, expenditure and consumption of Basotho households 145
Industrial development in peripheral small countries 319
Industrial relations in Lesotho in the 1980s and the challenges for the 1990s 408
Industrialisation and social change in South Africa: African class formation, culture and consciousness 1870-1930 81
Industries in the Southern African periphery: a study of industrial development in Botswana, Lesotho and Swaziland 319
Information and development research: the case of ISAS 455
Information sources as a factor of adults' occupational choice in selected non-formal educational institutions in Maseru 449
Integrated community forestry and agricultural resource management project 358
International migration and international trade 397
Introduction to the music of the Basotho 496
Iron Age communities of the southern highveld 52
Irrigation in Lesotho: bibliography 557
It depends: planning and managing induced innovation in uncertain environments; a contingency approach to extension reforms in Lesotho 256

J

Journal of Modern African Studies: a Quarterly Survey of Politics, Economics and Related Topics in Contemporary Africa 536
Journal of Southern African Studies 537
Justice of the Queen's Government: the Cape's administration of Basutoland 1871-1884 76

K

Keeping house in Lesotho 132
Key to families and Index to the genera of Southern African flowering plants 44
King or country: the Lesotho crisis of August 1994 223

L

Labour force of Lesotho 384
Labour market and trade unions at the South African periphery: Lesotho and Transkei 409
Labour migration and agricultural change: observations in Lesotho 1970-1982 344
Labour migration from Botswana, Lesotho, and Swaziland 398
Labour migration in Basutoland, c.1870-1885 81
Labour migration in South Africa and agricultural development: some lessons from Lesotho 399
Labour-related aspects of rural development in Lesotho 133
Land capability guide to safe land use and crop suitability ratings for Lesotho 9
Land degradation and class struggle in rural Lesotho 424
Land in African agrarian systems 355
Land reform and agricultural development 352
Land resources of Lesotho 10
Land tenure and agricultural development in Lesotho 353
Land tenure in Basutoland 82
Land use on irrigation schemes: case studies from the 'Malere and Rasekila II schemes, Butha-Buthe district, Lesotho 368
Language situation in Lesotho today: a preliminary survey 110
Law and natural-resource development: the case of water in Lesotho 241
Law and population growth in Lesotho 96
Legal constraints on women in development in Lesotho 163
Legal dualism in Lesotho: first supplement, up to date to 1st April 1986 242
Legal dualism in Lesotho: a study of the choice of law question in family matters 242
Legal situation of women in Lesotho 164
Legal situation of women in Southern Africa 164
Legal system of Lesotho 243
Leselinyana la Lesotho 528
Lesotho 2-3
Lesotho 1970: an African coup under the microscope 224
Lesotho Agricultural Situation Analysis Report 345
Lesotho and the inner periphery in the New South Africa 274
Lesotho and Nepal: the failure of western 'family planning' 188
Lesotho and the new South Africa: the question of reincorporation 275
Lesotho and the re-integration of South Africa 276
Lesotho and the struggle for Azania Africanist political movements in Lesotho and Azania: the origins and history of the Basutoland Congress Party and the Pan Africanist Congress 212
Lesotho, Botswana and Swaziland: the former High Commission Territories in Southern Africa 83
Lesotho: a comprehensive bibliography 558
Lesotho co-operative credit union movement 297
Lesotho: dilemmas of dependence in Southern Africa 288
Lesotho: a gender analysis 165
Lesotho general election of 1970 225
Lesotho: a geographical study 11
Lesotho Highlands Water Project 320
Lesotho Highlands Water Project: Environmental Action Plan. A synopsis of studies and proposed programmes 321
Lesotho Highlands Water Project: research opportunities beyond the year 2000 456
Lesotho Highlands Water Project: Vol 2 322
Lesotho: historical legacies of nationalism and nationhood 213
Lesotho: Investors Guide 547
Lesotho: land tenure and economic development 354
Lesotho Law Journal 538
Lesotho/Maseru map 14
Lesotho migration in post-apartheid South Africa: options and constraints 400
Lesotho National Development Corporation: Annual Report 323

Lesotho national fruit and vegetable production survey 369
Lesotho: the role of agriculture and migration 401
Lesotho small and microenterprise strategy – phase II: subsectoral analysis 324
Lesotho Statistical Yearbook 412
Lesotho: a strategy for survival after the Golden Seventies 289
Lesotho tapestry weaving 490
Lesotho Today 529
Lesotho woodlot project: progress, problems and prospects 359
Lesotho's economic policy and performance under the structural adjustment program: the external dependence 290
Lesotho's employment challenge: alternative scenarios, 1980-2000 AD 385
Lesotho's expensive border hoax 277
Lesotho's food priorities 153
Lesotho's heritage in jeopardy: report of the chairman of the Protection & Preservation Commission for the years 1980-1 and 1981-2 together with a survey of its past work and present challenges 510
Lesotho's land tenure: an analysis and annotated bibliography 559
Lesotho's long journey: hard choices at the crossroads 4
Lesotho's political crisis since independence: the role of South Africa 226
Lesotho's security policy in post-apartheid Southern Africa 278
Let my people play!: participatory theatre plays 498
Library and information science: an annotated bibliography of theses and dissertations on Botswana, Lesotho and Swaziland 560
List of climbs in the Natal Drakensberg 525
Literacy and cultural identity in Lesotho 435
Literature of Lesotho 463
Lithoko: Sotho praise-poems 467
Livestock development and range utilization in Lesotho 376, 380
Local initiatives: key to selfhelp in Lesotho 268
Local level institutional development for sustainable land use 425
Local participation, equity and popular support in Lesotho's Range Management Area programme 377
Look at the Lesotho Highlands Water Project 325
Longitudinal study of Basotho children, Volume 1. Off to a good start: a study of 400 Basotho one year olds 199
Low-cost urban sanitation in Lesotho 200
Low-input, sustainable agriculture (LISA) prescription: a bitter pill for farm-households in southern Africa 370

M

Mafeteng District 1
Main results from the household budget survey 1986/87 145
Maintenance in Lesotho 166
Maintenance payments for child-support in Southern Africa: using law to promote family planning 201
Making a fast buck: capital leakage and the public accounts of Lesotho 257
Manpower vs machinery: a case study of conservation works in Lesotho 415
Manure and fertilizer applications to three crops in Lesotho 1987-1991 371
Market for fresh vegetables in Leribe and Butha-Buthe, 1993 309
Market for fresh vegetables in Maseru and Teyateyaneng, 1992 310
Market for imported fresh dairy products in the lowland districts of Lesotho 311
Marketing channels utilised by Basotho livestock owners 312
Marotholi: theatre for another development 499
Maseru 1
Maseru: an illustrated history 99
Material culture 511
Meaning of Sesotho 111
Mediating effect of maternal nutrition knowledge on the association between maternal schooling and child nutritional-status in Lesotho 154

Medicine, magic and sorcery among the Southern Sotho 191
Men without work: unemployed migrant labour in Lesotho 402
Migrancy and male sexuality on the South African gold mines 202
Migrancy and militancy: the case of the National Union of Mineworkers of South Africa 410
Migrancy, dependency and urban formation in Lesotho: a case study 100
Migrant labour and colonial rule in Southern Africa: the case of Basutoland, 1870-1930 81
Migration and development. Dependence on South Africa: a study of Lesotho 291
Military kingdom: a case for restructuring the system of government in Lesotho in the 1990s 227
Ministry of Agriculture, Co-operatives and Marketing: Annual Reports 346
Missionary excursion 24
Missionary work and the Sotho in the gold mine compounds, 1920-1940 123
Modelling access to a basic need: the provision of primary health care in rural Lesotho 189
Moeletsi oa Basotho 530
Mohale's Hoek District 1
Mohlomi: Journal of Southern African Historical Studies 539
Mokhotlong District 1
Monetary and exchange rate management in tiny, open underdeveloped economies 298
More garden birds of Southern Africa 34
Morija museum and archives 527
Morija Sesuto Book Depot 532
Moshebi's Shelter: excavation and exploitation in eastern Lesotho 53
Moshoeshoe I: profile 92
Moshoeshoe, Chief of the Sotho 91
Mountain Bushmen of Basutoland 512
Mural art of the Bantu 477
Musical understanding: the ethnoaesthetics of migrant workers' poetic song in Lesotho 494
My life in Basutoland: a story of missionary enterprise in South Africa 93
Myths and legends of Botswana, Lesotho and Swaziland 503

N

Narrative of a visit to the Mauritius and South Africa 25
National environmental planning and sustainable development: theory and applications in the Lesotho context 416
National study of non-formal education in Lesotho: first report to the Lesotho Distance Teaching Centre, February 1982 450
National survey of biomass and woodfuel activities in Lesotho 333
National transport study: first interim report on roads sector 326
Needs of dairy farmers: the farmer's perspective 378
New radiocarbon dates from Sehonghong rock shelter, Lesotho 54
New sanctions against South Africa 315
Note on women, conflict and migrant labour 167
Notes on Aloe polyphylla 47
Notes on the social costs of migrant labour from Lesotho 389
Ntloana Tsoana: a Middle Stone Age sequence from western Lesotho 55
NUL Journal of Research 540

O

Old clothing of the Basotho 513
Oral evidence in historical environmental impact assessment: soil conservation in Lesotho in the 1930s and 1940s 428
Orthographical rules for Sesuto together with the report of the conference on Sesuto orthography, 1906 112

P

Passing of Sotho independence, 1865-1870 68
Patterns of infant care in Lesotho 203

P. E. M. S.: Church of Basutoland origin 124
Persistence of women's invisibility in agriculture: theoretical and policy lessons from Lesotho and Sierra Leone 168
Pestles, mullers and querns from the Orange Free State and Basutoland 491
Pinto beans in Lesotho: the farmer's perspective 372
Place of the Laws of Lerotholi in the legal system of Lesotho 244
Planting of Christianity in Africa 125
Poets of Lesotho: first steps of a brief incursion into Sesotho literature 468
Political dilemma of chieftainship in colonial Lesotho with reference to the administration and court reforms of 1938 217
Political economy of small states in southern Africa - dependency and development options – towards regionalism in the inner periphery 279
Political economy of the Southern African periphery: cottage industries, factories and female wage labour in Swaziland compared 386
Politics and government in African states, 1960-1985 258
Polygyny as myth: towards understanding extramarital relations in Lesotho 514
Population and development in Southern Africa: the 1980s and beyond 97
Population census analysis report, 1986 98
Portfolio of black business in Southern Africa 548
Pottery guide: Lesotho 492
Poverty and remittances in Lesotho 134
Poverty eats my blanket: a poverty study: the case of Lesotho 135
Poverty in Lesotho: a mapping exercise 136
Poverty in Lesotho, 1994: a mapping exercise 137
Power of oral poetry: narrative songs of the Basotho Migrants 494
Practical method to learn Sesotho, with exercises and a short vocabulary 113
Practical studies curriculum in Lesotho: some reflections 440
Predicament of Lesotho's security in the 1990s 280
Preliminary findings from the national database on rural water supply 204
Preliminary fish survey of the Caledon River system 35
Preliminary list of the ecological sites of Lesotho 417
Press at Morija, Basutoland 533
Primary agricultural curriculum in Lesotho – a demarcation of imperatives 441
Primary school enrolment in Lesotho 442
Private herds and common land: issues in the management of communal grazing land in Lesotho, Southern Africa 374
Proceedings of the Volksraad 122
PRODDER's development directory 1992/93 549
Production through conservation: a strategy towards village-based participatory rural development 426
Prophets with honour: a documentary history of Lekhotla la Bafo 218
Public administration and community development: Lesotho's experience 259
Public Lecture Series 541
Purchasing patterns of milk and poultry in rural lowlands of Lesotho 313

Q

Qacha's Nek District 1
Quarterly Review 300
Quarterly Statistical Bulletin 413

R

Rainfall oscillations in Lesotho and the possible impact of drought in the 1980s 12
Ramabanta's 1
Ramabanta-Semonkong road project in Lesotho: a case study on community development and national planning 260
Recent Holocene archaeology in Western and Southern Lesotho 56
Recent political crisis in Lesotho 228
Reconstructing Babylon: essays on women and technology 188

Re-evaluating modernisation and dependency in Lesotho 292
Regional cooperation and integraton in Southern Africa: the case of the SADCC industrial sector 281
Religion and social change in Southern Africa: anthropological essays in honour of Monica Wilson 516
Reluctant empire: British policy on the South African frontier, 1834-1854 69
Renegotiating dependency: the case of the Southern Africa customs union 316
Renewable and conservation energy technology in the Kingdom of Lesotho: a socio-economic study of constraints to wider adoption by households and in residential buildings 334
Report on the effects of Sesotho culture, traditions and attitudes on agricultural development in Lesotho 515
Report on the evaluation of attitudes of farmers to demonstrations of the 1990/91 season 457
Report on an evaluation of the Seforong Women's Integrated Rural Development Project 269
Report on the geology of Basutoland 16
Report on range and livestock management in four sub-areas of the Matelile Project area 379
Report on research in Lesotho 497
Report on the socio-economic conditions and needs of the people in the Ketane valley of Lesotho 146
Report on the socio-economic study carried out in Leribe town for the Urban Upgrading Project 101
Report on the socio-economic study carried out in Mohales Hoek town for the Urban Upgrading Project 102
Report on the socio-economic survey carried out in Butha-Buthe Town for the department of Housing of Ministry of Interior, Chieftainship Affairs and Rural Development 103
Report on the socio-economic survey carried out in Maputsoe for the Department of Housing of Ministry of Interior, Chieftainship Affairs and Rural Development 104
Report on a survey of primary producer cooperatives, village development councils and other organisations 261
Reptile fauna of the Katse Dam catchment area and a biogeographical assessment of species composition in the Lesotho Highlands 36
Research on rural non farm employment in Lesotho: results of a baseline survey 387
Research on the rural poor of Lesotho: preliminary indicators and future directions 138
Resettlement and rural development aspects of the Lesotho Highlands Water Project 327
Resource guide for nutrition planning in Lesotho 155
Review of Lesotho's agricultural policies and strategies 347
Review of Southern African Studies 542
Revisiting the Robberg: new results and a revision of old ideas at the Sehonghong rock shelter, Lesotho 57
Rise of the Basuto 61
Ritual and medicines: indigenous healing in South Africa 192
Rock-painting sites in the upper Senqu Valley, Lesotho 474
Rock paintings of Lesotho, their contents and characteristics 475
Role of adult education in development at the Institute of Extra Mural Studies of the National University of Lesotho, Africa 451
Roma 1
'Runaway wives': Basotho women, chiefs and the colonial state, c 1890-1920 84
Rural development and women: lessons from the field, vol. II 170
Rural development in Lesotho 139-40
Rural differentiation and the diffusion of migrant labour remittances in Lesotho 141

Rural electrification in Lesotho 335
Rural energy and poverty in Kenya and Lesotho: all roads lead to ruin 336
Rural rehabilitation in the Basotho labour reserve 262
Rural water supply systems in Lesotho: findings from a nation-wide inspection 205

S

Secondary mineral zonation in the Drakensberg Basalt Formation, South Africa 17
Security and small states: the political economy of Lesotho's foreign policy – 1966-1985 272
Sefela sa Liate Kometsi: human rights and civil justice 469
Semonkong 1
Sex, smoking and the shades: a Sotho symbolic idiom 516
Sexual behaviour and attitudes to AIDS of soccer players in Lesotho 190
Short general report on the geology of the extreme northern and north-eastern portion of Basutoland 18
Short history of Lesotho: from the late Stone Age until the 1993 elections 5
Silent language of stone 483
Situation of children and women in Lesotho, 1994 206
Situation of women and children in Lesotho, 1991 207
Sketches of life and sport in South-Eastern Africa 94
Small and the new in Southern Africa: the foreign relations of Botswana, Lesotho, Namibia and Swaziland since their independence: a select and annotated bibliography 561
Social change and economic reform in Africa 294
Social forestry manual – an aid to rural development in Lesotho 360
Sociocultural environment in Lesotho as it impinges on development: focus on children 208
Socio-economic analysis of the Hololo Valley, Lesotho, 1978-1988 147
Sociological sketch of Sotho diet 156
Soil conservation: administrative and extension approaches in Lesotho 427
Soil erosion in the Kingdom of Lesotho: origin and colonial response, 1830s-1950s 428
Some anomalies in the marriage laws of Lesotho 245
Some aspects of circumcision in Basutoland 517
Some characteristics of the urban informal sector in Southern Africa: the case of Lesotho 105
Some economic and technological factors behind the adoption of the blanket as Basotho dress 518
Some legal and political issues in respect of Lesotho's options in the context of a future democratic South Africa 229
Some medicinal, magic and edible plants of Lesotho 48
Some MS notes on Basutoland birds 31
Some notes on the concept of custom in Lesotho 246
Sotho cattle kraals 484
Sotho fertility symbolism 519
Sotho laws and customs: a handbook based on decided cases in Basutoland together with the Laws of Lerotholi 247
Sotho medicine 193
Sotho-Tswana peoples before 1800 64
South Africa: a reprint of the 1878 edition 70
South African kingdom: the pursuit of security in nineteenth-century Lesotho 71
South African mine wages in the seventies and their effects on Lesotho's economy 293
South African peasant architecture: Southern Sotho folk building 485
South-North partnership in strengthening higher education in agriculture 452
Southern Africa after apartheid: prospects for the inner periphery in 1990s 213, 222, 227, 229, 272, 276, 279, 317, 330, 347, 391, 396, 400, 407

Southern Africa in the 1980s and beyond: Institute of Southern African Studies 1980-1990 97, 162, 208, 281, 301, 381, 395, 408, 414, 455-56
Southern Africa, Lesotho & Swaziland: a travel survival kit 19
Southern Africa on a budget: the essential guide for the adventurous traveller 20
Southern African Customs Union (SACU) and the post-apartheid South Africa: prospects for closer integration in the region 317
Southern African environment: profiles of the SADC countries 418
Southern Basutoland 526
Southern Sotho (Ethnographic survey of Africa, Southern Africa, Part II) 520
Spatial analysis of agricultural intensity in a Basotho village of southern Africa 348
'Stabilization' and structural unemployment 403
State and development: an analysis of agricultural development in Lesotho 349
State of dependence 328
Statistical Yearbook 413
Statutory regulation and supervision of banks and banking services in Lesotho 299
Strategic review 329
Structure and philosophy of Sotho indigenous poetry 470
Structuring agricultural education in Lesotho 452
Struggling over scarce resources: women and maintenance in Southern Africa 169
Student academic workload: are students overloaded? 445
Studies in the economic history of Southern Africa, Volume II: South Africa, Lesotho and Swaziland 401
Study of village development committees: the case of Lesotho 263
Study on adoption of improved crop technologies promoted by the Local Initiatives Support Project 458
Study on a dairy information system 375
Successful women's projects: the case of the Lesotho National Council of Women 170
Sun Chief: legends of Basutoland 502
Survey of the production, utilization and marketing of livestock and livestock products in Lesotho 380
Survival in two worlds: Moshoeshoe of Lesotho 1786-1879 95
Suto (Basuto) medicines 194

T

Tabulation report 145
Take out hunger: two case studies of rural development in Basutoland 270
Tales from the Basotho 504
Teacher education and the teaching profession in Lesotho: the state of the art 443
Teacher learning strategies in Lesotho: an empirical perspective on primary school classrooms 444
Teacher learning strategies in Lesotho primary school classrooms 444
Teacher-Researcher 543
Technology, ethnicity and ideology: Basotho miners and shaft-sinking on the South African gold mines 404
Tentative history of Lesotho palaeontology 58
Textbook of Southern Sotho grammar 114
Teyateyaneng and Berea District 1
Then and now: the praise poem in Southern Sotho 471
Thomas Mofolo and the emergence of written Sesotho prose 464
Tour in South Africa 26
Toward the year 2000: strategies for Lesotho's agriculture 350
Towards a political economy of adjustment in a labour-reserve economy: the case of Lesotho 294
Towards a redefined role of the Lesotho Highlands Water Project in the post-apartheid Southern Africa 330
Towards an understanding of the political economy of Lesotho: the origins of commodity production and migrant labour 1830- c.1885 72

Trade, accumulation and impoverishment: mercantile capital and the economic transformation of Lesotho and the conquered territory, 1870-1920 85
Tradition and transition in Southern Africa 514
Transactions in cropland held under customary tenure in Lesotho 355
Transformations on the Highveld: the Tswana and Southern Sotho 62
Treasury of Ba-Suto lore being original Se-Suto texts, with a literal English translation and notes, Vol. I 505
Trees of Southern Africa covering all known indigenous species in the Republic of South Africa, South-West Africa, Botswana, Lesotho and Swaziland 49
Twelve hundred miles in a waggon 27

U

Unemployment and casual labour in Maseru: the impact of changing employment strategies on migrant labourers in Lesotho 405
Unemployment, migration and changing gender relations in Lesotho 406
Update of the village drought survey: revised edition 157

V

Vandalism and uneven development: lessons from the experiences of the Lesotho Electricity Corporation and the Lesotho Telecommunications Corporation 142
Vanishing bogs of the mountain kingdom 419
Vegetable growing for home consumption and cash. Implementation manual 373
Vegetables for all seasons: a grow-hole user's guide 459
Veld types of South Africa with accompanying veld type map 50
Village drought assessment survey: a report based on a survey of 213 villages in the ten districts of Lesotho 157
Visitor's guide to Lesotho: how to get there, what to see, where to stay 21
Visual art in the Southern African Development Community: the argument for a regional school of art and design 478

W

Wage employment of rural Basotho women: a case study 388
Water, sanitation, hygiene and health in the Qabane Valley, Lesotho 209
Waterbirds of Southern Africa 37
Weaving guide, Lesotho 493
When people play people: development communication through theatre 500
Women and development in Lesotho 171
Women and gender in Southern Africa to 1945 74, 78
Women in the Church of Basutoland 126
Women in development in Southern Africa: a annotated bibliography. Vol. II: Lesotho 562
Women in production: the economic role of women in 19th-century Lesotho 73
Women in Southern Africa 172
Women in Southern Africa: a bibliography 563
Women, land and agriculture in Lesotho 173
Women's 'conservatism' and the politics of gender in late colonial Lesotho 219
Workers' collective rights under the Lesotho Labour Code 248

Index of Subjects

A

Abortion *see* Women
Accommodation 1, 20-21, 522
Administration *see* Government
African Methodist Episcopal Church 122
Agriculture 1-2, 6, 8-10, 13, 16, 77, 80, 132-33, 137, 141, 149, 230, 268, 282-83, 340, 352, 358, 418, 511, 550-51
- Agricultural Marketing Research Project 301, 350
- census 341
- contract farmers 366
- crop production 9, 77, 143
- dairy farming 301-02, 307, 375, 378
- demonstrations 457
- development 349, 351-53, 515
- economics 342-43
- education 346
- farming 77, 127, 141
- grow-holes 459
- hazards 339
- household gardens 152, 367, 369-70
- imports (dairy and vegetable) 309-11
- intercropping 453
- land use 9, 11, 13
- livestock 11, 77, 264, 301-02, 304, 312, 342-43, 345, 350, 354, 374, 376, 379-80, 508
- maize 454
- marketing 301-06, 308, 309-10, 312, 338, 346, 365
- mechanization 270
- milk marketing 306, 313
- overgrazing 79
- pinto beans 372
- policy 337-38, 340, 347, 349-50, 365
- poultry 77, 313, 342
- production 8, 131, 138, 337-38, 345, 348, 355, 401
- research 455
- share-cropping 294, 355
- soil 10
- erosion 9, 11, 27, 143, 352, 419, 422, 428
- storage facilities 77
- technology 458
- vegetable production 302, 305, 309-10, 361, 364, 373, 459
- *see also* Conservation: soil erosion

AIDS *see* Health and medicine: HIV
Alcohol abuse *see* Health and medicine
Aloes 38, 47
Amahlophe (people) 520
Amahlubi (people) 520
Amavundle (people) 520
Amphibians *see* Frogs; Toads
Anglican Church 120
- *see also* History

Animal husbandry *see* History
Arbousset, T. *see* History
Archaeology 51, 510, 526
- excavations 53-54, 56-57
- fossils 58
- rock shelters 51, 54, 56-57

Architecture 479-83, 485
- cattle kraals 484
- *see also* History

Arts and crafts 2, 71, 486, 511
- *dagga* pipes 489
- house decoration 476-77
- mullers 491
- music 494-97, 511
- pestles 491
- pottery 487, 492
- querns 491
- rock paintings 53, 472-75, 510, 512
- schools 478
- shields 488
- theatre 498-500
- weaving 324, 490-91, 493
- wool and mohair 302, 308, 324

Asparagus farming 363, 365
Atlases *see* Maps

B

Backhouse, James *see* History
Bakholokoe (people) 520
Banjul Charter 239
Banking 300
- development 295, 300
- exchange rates 298, 300
- interest rates 300
- regulation 299
- savings 296

Baphuthi (people) 520
Barolong (people) 118
Basotho Farm Produce 363
Basuto (people) *see* History
Basutoland 15-16, 18, 23, 42

Basutoland Congress Party (BCP) 212
Basutoland National Council (BNC) 244
Basutoland National Party (BNP) 251
Basutoland Scientific Association 481
Batlokoa (people) 156, 488, 520
Battles *see* History
BCP *see* Basutoland Congress Party
Beer brewing *see* Women
Berea (place) 27
Bereng, D. C. T. (poet) 468
Bibliographies 550-63
Bigamy 245
Birds 30-31, 33-34
  birdwatching 1, 30
  waterbirds 37
Blue Mountain tapestries 490
BNC *see* Basutoland National Council
BNP *see* Basutoland National Party
Boers 86
Bogs and wetlands 39, 419
Border disputes 59, 68-69, 277
Botany 38, 40, 43
Botswana 49, 62, 83, 216, 239-40, 279, 298, 317-18, 393, 398, 486, 503, 560-62
Bride wealth *see* Customs and folklore
British Rule *see* History
Butha-Buthe 103, 309, 362, 472

C

Caledon River 35
Cambridge Overseas School Certificate Examinations 448
Canoeing *see* Sports and recreation
Cape Rule *see* History
Cape Town 65
Casalis, Eugène (missionary) *see* History
Cathcart, Sir George 89
Catholic Church 530
  see also History
Census *see* Surveys
Chiefs 1, 26, 81, 88, 103, 211, 215-17, 222, 227, 231, 255, 263, 520
  see also History
Children
  child care 196, 199, 203, 207-08
  diseases 208
  education 196, 199, 207
  in society 208
  legal issues 206-08
  morbidity 176, 178, 180
  speech development 106
  support 201
Christianity 118, 121-22, 125
Circumcision *see* Customs and folklore
Clans 52
Class 128
Climate 1, 6-8, 12-13, 43
Coal 16
Colonialism 5, 22-23, 60, 62, 71-72, 84, 119, 214-16, 534, 558
  guides and accounts 24-25
  maps 24
Common law 232-33, 242-43
Communal grazing 374
  see also Range Management
Communications 11
Community development 259-60
Condoms *see* Health and medicine
Conquered Territories 26
Conservation 9, 350, 415, 417, 421, 424-26
  community participation 421, 425-27
  soil erosion 420-21, 423, 427
  reclamation 270
Constitution 234, 243
Continuing Education Programme 448
Contraception *see* Health and medicine
Cooperatives 261, 297, 329, 346, 363
Councils 252
Courts 243, 246
Crafts *see* Arts and crafts; History
Crops *see* Agriculture
Culture 3, 5
Customary law 163, 169, 231, 237, 242-43, 246-47
  see also Women: law
Customary marriage *see* Marriage
Customs and folklore 22, 87, 501-05, 507, 512, 514, 519, 535
  bride wealth 509
  circumcision 517
  dress 502, 506, 511, 513, 518
  food 513
  initiation 495, 517
  see also History

D

Dagga pipes *see* Arts and crafts
Dairy farming *see* Agriculture
Dams 15
  see also Lesotho Highlands Water Project
Decentralization *see* Government
Democracy 4, 206, 216, 228, 236, 252, 255

Demonstrations *see* Agriculture
Development projects 264, 267, 269-70, 283, 515
Diarrhoea *see* Health and medicine
Dicotyledons *see* Plants
Dictionaries 109
Diet *see* Health and medicine; Surveys
Directories 544
Disease *see* Health and medicine
Districts 1
Divination 495, 516
Domestic production 150
Donor agencies 4, 264, 549
Drakensberg Escarpment 17, 523, 525-26
Dress *see* Customs and folklore
Drinking water *see* Health and medicine: water
Drought and drought relief 12, 148
  see also Surveys: Village Drought Survey
Drugs 489

E

Eastern Mountains 42
Ecological sites 417
Ecology 18, 43, 79
Economics 105, 536, 542
  macro-economics 127
  see also History
Economy 1-2, 4, 60, 80, 83, 134, 139, 221, 282, 287, 289, 291-92, 318, 325, 386, 418, 520, 537
  dependency 100, 210, 213, 285, 288, 290, 292, 315-16, 318
  development 62, 128-29, 133, 283-84, 289, 291, 549, 551
  policy 290
  regional 279
  statistics 135
  see also Agriculture; Banking; History; Socio-economic conditions; Women
Education 554
  adult 451
  agriculture 447, 452
  basic education 447
  and employment 434
  formal 435
  literacy 429, 450
  mass media 447
  non-formal 435, 448-50
  policy 433
  practical studies 440-41
  primary 431, 442
  schools 546
  secondary 431
  selection policy 439
  social effects 412, 434
  statistics 430
  teacher organizations 443
  teacher training 436, 438, 443-44
  teaching 437, 543
  university courses 445
  university enrolment 445
  vocational 447-49, 546
  see also History
Elections 5, 224-25
Electoral law 236
Electricity *see* Energy
Employment 137-38, 286, 289, 324, 384-85
  see also Labour; Women
Encyclopaedias 545
Energy 331-36
Enterprises
  small 324, 329
Environment 6, 10, 36, 319, 321-22, 327, 416, 418, 551
  acid precipitation 414
  see also Agriculture
Ethnographic surveys 520
Europe 106
Evangelical Church 15, 124-26
Excavations *see* Archaeology
Exchange rates *see* Banking

F

Family law 235, 237
FAO *see* Food Agriculture Organization
Farm Improvement with Soil Conservation (FISC) Programme 422
Farming *see* Agriculture
Fauna *see* Flora and Fauna
Fertilizer *see* Agriculture
Financial mismanagement 257
Fish 32, 35
Flora and fauna 1, 19, 36, 42-44, 510, 524
  see also Ecological sites; Plants; individual species by name, i.e. Frogs
Folklore *see* Customs and folklore
Food and nutrition 8, 150-52, 154-55
  marketing 153
  production 149, 153
  see also Customs and folklore
Food Agriculture Organization (FAO) 77
Food Management Unit 136
Food Self-Sufficiency Programme 347, 350
Foreign relations 271-74, 277-80, 287, 561
Forestry 45, 262, 333, 342-43, 356-60
Fossils *see* Archaeology
Frogs 28

G

Gardens *see* Agriculture: household gardens

Garment industry 324
Gender issues *see* Women
Geography 1-3, 22
 see also Climate
Geology 1, 11, 15-18
 agroclimatology 6
 dykes 15
Gold mines 123
 see also Migrant labour
Government 1
 administration 249-51, 254
 central planning 260
 decentralization 250-52, 254
 development policy 284
 planning 249, 255
Grammar *see* Language: Sesotho
Grass 46
Gun War *see* History
Gymnosperms *see* Plants

H

Health and medicine 186, 207, 209
 alcohol abuse 197-98
 condoms 190
 contraception 181-82, 185, 188, 201
 diarrhoea 176, 180
 diet 48, 195
 disease 178-79, 184, 186
 health care 179, 183
 herbalists 48
 HIV 187, 190
 medical statistics 174
 miners 202
 planners 189
 primary health care 177, 183, 189
 respiratory infections 178
 sanitation 176, 200, 209
 traditional healers 186, 191-92, 194
 traditional medicine 48-49, 191-94
 water 180
 see also Socio-economic conditions
Herbalists *see* Health and medicine
Herbarium 44
Heritage 510
Hiking *see* Sports and recreation
History 1-2, 4-5, 19, 43, 52, 58-59, 63-64, 67, 71, 82-83, 87, 116-17, 120, 139, 275, 285, 502, 512, 527-28, 535, 545, 555, 558
 19th-century wars 59
 agriculture 71, 82, 507
 Anglican Church 125
 animal husbandry 82
 Arbousset, T. 24
 architecture 480-83, 485
 Backhouse, James 25
 Basuto society 71
 battles 89
 British Rule 69, 214-15, 217
 Cape Rule 68, 74-76
 Casalis, Eugène (missionary) 22, 70
 Catholic Church 125
 chiefs 72, 84
 colonial rule 253
 colonial travellers' accounts 22-27, 38
 crafts 71
 customs 87
 economics 288
 economy 66, 71-72, 75, 83, 85
 education 75
 Gun War 75, 86, 90, 214
 historical buildings 510
 historical sites 524
 hunters 51, 56-57
 Iron Age 5, 52, 71
 Kafir War 89
 lifaqane 63
 Maseru 99
 medicine 507
 migrant labour 71-72, 401
 migration 81
 military 61, 89
 missionaries 24, 75, 87, 90, 93, 117-18, 122-23, 125, 214, 555
 Moorosi Wars 76, 86
 Moshoeshoe I (King) 5, 22, 24-25, 65, 67, 69, 89, 91-92, 94-95, 211, 215, 467
 Napier Treaty 69
 oral tradition 91-92
 Orange Free State Wars 70
 poetry 467
 politics 66, 72, 83, 224, 507
 religion 125
 Siege of Hlotse 90
 social structure 81-82, 288
 Stone Age 5, 51, 53, 55
 trade 71, 85, 507
 traders 82
 traditional literature 460, 462-63
 Walker, G. W. 25
 wars 70
 women
  the Church 126
  economic roles 73
  legal rights 74, 84
  migrancy 84
  politics 119, 219
  religious groups 119
  society 71, 73, 84
 see also Basutoland; Colonialism
HIV *see* Health and medicine
Hlotse (place) 90, 481
 see also History: Siege of Hlotse
Holocene Period 56
Hololo Valley 147
Hotels 1, 21
 see also Accommodation
House decoration *see* Arts and crafts

Household gardens *see* Agriculture
Households 101, 103-04, 128-30, 138, 144
 income 144
 structure 144
 see also Surveys
Human rights 234, 238-40, 243, 556
Hydropower 335
 see also Lesotho Highlands Water Project
Hygiene 209

I

Imports 150, 283
 permits and levies 375
 see also Agriculture
Income 27, 105, 127
 see also Surveys
Independence 5
 see also History
Industrialization 80, 281, 386, 408-09
Industry 318, 547-48
 see also individual industries by name, i.e. Garment industry
Infections *see* Health and medicine
Infidelity 514
Influx control 159
Informal sector 105
 see also Labour
Inheritance 231
 see also Customary law
Initiation *see* Customs and folklore
Institute of Extra Mural Studies 451
Institute of Southern African Studies 455, 538
Integration into South Africa 274-76, 278-81
Intercropping *see* Agriculture
Interest rates *see* Banking
Interim National Council 211
International relations *see* Foreign relations
Investment 547-48
 foreign 221
Iron Age *see* History
Irrigation 161, 361-62, 364, 368, 557

K

Kafir War *see* History
Kalahari Desert 42
Katse Dam 36
 see also Lesotho Highlands Water Project
Kenya 336
Kerea ea Lesotho 124
Ketane Valley 146
Khaketla, B. M. (poet) 466, 468
Khooanyane (place) 474
Kimberlite 16
Koeneng (place) 88
Kometsi, L. (poet) 469
Kopano (religious groups) 119
Kraals *see* Architecture

L

Labour 60, 81, 133, 383-84
 agriculture 382
 informal sectors 387
 markets 409
 rehabilitation 262
 skilled and unskilled 381
 unemployment 402-03, 405-06
 see also Migrant labour; Women
Labour Code 248
Land
 degradation 424
 legislation 234
 reform 352, 354
 resources 10
 tenure 80, 82, 173, 230-31, 351-55, 359, 424, 507, 520, 559
 use 4, 9, 51, 230, 345, 354, 368, 425
 see also Agriculture
Language 1, 19-20, 106-07, 110-11, 503
 Sesotho 108, 110, 113
  grammar 109
  orthography 112
 translations 107
 see also Dictionaries
Latrines *see* Health and medicine
Law *see* Legal systems
Leather industry 324
Legal systems 96, 244, 507, 538
 see also Common law; Customary law; Electoral law; Family law; Women
Legislation 243
Lekhotla la Bafo (protest movement) 218
Leribe 101, 309, 362
 Leribe Mission 42
 Plateau 42
Lerotholi's Law 244, 247, 559
Lesotho Church 117
Lesotho Cooperative College 329
Lesotho Distance Teaching Centre 447, 450
Lesotho Electricity Corporation 142
Lesotho Highlands Water Project 36, 319-22, 327, 330, 456
Lesotho National Development Corporation 323
Lesotho Planned Parenthood 181
Lesotho Red Cross Society 265
Lesotho Telecommunications Corporation 142
Lesotho Woodlot Project 359
Libesoaneng (place) 474
Lifaqane see History

Literacy *see* Education
Literature 107, 109, 462, 464, 533
- criticism 460-61
- poetry 465-71
- *see also* History: poetry; History: traditional literature

Livestock *see* Agriculture
Local Initiatives Support Program (LISP) 131, 268

M

Machobane, J. J. (poet) 466
Mafeteng District 86, 149, 270, 360
Magic 48, 191
Maintenance 201
- *see also* Women

Maize *see* Agriculture
Makara, A. (poet) 468
Makhaleng District 453
Makhoakhoa (people) 520
Makomereng (mountain) 526
Malawi 393, 562
Maliba-Matso river 24
Mangoaela, A. D. (poet) 466
Mangolong 474
Mapoteng (place) 88
Maps 13-14
- atlases 13

Maputsoe (town) 104, 309
Marketing *see* Agriculture
Marriage
- ceremonies and laws 245, 247
- customary 235, 245
- *see also* Women

Maseru 14, 27, 99-100, 135, 310, 387, 414, 449, 472, 481
- *see also* History

Maseru City Council 252
Matelile District 143, 379
Matelile Rural Development Project 143, 267, 360
Mauritius 25
Media *see* Newspapers and the media
Medicine *see* Health and medicine; History
Melikane (place) 474
Middle Sister (mountain) 526
Migrant labour 4, 11, 78, 81, 100, 130, 132-33, 138-39, 141, 187, 227, 238, 262, 285-86, 289, 291, 293, 337, 344, 353, 389, 391-93, 395, 397, 399, 401, 403-04, 406-07, 410, 509
- effect on South Africa's labour market 394, 396, 400
- migrant remittances 127, 134, 138, 141, 144, 153, 227, 285, 293, 392-93, 397
- sexual practices 202
- skilled labour migration 390
- social impact 389, 398, 406
- *see also* History; Socio-economic conditions; Women

Military *see* History
Military Rule 226-28, 287
Milk *see* Agriculture
Minerals 16-18
Miners *see* Health and medicine; Migrant labour
Ministry of Education 433
Missionaries *see* History
Mofolo, Thomas (author) 464, 466
Mohair *see* Arts and crafts: wool and mohair
Mohale's Hoek 86, 101, 176, 255, 270, 453, 482
Mohapeloa, J. M. (poet) 466
Mojela, Lerotholi (poet) 466
Mokhomo, M. A. (poet) 466
Monocotyledons *see* Plants
Moorosi Wars *see* History
Morija 22, 26, 389, 481, 524, 531-32
Morija Museum 527
Morija Printing Works 531, 533
Morija Sesuto Book Depot 532
Moshoeshoe I (King) *see* History
Moshoeshoe II (King) 220, 223, 467, 499
Mountaineering 1, 59, 523, 525-26
Mozambique 393
Museums and archives 527

N

Namibia 279, 561
- *see also* South West Africa

Napier Treaty *see* History
National Council of Women 170
National Environmental Action Plan 416
National identity 210
National parks *see* Sports and recreation
National University of Lesotho 446, 451
Nationalism 213
Natural Resource Management 241, 425
Nepal 188
Newspapers and the media 528-30
NGOs *see* Non-Governmental Organizations
Nigeria 448
Non-Governmental Organizations (NGOs) 120, 148, 549
Ntsane, K. (poet) 468
Nutrition *see* Food and nutrition

O

OAU *see* Organization of African Unity
Oral tradition *see* History
Orange Free State 67, 70, 329, 477, 491
see also History
Orange Free State Volksraad 122
Orange River 26, 32
Organization of African Unity (OAU) 239
Orpen 474
Orthography *see* Language: Sesotho

P

Painting *see* Arts and crafts: rock paintings
Palaeontology 16, 58, 510
Pan Africanist Congress 212
Paris Evangelical Mission Society (PEMS) 117, 122-23, 125, 528
Peat *see* Bogs and wetlands
PEMS *see* Paris Evangelical Mission Society
Periodicals 534-43
Pinto beans *see* Agriculture
Planning *see* Government
Plants 39-40, 42-44, 48
see also Flora and fauna
Pleistocene Period 57
Poetry *see* History; Literature
Politics 4-5, 62, 83, 206, 210-12, 225-26, 236, 240, 271, 294, 418, 536-37, 542
political institutions 253
political parties 271
unrest 221, 224, 226, 228
see also History; Women; individual political parties by name, i.e. Basutoland Congress Party
Polygyny 514
Pony trekking *see* Sports and recreation
Population 1, 11, 13, 96-97, 100-01, 418
see also Surveys
Pottery *see* Arts and crafts
Poultry *see* Agriculture
Poverty 127, 130-31, 134, 138, 141, 150, 152, 268, 292, 340
see also Surveys
Primary health care *see* Health and medicine
Primary Producer Co-operatives 261
Prostitution 78, 187
Protection and Preservation Commission 510
Publishing 109, 531-33, 553

Q

Qabane Valley 209
Qacha's Nek District 472, 526
Qiloane (place) 27
Quthing Distict 268, 472, 482
Qutu (place) 474

R

Ramabanta-Semonkong Roads Project 260
Range Management 374, 376-77, 379, 425
Regional cooperation 281
Regional economies 279
Regulation *see* Banking
Religion 5, 123, 520
traditional 506
see also History; individual religions by name, i.e. Christianity
Reptiles 36
Resistance movements 218
Riots 221
Ritual beliefs 62
Roads *see* Transport
Rock paintings *see* Arts and crafts
Rock shelters *see* Archaeology
Roma 27, 389, 414
Royal Lesotho Tapestry Weavers 490
Rural communities 127-31, 133, 138-39, 141
Rural development 139-40, 255
see also Surveys

S

San (people) 512
Sanctions on South Africa 315
Sani Pass 17
Sanitation *see* Health and medicine
Savings *see* Banking
Schools *see* Education
Scott Hospital 148, 182, 197
Security 278
Seforong (place) 269
Segoete, E. L. (poet) 466
Sehlabethebe National Park 53, 521
Sehonglong (place) 54, 57, 474
Selfhelp projects 268
Senqu Valley 9, 52, 474, 526
Sesotho *see* Language
Setsoasi Valley 473
Sex 516, 519
Share-cropping *see* Agriculture
Shava, P. (theatre critic) 498

Shields *see* Arts and crafts
Shrubs 45
Siege of Hlotse *see* History
Small-Scale Intensive Agricultural Project 266
Small Scale Irrigated Vegetable Project 362, 557
Smithfield (place) 67
Snakes 29
Soccer players 190
Social organizations 520
Social services 4
Social structure *see* History
Social welfare 134
Société des Missions Evangéliques de Paris *see* Paris Evangelical Mission Society
Socio-economic conditions 127, 412-13
Socio-economics 146-47, 294
  see also Surveys
Sociology 537, 542
Soil *see* Agriculture; Conservation
Sorcery *see* Magic
South Africa 8, 17, 25, 38, 49-50, 62, 78
  integration into 274-76, 278-81
  sanctions 315
  trade links 302, 315-17
South African Customs Union 314, 316-17
South African Home Lands 62
South African National Union of Mineworkers 391, 407, 410
South West Africa (now Namibia) 49
  see also Namibia
Southern Africa 8, 19-20, 33-34, 37, 44, 46, 49, 51, 81, 83
  settlement 5
Southern African Development Coordinating Conference (SADCC) 281, 550
Southern Sotho (people) 62
Speech *see* Children
Sports and recreation 20
  canoeing 526
  hiking 21, 522, 524
  mountaineering 1, 59, 523, 525-26
  national parks 521
  pony trekking 21, 522
Statistics 413
  see also Surveys
Stone Age *see* History
Storage facilities *see* Agriculture
Street maps *see* Maps
Structural Adjustment Programme 290, 294
Surveys 102
  censuses 77, 98
  Household Budget Survey 134, 145
  Household Data – Mafeteng District 143
  Household Income and Expenditure 144
  language 110
  Poverty Mapping 136-37
  Poverty Study 135
  rural surveys 138
  socio-economic 101-04
  Socio-economic survey – Thaba-Tseka and Qacha's Nek 152
  Socio-economic survey – Hololo Valley 147
  Socio-economic survey – Ketane Valley 146
  Sotho Diet Survey 156
  Vegetable National Survey 369
  Village Drought Survey 157
Swaziland 8, 19, 49, 83, 149, 239-40, 272, 279, 298, 317-18, 337, 386, 398, 503, 560-61
Synod (church) 124

T

Teaching *see* Education
Tebellong Hospital 148
Territory claims 229
Textbooks 107
  Sesotho grammar 114
Teyateyaneng (place) 310
Thaba-Bosiu (place) 22, 24, 26, 94
Thaba-Bosiu Rural Development Project 9
Thaba-Tseka (place) 264
Thaba-Tseka Project 9
Thabana Li Mele Handicraft Project 492
Thabong Weavers 490
Theatre *see* Arts and crafts
Tloutle (place) 51
Toads 28
Topography 43
Tourism 20, 328
Towns 1, 19
Trade 314
  with South Africa 302, 315-17
  see also History
Trade unions 407, 409-10
Traders *see* History
Traditional healers *see* Health and medicine
Traditional medicine *see* Health and medicine
Traditional religion *see* Religion
Transport 326, 332, 522
Transvaal (district) 477
Travel guides
  historical 22
  modern 1, 19-21
Travellers' accounts
  colonial 22-27, 38

Trees 45, 49
see also Flora and fauna
Tsoelike Valley 473
Tswana (people) 62, 64

U

United Nations Environmental Programme 544
United States of America 106
University education *see* Education
University of Botswana, Lesotho and Swaziland 446
Urban planning 99-100

V

Vaal Triangle 52, 414
Vandalism 142
Vegetables *see* Agriculture
Vegetation 41, 79
Village Development Committee 255, 263
Village health workers 181, 185
Village life 1, 52
Violence 175

W

Wars *see* History
Water resources 11-12, 16, 241, 319-21
see also Lesotho Highlands Water Project
Water supply 131, 204-05
see also Health and medicine: water; Lesotho Highlands Water Project
Wealth 129
Weaving *see* Arts and crafts
Wetlands *see* Bogs and wetlands
Wildlife *see* Flora and fauna; individual species by name, i.e. Frogs
Witchcraft *see* Magic
Women 74, 132-33, 161-62, 165
abortion 96
agriculture 161, 173, 365, 458
beer brewing 78
church 126
customs 4
development 171, 562
education 162
employment 384
female-headed households 134, 138
labour migration 78, 158-60, 167, 388, 563
law 4, 563
legal and social constraints 163-66, 168-69, 173, 201, 206, 235
maintenance 166, 169
marital careers 160
marriage 563
nutritional education 154
organizations 170, 172
politics 219, 563
position in society 143
prostitution 78
Rural Development Project 269
self-development 170
society 172, 255, 509
statistics 411
textiles and clothing 383, 386
Woodfuel *see* Energy
Woodlots *see* Forestry
Wool *see* Arts and crafts
Workers' rights 238, 248

Z

Zambia 562

Map of Lesotho

This map shows the more important towns and other features.

Harrismith
Clarens
(Phofung)
Ladysmith
Mohokare (Caledon)
BUTHA-
BUTHE
Butha-Buthe
Oxbow
MONT-AUX-
SOURCES 3282 M
NATAL
Letseng-
la-Terae
Estcourt
MOKHOTLONG
Malibamatšo
Senqu (Orange)
Mokhotlong
THABANA-
NTLENYANA
3482 M
Mantšonyane
Thaba-Tseka
Senqunyane
Sehonghong
QACHA'S NEK
Underberg
Sehlabathebe
Qacha's Nek
Cedarville
Kokstad
PROVINCE

ALSO FROM CLIO PRESS

INTERNATIONAL ORGANIZATIONS SERIES

Each volume in the International Organizations Series is either devoted to one specific organization, or to a number of different organizations operating in a particular region, or engaged in a specific field of activity. The scope of the series is wide-ranging and includes intergovernmental organizations, international non-governmental organizations, and national bodies dealing with international issues. The series is aimed mainly at the English-speaker and each volume provides a selective, annotated, critical bibliography of the organization, or organizations, concerned. The bibliographies cover books, articles, pamphlets, directories, databases and theses and, wherever possible, attention is focused on material about the organizations rather than on the organizations' own publications. Notwithstanding this, the most important official publications, and guides to those publications, will be included. The views expressed in individual volumes, however, are not necessarily those of the publishers.

VOLUMES IN THE SERIES

1 *European Communities*, John Paxton
2 *Arab Regional Organizations*, Frank A. Clements
3 *Comecon: The Rise and Fall of an International Socialist Organization*, Jenny Brine
4 *International Monetary Fund*, Anne C. M. Salda
5 *The Commonwealth*, Patricia M. Larby and Harry Hannam
6 *The French Secret Services*, Martyn Cornick and Peter Morris
7 *Organization of African Unity*, Gordon Harris
8 *North Atlantic Treaty Organization*, Phil Williams
9 *World Bank*, Anne C. M. Salda
10 *United Nations System*, Joseph P. Baratta
11 *Organization of American States*, David Sheinin
12 *The British Secret Services*, Philip H. J. Davies
13 *The Israeli Secret Services*, Frank A. Clements